don't stop
believin'

the unofficial guide to

erin balser & suzanne gardner

don't stop believin'

the unofficial guide to

ecw press

Published by ECW Press
2120 Queen Street East, Suite 200, Toronto, Ontario, Canada M4E 1E2
416-694-3348 / info@ecwpress.com

LIBRARY AND ARCHIVES CANADA CATALOGUING IN PUBLICATION

Balser, Erin
Don't stop believin' : the unofficial guide to Glee / Erin Balser and
Suzanne Gardner.

ISBN 978-1-55022-938-7

1. Glee (Television program). I. Gardner, Suzanne II. Title.

PN1992.77.G578B34 2010   791.45'72   C2010-901394-8

Developing editor: Jen Hale
Copy editor: Jen Knoch
Cover and color section design: Cyanotype
Text design: Melissa Kaita
Typesetting: Rachel Ironstone
Production: Troy Cunningham
Printing: Lake Book Manufacturing   2 3 4 5

Cover photo: Ian Daniels/startraksphoto.com
Author photo: Mohammad Jangda
Color photo section: All photos © Fox/Shooting Star,
except page 5 (bottom) and page 7 (bottom), © AP Photo/Ross D. Franklin.
Interior black and white photos: page 2: AP Photo/Jennifer Graylock; 8, 10, 15: Courtesy Lauren Pon; 6: Gregg DeGuire/PictureGroup; 12: Mark Davis/PictureGroup; 19, 24, 49, 88, 200, 241: Sthanlee Mirador/Shooting Star; 22, 41: Joe Martinez/Shooting Star; 26: Aundray Cheam; 28, 30, 52, 206: ML/Agency Photo; 32, 131: Grady/Agency Photo; 33: Courtesy Genevieve Collins; 35, 40: Marc Sterling/Shooting Star; 37: Kyle Rover/startraksphoto.com; 38: Christina Radish/Agency Photo; 43, 45, 46, 48: Michael Williams/startraksphoto.com; 51: Pseudo Image/Shooting Star; 56: Scott Gries/PictureGroup; 80, 161, 219: Courtesy Stephen Tobolowsky; 94, 106, 114, 123: Fox/Shooting Star; 140: AP Photo/Chris Pizzello; 155: Courtesy Lisa Djakalovic; 169: AP Photo/Ross D. Franklin; 184: Kristian Dowling/PictureGroup

The publication of Don't Stop Believin': The Unofficial Guide to Glee has been generously supported by the Government of Ontario through the Ontario Book Publishing Tax Credit, by the OMDC Book Fund, an initiative of the Ontario Media Development Corporation, and by the Government of Canada through the Canada Book Fund.

Canada

PRINTED AND BOUND IN THE UNITED STATES

ECW PRESS
ecwpress.com

table of contents

hello, i love you: introduction

The opening riffs from an epic 1980s power ballad hit the hallways, piquing the interest of a dejected teacher, a malicious cheerleading coach and the resident bad boy. In the auditorium six misfit kids in matching red shirts and Converse sneakers twirl and wheel (literally!) to a song they have not only made their own but taken to heart — Journey's "Don't Stop Believin'." They radiate joy with every note, much to the delight of the teacher and to the dismay of the cheerleading coach. William McKinley High School's glee club has arrived. And so has *Glee*, becoming must-see TV for millions of self-proclaimed gleeks around the world.

Glee, the show about a misfit show choir, is a celebration of freaks, geeks and underdogs, and of passion, pride and creativity. It's about doing what you love and being proud of who you are, even if you don't always fit in. "You know, the show choir thing, I think, is a metaphor for being different and embracing your difference and being able to express yourself no matter how hard or how much pain you're in," *Glee*'s creator Ryan Murphy says. It's this metaphor that viewers everywhere connect with, looking at Rachel, Finn, Quinn, Kurt, Artie, Puck, Mercedes and Tina and seeing themselves (albeit with killer singing and dancing skills).

Glee is often compared to *High School Musical*, but it's darker and more complex, and while the musical performances are similar to *American Idol*'s, that's where that comparison ends too. *Glee* is a comedy, drama and musical all rolled into one. To find a comparable show, you need to go back to the 1980s and the success of *Fame*, which aired for one season on NBC before being syndicated for its five remaining seasons. *Fame*, like *Glee*, put the spotlight on a group of talented high school students aspiring to stardom. It explored mature themes, dealt with the difficulties of growing up and addressed the sacrifices we make for our dreams, highlighting these issues with a dynamic musical element. After *Fame*'s television run ended, shows with a performing arts focus experienced a bit of a lull, but in the last decade they've regained their place at center stage. And with Rachel Berry–esque determination, they're not giving up their marquee status any time soon. With the success of shows and movies like *American Idol, So You Think You Can Dance, America's Got Talent, Stomp the Yard, Step Up* and the *Fame* film remake, it was only a matter of time before someone channeled the movement into a scripted television show.

When writer/director Ryan Murphy did just that in 2009, his show became an unstoppable force, with an average of 9.77 million viewers per episode, millions of song downloads, a live concert tour, a clothing line and so much more. The fans are in on the spin-off action too. From YouTube mash-up videos to fan cover songs, from Twitter trending to fan fiction: there's nothing *Glee* hasn't touched. Including us, the lucky gals writing this book.

We both became enamored of the show, mysteriously unavailable on each Wednesday (and then Tuesday) night, wearing Emma-inspired monochromatic outfits around town, dancing to "Don't Stop Believin'" in the subway and suggesting *Glee*-only karaoke nights with friends. We went online to find people who felt the same way, started our own blogs and connected with fans, including role players, other bloggers and frequent forum users.

In fact, it was *Glee* that brought us together. We're both writers who pitched the idea of a *Glee* companion guide to ECW Press, a publishing house known for their great television books. ECW loved both proposals and thought that, together, we could create a book that every gleek would love to read. Mash-ups, as *Glee* has taught us, can be a beautiful thing.

As much as we love *Glee*, we're the first to admit the show isn't perfect. Some lessons can be heavy-handed and some plot points fall flat. But *Glee* has guts and isn't afraid to make mistakes. Just like their characters, the creative minds behind the show push forward with originality, spunk and heart, knowing that doing what they believe in is worth the occasional slushie facial from their critics. Besides, emotional peaks and valleys are all part of a regular episode of *Glee*. Inspiring laughter one minute and tears the next (and sometime tears of laughter!), one episode of *Glee* takes viewers through more emotions than some television shows do over a whole season. No wonder we finish every episode with a song in our hearts!

Glee is a huge, complicated and fascinating world, both on-screen and off. It has an eclectic cast of Broadway stars and previously unknown actors, a complicated production process, tons of musical numbers and references to everything from 1930s Broadway to Justin Timberlake. *Glee* moves at a breakneck pace and it's sometimes hard to keep up, let alone take it all in. But don't worry, we're here to help you successfully navigate the halls of McKinley High.

Don't Stop Believin' acts as a companion to this brilliant show, something you can read while watching (or rewatching!) each episode. The book delves into the history of the music, offers behind-the-scenes information, and explains the Broadway, pop culture and history references. Think of it as *Pop-Up Video* in book form. *Glee*'s history, production process and cast biographies open this book, followed by episode guides so detailed that they make Emma Pillsbury's sanitation look sloppy. If you're reading along while watching the show for the first time, never fear! No spoilers for future episodes will be revealed. Each guide opens with a quote that captures the episode's major themes, followed by the essential who, what, where and when of its original U.S. airing. After that, we'll supply you with a full analysis of the episode and several juicy extras, such as:

Star Rating: A lot happens during an episode of *Glee*. You laugh, you cry, you get up and dance — sometimes all at once. By giving each element (the Music, the Drama, the Laughs) a star rating out of four, you'll know how much Kleenex you're going to need, or if you'll want to break out the spandex.

High Note: So much happens in a single episode of *Glee*, but for us, this was the moment most deserving of a Rachel Berry gold star.

Low Note: And, on the other hand, while we love the show, we know it isn't perfect, so we'll also mention the episode's biggest sore spot.

Behind the Music: Music is the heart of *Glee*. We'll focus on the music heard in each episode, giving a brief history for the original song (or the version covered on *Glee*) and examining the connections between the song and what's happening on-screen.

The Sound of Music: Some episodes are based on a specific musical style or genre, or on the influence of a legendary performer, so here we'll give you a fun mini–music history lesson.

Give My Regards to Broadway: A lot of Broadway shows get the *Glee* treatment, whether it's New Directions singing a song from an acclaimed play or Sandy Ryerson directing a high school production of it. In this section, we will give you some background on these shows.

That's Pretty *Popular*: Ryan Murphy brought a lot of his best stuff — singing jocks, bitchy cheerleaders, social outcasts — with him from the halls of Jacqueline Kennedy Onassis High School to McKinley. We'll point them out for you so you can find them more easily when you rent the *Popular* DVDs.

Slushie Facials: All the pranks and dirty deeds performed (on- or off-screen) at McKinley High are cataloged here.

Off-Key: Even the great Ryan Murphy makes mistakes sometimes, and this is where you'll find them, whether it's a blooper, an error in continuity or just something that didn't make sense.

Behind the Scenes: Sometimes fact is more interesting than fiction, and here we'll give you a backstage pass to the cool real-life stories with connections to *Glee*.

Center Stage: *Glee* is chock full of references to rock stars, stage stars, movies, songs, TV shows and more. Center Stage is a handy guide to the show's entertainment references.

Jazz Hands: The *Glee* world is filled with funny little details, quirks and references that give each episode an added sparkle, and here we'll point out some of the best ones.

The Buckeye State: The propmasters and writers do their best to make *Glee*'s version of Lima, Ohio, feel authentic. They (and the Ohioans who put up with this show!) deserve a few shout-outs now and then and we'll highlight them here.

How Sue Cs It: Sue Sylvester is one of the most quotable characters on television. Every episode, we pick a favorite quote and put it here!

As jam-packed as each episode guide may seem, that's not all! We've got exciting extras such as biographies of the greatest guest stars, exclusive interviews and a sidebar we call Gleek Speak, where we chat with the biggest gleeks around or people doing awesome *Glee*-related things.

While we did our best to make this the most comprehensive *Glee* guide out there, you may spot something completely new or disagree with our interpretations of certain episodes. Good, bad, happy or sad, we'd love to hear from you. Erin can be found at embalser@gmail.com and Suzanne's email is suzie.gardner@gmail.com. Don't forget to stop by our blogs, Glee Dork (gleedork.com) and Gleeks United (gleeksunited.wordpress.com), where you can find weekly Gleecaps, *Glee* gossip and more!

Don't stop believin',
Erin & Suzanne

can't fight this feeling: the origins of *glee*

With top 40 hits and Broadway show tunes, lightning-fast plotlines and a large cast of characters, dark social commentary and heartwarming moments, *Glee* itself is a mash-up more complex than the New Directions team could ever dream of. With so much going on, every element needed to be dynamite in order for *Glee* to work. One miscast character or poorly selected song and the pilot would have been criticized for being overly cheesy. But the final product was pitch perfect. *Glee* is the brainchild of three different men, Ryan Murphy, Brad Falchuk and Ian Brennan, who, with the help of a large cast and crew, make the world of *Glee* come alive every week.

Even the best show choir needs a leader and *Glee*'s is none other than television veteran Ryan Murphy. Ryan was born on November 30, 1965, to an Irish-Catholic family in Indianapolis, Indiana. Considered a high-strung and precocious child, Ryan was always imaginative, immersing himself in movies, television, music and books as a form of escape. He even obsessed about becoming the Pope. "You just wanted a way out. You wanted a way to express yourself and just sort of not stay in Indiana and be an insurance salesman or a farmer," he says. Despite his aspirations to papal glory and his family's devout influence, Ryan never felt a connection with the church or with God. Yet his Catholic education would influence a major part of his future career — his storytelling. Ryan explains, "I'm very, very glad that I had that religious upbringing because, you know, it really taught me about

1

The man who makes dreams come true, Ryan Murphy.

storytelling and it really taught me about theatricality."

Even with his strict Catholic upbringing, Ryan, who is openly gay, never struggled with his sexuality. "My sexuality was always just a given and I always accepted it," he told *After Elton*. "I never really had a coming out. I was out in utero, I think. I had a very strong sense of self. It was never an issue for me. I never struggled with it." Despite Ryan's keen self-awareness, his parents worried about his well-being and sent him to a psychiatrist at 15. However, the psychiatrist deemed him simply "too precocious for his own good" and sent him home. Ryan's experience growing up gay in the Midwest would inform his future television shows, including *Glee*, and many of Kurt Hummel's experiences are based on Ryan's high school days.

Growing up, Ryan was always on the lookout for creative outlets to channel his energy. Ryan applied — and was accepted — to film school but couldn't afford to go. Instead he attended Indiana University in Bloomington, where he majored in journalism, worked at the *Indiana Daily Student*, starred in productions of *Bye Bye Birdie* and *South Pacific* and sang in the choir. He flirted with the idea of being a professional actor, but decided to put his journalism degree to use by writing headlines instead of becoming a headliner. After graduating, Ryan moved to star-studded Los Angeles where he penned entertainment stories for the *Miami Herald*. The writer's boundless energy and passion for showbiz led to freelance opportunities with such entertainment news heavyweights as the *Los Angeles Times*, the *New York Daily News* and *Entertainment Weekly*.

It was only a matter of time before Ryan shifted his focus from chasing stories to making up his own. He started scriptwriting in the late 1990s, after he became bored with writing about Hollywood and celebrities. "I had interviewed Cher for the fifth time and I was like, 'Okay, you got to do something else,'" Ryan says. "Even though I love her, I can't keep writing about her." The journalist began to write a screenplay about a woman who meets a man who loves Audrey Hepburn as much as she does, writing late into the night after work. He eventually sold that script, *Why Can't I Be Audrey Hepburn?*, to Steven Spielberg. Despite the big-name buy, the project (which had both Téa Leoni and Jennifer Love Hewitt attached to star at different points) was never put into production. Hollywood's many hurdles didn't faze Ryan, and he eagerly launched into his new career as a screenwriter with his next project, the dark teen drama *Popular*.

Popular, which ran for two seasons from 1999 to 2001 on the WB (now the CW), brought a caustic edge to teen drama, a genre that was experiencing a surge in viewership at the time. The show was originally conceived as a movie, but, after getting some feedback, Ryan teamed up with television producer Gina Matthews and turned the concept into a series. They shopped it around and four networks bid on it, but they signed with teen television powerhouse the WB. "We went with the WB because they seem to give shows more of a chance," Ryan says. At the time, the WB aired *Buffy the Vampire Slayer*, *Dawson's Creek*, *7th Heaven*, *Felicity*, *Roswell* and *Charmed* and appeared to be the perfect home for *Popular*.

When *Popular* premiered on September 29, 1999, it enhanced the WB's teen line-up with its honest, and often brutal, portrayal of surviving high school. Cynical, funny and over-the-top, the show looked at high school through the eyes of two girls who were the heads of their own cliques: popular cheerleader Brooke McQueen and unpopular journalist Sam McPherson. "It was sort of *Heathers*-esque," Ryan explains, referring to the 1989 black comedy starring Winona Ryder and Christian Slater about a murderous, popular clique of girls, all named Heather. "I always thought that that was a culty, darker thing that had a very cynical tone to it." Ryan claims that *Popular* and *Glee* are two very different shows, but it's obvious that many ideas and themes found their way from *Popular* to *Glee*. (We'll take a closer look at these comparisons in the section That's Pretty *Popular*.) *Popular* was a hit in its first season but failed to hold on to its audience after being moved to Friday nights for the second season. In a dark, real-life plot twist, *Popular* was abruptly and unexpectedly canceled, leaving the audience with a deadly cliffhanger.

Ryan's next project was the 2002 WB TV pilot *St. Sass*. Delta Burke was set to star as the new headmistress of an exclusive all-girls prep school, but the show (which had future *Glee* star Amber Riley in its cast) wasn't picked up. Yet this small step back would lead to a much bigger step forward as the writer refocused his time and energy on a new project that would establish him as a top-notch creative force. That project was the F/X drama *Nip/Tuck*, a show about two plastic surgeons practicing in Miami and, later, Los Angeles. Ryan was inspired to create *Nip/Tuck* after visiting a plastic surgeon for research for an article about men's calf implants. He was so appalled and intrigued by the experience that he knew he had to turn it into a television show. "I went into my consultation with this plastic surgeon, and, within five minutes, he told me five things I could do to improve my face and my body, and thus my life," he recalls. The article never got written; instead, *Nip/Tuck* was born.

Nip/Tuck was a huge departure from *Popular* but contained the same dark humor, cynical tone and biting commentary on contemporary culture. With Dr. Sean McNamara or Dr. Christian Troy urging patients, "Tell me what you don't like about yourself," *Nip/Tuck* asserts that we don't grow out of the teenage insecurities that plague the kids in *Popular*, and that the *Glee* kids strive so hard to overcome. Premiering on July 22, 2003, *Nip/Tuck*, a gruesome and graphic show, explores the ugly side of beauty, wealth and plastic surgery. "I think the public thinks that this is delicate surgery, and these surgeons treat the face as if it were porcelain," Ryan explains. "And in fact they treat it like it was sirloin." Ryan was an executive producer on *Popular* but came into his own with *Nip/Tuck*. He became more hands-on and began to direct for the first time in his career, a skill he'd take with him to movie sets and to *Glee*. The series won a Golden Globe for Best Drama in 2005 and received an order of 22 episodes, unprecedented for a cable TV show, for its fifth season.

Once *Nip/Tuck* became a well-oiled machine, Ryan started working on other projects, including co-writing and directing the 2006 film *Running with Scissors* and penning the 2008 pilot for *Pretty Handsome* (a show about a transgendered gynecologist that co-starred Jonathan Groff, Lea Michele's *Spring Awakening* co-star and Vocal Adrenaline's Jesse St. James). *Nip/Tuck* ended its remarkable six-season run with its 100th episode on March 3, 2010. The show's success had given Ryan's career a transformative facelift, and, in 2007, Ryan signed an eight-figure multi-year deal with Fox that included developing new series for 20th Century Fox Television and giving the network the first look at any project, including *Glee*.

It was a tremendous opportunity, but one that came with significant pressure. Luckily, Ryan wasn't working alone. Originally hired as a writer for *Nip/Tuck* in its first season, Brad Falchuk (currently one of *Glee*'s executive producers, who writes, produces and directs for the show) quickly worked his way up to producer on the F/X drama. In fact, Ryan liked Brad's work so much that the two developed *Pretty Handsome* together before teaming up again for *Glee*.

If Ryan was Kurt Hummel in high school, the gay drama and choir geek, Brad was Finn Hudson, the jock trying to figure out where he belonged. Brad played baseball, basketball and lacrosse in high school, and, despite being relatively popular, he always felt the need to stand out and be different. Brad, like Ryan, was driven by a need to move on to bigger and better things. He struggled in school (and later discovered he was dyslexic), and, to distract his classmates from his difficulties and to stand out from the crowd, he wore a tie every day and told everyone at his liberal-leaning school that he was a Republican. "Everyone is searching for something," he says. "And usually

Ryan's right-hand man, writer and producer Brad Falchuk.

what they're searching for is to be heard or to be seen. . . . I was desperate to be seen."

After graduating from high school, Brad attended the American Film Institute in Los Angeles. He struggled as a film scriptwriter and worked as a personal trainer for four years before his wife prompted him to give writing for television a try. After short stints as a writer on *Mutant X*, *Earth: Final Conflict* and *Veritas: The Quest*, Brad asked his agent to set up a meeting with Ryan Murphy. Ryan liked his work and hired him for *Nip/Tuck*. "Ryan took me under his wing and said, 'Let's see what happens. Let's do this ride together and I'm going to open these things up to you and all I expect of you is that you work your ass off and you bring your voice," Brad recalls. The duo achieved a beautiful harmony and have been working together ever since.

Brad may relate the most to Finn, but Artie Abrams is the character most inspired by his life. Artie is named after one of Brad's childhood best friends and a spinal scare Brad had was the catalyst for the story in "Wheels." In 2008, Brad was diagnosed with a malformed blood vessel on his spinal cord, otherwise known as hemangioma, and it required emergency surgery. He spent months in recovery, and the former personal trainer was wheelchair bound. Brad is now back on his feet, but the ordeal inspired him to use *Glee* as an accessible approach to disability issues.

Fox was so impressed with Brad's work on *Glee* that they signed him to his own seven-figure development deal. He'll work on multiple projects for the network as a writer, director and producer. "Brad is an extremely versatile and talented team player," praised 20th Century Fox Television chairman Dana Walden. "The tone of *Glee* is so specific, it takes delicate balance. If you can direct *Glee* successfully, you can probably direct anything."

But as Ryan Murphy had already discovered, talent and a multi-million-dollar development deal don't guarantee all your work will be produced, and after the *Pretty Handsome* pilot failed to get picked up by F/X, Ryan and Brad wanted to do something completely different and the notion of doing a television musical kept popping up. However, they needed to figure out how to make the format work. No musical television show had succeeded since *Fame* in the 1980s. *Cop Rock* lasted for one widely panned season in 1990, and *Viva Laughlin*, the 2007 television musical starring Hugh Jackman, was canceled after two episodes. Even the sometimes-musical *Eli Stone* and *Pushing Daisies* didn't get very far. But with shows like *American Idol* and *So You Think You Can Dance* soaring in the ratings and *High School Musical* and *Hannah Montana* becoming pop culture phenoms, audiences seemed primed and ready for this genre — if it was the right show.

While Ryan searched for this elusive project, television producer Mike Novick, a member of Ryan's gym and a casual acquaintance, coincidentally approached Ryan with a movie script about a high school glee club, written by Mike's friend Ian Brennan in 2005. After the script was turned down by several Hollywood producers, Mike realized there was only one person who could do justice to such a creative and original project: Ryan Murphy. "From

It was Ian's Brennan's original film script that started it all.

getting to know him and being a fan of his work on *Nip/Tuck* and *Popular* and *Running With Scissors*, I knew that there's a comedic tone and sensibility that's very unique in Ryan," Mike explained to the *Los Angeles Times*. "A lot of writers, directors and producers out here come up through the high school musical bubble world, and I just felt it was a world that Ryan could get. Creatively, it all starts with him." Ryan read the script and loved it, and the partnership between him, Brad and Ian began.

Growing up in Mount Prospect, Illinois, Ian Brennan was a wannabe actor who dabbled in show choir. He admittedly hated everything about the choir but joined because its director doubled as the drama club director and Ian thought that by signing up he'd have a better shot at scoring great acting roles. It worked, and Ian starred in several high school productions, all while donning sequined tuxedos for his glee club performances. Ian's drama teacher, John Marquette, influenced more than his participation in glee club: the character of Will Schuester is based on this encouraging teacher.

Ian's interest in acting stemmed from the same place Ryan's and Brad's did — a desire to escape his small town and search for something better. Growing up, Ian couldn't wait to get out of Mount Prospect and achieve fame and fortune. "I find it interesting that there is something in everybody, a longing for something transcendent, particularly in a place like Mount Prospect, a place that's very suburban and normal and plain," he says. "Even in places like that, there's this desire to shine."

Ian's love for acting stayed with him, and, after high school, he headed to Loyola University in Chicago to study theater. Once he graduated, Ian struggled to make ends meet as an actor in Chicago and New York before he tried his hand at screenwriting. The actor couldn't ignore his idea for a film about show choirs inspired by his high school days and the horrors of his own glee club experience. "It's such a strange phenomenon," he says. "It doesn't really exist except in high schools and maybe cruise ships. I figured there was the potential for some really good stories there." A lot of what you see on *Glee* — Sandy's firing, the bullying, the eggings — is taken directly from Ian's own life. "When I'm writing scenes, I invariably picture Prospect High School," he explains. "Like one of my classmates got rolled down a hill in a Porta-Potty, which is terrible."

The original *Glee* script was the first screenplay Ian ever wrote, other than simple sketch pieces in college, and it resonated with Ryan. "I read it, and I said, 'Well, I don't think this is a movie for me, but I love the title, and I love the idea. Let's just do that, and maybe we can turn that into a TV show,'" Ryan explains. After tossing the original film script, Ian sat down with Ryan and Brad and rewrote it for television.

The result may have come from Ian's idea, but it has Ryan Murphy's signature all over it. *Glee*, despite its heart and happy endings, is sprinkled with dark humor and cynical observations. "I want[ed] to do a show that has a bigger heart and is kinder," Ryan says. "But make no mistake. It still has an edge." Star Cory Monteith, who plays the vulnerable jock Finn Hudson, said it best at the 2009 Comic-Con panel: "It's like as if *High School Musical* had been punched in the stomach and had its lunch money stolen."

Ryan, Brad and Ian pitched the show idea to Fox in spring 2008, and the network picked it up the very same day. Four additional episodes were ordered and the crew needed to get to work. Casting was difficult, as everyone on the show needed to pass as a triple threat *and* as a high school kid. To emphasize the idea that anyone can be a star, Ryan was insistent that they cast only unknown actors in the lead roles. The casting team saw nearly 3,000 hopefuls before landing their dream team, plucking stars like Matthew Morrison, Lea Michele and Jenna Ushkowitz from Broadway, and others like

Cory Monteith, Chris Colfer, Amber Riley, Dianna Agron and Mark Salling from relative obscurity.

After the cast was picked, the music rights were secured, and the pilot was filmed, Fox arranged for a sneak peek of the premiere episode to air on May 19, 2009, after the *American Idol* season finale, months before any other show in the fall schedule was slated to premiere. At first, Ryan, Brad and Ian were reluctant to pull such a risky move, but eventually they came around to the idea. It had never been done before and would create tons of buzz for the show, hopefully fueling a word of mouth campaign that would last through the summer. Millions of people watch *American Idol* and pairing *Glee* with it gave Ryan's unusual show a built-in audience. Ryan admits,

Glee's biggest (gold!) star is Broadway veteran Lea Michele.

"It's like having a movie trailer before James Cameron's *Titanic*."

American Idol may be a ratings juggernaut, but only 9.62 million people tuned in to see the spring preview of Fox's newest show — a respectable but not jaw-dropping number — and reactions were mixed. Some critics loved it, some hated it and some saw its potential but wondered if it would find an audience. But its fans had faith and were already crying out for an encore. They were encouraged by the endorsements of established entertainment writers. *Entertainment Weekly* television critic Ken Tucker wrote, "[*Glee*] is so good — so funny, so bulging with vibrant characters — that it blasts past any defenses you might put up against it. *Glee* will not stop until it wins you over utterly." The *Los Angeles Times* concurred: "The only real problem with *Glee*, Fox's new musical comedy, which premieres tonight, is that viewers will have to wait four whole months for the next episode."

The show itself wasn't *Glee*'s only buzzworthy factor. The music scored with audiences as well. *Glee*'s version of "Don't Stop Believin'" debuted at #2 on iTunes when it was released in May and was downloaded 177,000 times the week after the preview. Journey's original version received a surprising boost as well, with downloads increasing by 48% that same week. Undoubtedly television execs at Fox were feeling the glee as well — they'd hit the pop culture jackpot. Like commercial juggernauts *High School Musical* and *Hannah Montana*, *Glee* had built-in opportunities for related products (albums, live tours, etc.), and a ravenous audience that wanted as much *Glee* in their lives as they could get. Fox had also seen significant success selling *American Idol* performances as iTunes singles, and it looked like *Glee* could repeat, or even outstrip, that success. The network quickly ordered eight additional episodes, bringing the total order from five episodes to 13.

Never before has a show developed such a rabid fan base before the official fall premiere. *Glee* fan websites and online communities popped up everywhere. Fox launched a "Biggest Gleek" contest and made the pilot available for live-streaming on their website and through Hulu.com so that fans could discover the show before it returned in September. They also offered videos of the pilot's other big song, "Rehab," as well as a free preview of the "Gold Digger" performance scene from the show's second episode, on iTunes, and several behind-the-scenes videos were released throughout the summer. The *Glee* cast went on a nationwide tour to Hot Topic stores in Boston, New York, Philadelphia, Chicago, Minneapolis, Houston, Dallas,

Glee's great cast with their first gold record! And there are many more to come!

Denver, Los Angeles and Washington, D.C., in late August to amp up buzz for the official fall premiere. Hundreds of fans came out to see their favorite cast members, and everyone was overwhelmed by the response. It looked like this band of misfits had a real shot at becoming popular.

When *Glee* made its long-awaited return on September 9th, it didn't disappoint. The episode was Fox's highest-rated scripted premiere that season, and Fox ordered a full 22-episode season pick-up the following week. In its first season, *Glee* averaged eight to ten million viewers an episode, but the show has already exploded beyond its medium into a true phenomenon. By the time *Glee* took a mid-season break in December 2009, over four million *Glee* songs had been downloaded. The first soundtrack, *Glee: The Music, Volume 1*, debuted at #4 on the Billboard Hot 200 when it was released on November 3, 2009, and went on to be certified gold before the end of the year. The cast of *Glee* had 25 songs in the Billboard Hot 100 in 2009, an accomplishment surpassed only by The Beatles, who had 31 songs make the list in 1964. The remaining soundtracks and singles continue to fly off the shelves as the *Glee* cast has solidified itself as one of the most popular musical acts ever, and its members are fielding offers for movies, Broadway shows, endorsements deals, recording contracts and more. Truly a pop culture sensation, *Glee's* second season was ordered on January 11, 2010, making it the first show of the season on any network to get renewed and reasserting itself as one of the season's hottest shows. In an unprecedented move, Fox ordered the third season of *Glee* before all of the first season had aired. *Glee* had become a force that couldn't be stopped.

this is how we do it:
the making of *glee*

According to the *New York Times*, each episode of *Glee* takes ten days to shoot and costs over $3 million to make. That's three days longer and 50% more expensive than the cost of a regular hour-long prime-time drama. The show has a large and talented team that works together to bring each episode from a few stray notes to a TV symphony.

It all starts with the writing. Ryan, Brad and Ian pen every single episode of *Glee* (although one man takes the lead writing credit for each), distinguishing themselves as an abnormally small writing team for an hour-long television show. During production, the talented trio meets at the Chateau Marmont in West Hollywood every Sunday evening to pitch ideas for the next episode. From there, they sketch out the plot and different story arcs, creating a first draft to take to rehearsals. Afternoons (and the occasional evening) on the *Glee* set are usually reserved for table reads, rehearsing or filming scenes. When it's time to film, every scene is run through four or five times before it's good to go. The writing changes all the time as they throw out something that doesn't work, add stuff that does or keep a great ad-libbed one-liner from a cast member.

Ryan, Brad and Ian are the creative arm of *Glee*, but it's Dante Di Loreto, an American Film Institute graduate, who keeps things on schedule and deals with any creative, personal and legal conflicts that arise. Dante originally worked with Ryan and Brad on *Pretty Handsome*, and he followed them to

Dante Di Loreto, one of *Glee*'s executive producers,
is the behind-the-scenes magic maker.

Glee. As one of *Glee*'s executive producers, Dante takes what Ryan, Brad and Ian come up with and makes it reality. "I like to describe it as a human body," Brad explains. "Ian and Ryan and I write all the scripts, and in that configuration, Ryan's sort of the brain, I bring the heart and Ian brings the funny bone. Ian's all the fun. So we write the scripts, Ryan and I direct episodes, Dante deals with all of the shit, I like to say, all of the very huge amount of legal stuff."

Once the episode is sketched out, Ryan chooses the musical numbers that will appear. Brad and Ian readily admit that Ryan is the driving force behind the music on the show. "If we did the music I wanted to listen to, no one would watch the show," Ian jokes. Brad does takes credit for some of the classic rock that makes it on the show but points to Ryan as *Glee*'s official DJ. His music knowledge and ear for what works and what doesn't is uncanny, but even Ryan himself is unsure as to why he's good at this. "The best part of my job is I pick all the songs. People ask me how I do it, and it's just bizarre. I don't really know," he says. Lea Michele, who has been singing and dancing on Broadway since she was eight years old, has high praise for the musical mastermind. "Ryan Murphy's brain is iTunes. I've never met anyone with a music vocabulary as incredible as his."

It's not just having a massive mental playlist that makes what Ryan does so special, but that he has the vision to throw all kinds of music into the mix. Rap, pop, R&B, show tunes, country: it all finds a home on *Glee*. While Ryan gets the final say, everyone on the cast and crew is encouraged to pitch songs. Sometimes the songs are drawn from real life experiences, personal favorites or overheard in one of the cast's impromptu jam sessions. "Bust Your Windows," "Sweet Caroline" and "Ride Wit Me" were all written into the show after being heard on set. But the story always comes first. "We'll know the story and the scenes first, and normally we just know, 'Oh, the song that needs to go here is "blank,"'" Brad explains. Ryan agrees: It's story first, songs second. "Brad, Ian and I write the show, we write all the scripts, and first of all what we do is thematically come up with what is the episode about? What are the characters doing?" Ryan says. "And then, to be quite honest, I just go home and swan around the house until two in the morning and try and remember what my mother was doing when she had her nervous breakdown when I was in fifth grade and what songs I remember. It's very personal."

Once the songs are chosen, music supervisor P.J. Bloom acquires the rights to use them on the show, include them in soundtracks and sell them on iTunes. Originally, acquiring rights was difficult and the producers had to sell *Glee* to artists and record labels to get them to agree to license them. Artists that originally refused to have their songs on the show included Bryan Adams and Coldplay (although the latter has since offered full use of their catalog). As *Glee* became more popular, acquiring rights became easier, with artists like Rihanna, Beyoncé and Madonna offering their catalogs at reduced licensing rates.

With the rights secured, *Glee*'s music team, led by producer Adam Anders, gets its cue to take over. Born in Stockholm, Sweden, to classically trained musicians, Adam spent most of his teen years in Tampa, Florida. He was a dedicated music lover from a very young age, starting a band with his brother and sister at age 12 and enrolling in music courses at the University of South Florida while still attending high school. When he was 17, Adam moved to Nashville and tried to make it in the country music business, spending his nights working in factories and his days searching for music gigs. In 1997, he met his future wife (and future music producing partner) Nikki Hassman. Adam starting working with Nikki, an aspiring musician, and realized that his talents were best served in the studio rather than onstage. The couple made the move to Los Angeles, and Adam began mixing music for film, television and pop acts. In 2000, Adam scored his first big hit with the Backstreet Boys' "More Than That" and hasn't looked back. His ear for tween tunes has brought him much success, having written or produced hits for *Camp Rock*, *High School Musical 3* and *Hannah Montana: The Movie*.

After writing theme songs for Fox television shows such as *Back to You* and *K-Ville*, Adam got his chance to work on *Glee*. Ryan was on the hunt for a music producer with the magic touch, and, after trying several people who just didn't work, Fox hooked Ryan up with Adam. The producer's *High School Musical* background made Ryan wary, but after Adam turned "Rehab" into Vocal Adrenaline's signature smash, he got the gig.

Hiring Adam did come with one complication — his music partner, producer Peer Åström, telecommutes from Sweden! Adam makes the trans-atlantic telecommuting possible by working with studios in New York and Los Angeles. He swears the different time zones actually make the process easier. Adam explains, "We use the time change to our advantage, so when I go to bed he keeps working and vice versa — basically, 24 hours a day, six days a week."

Adam and his team work on the music for anywhere between a few days to several weeks, depending on how complicated the arrangement is. During this process, Adam and his wife lay down the temporary vocals while the cast focuses on other things. "She's my secret weapon on *Glee*," Adam says. When the arrangement is finalized and approved, the cast replaces the vocals for the final production. The lead vocals are each recorded separately, but the group records together to fill in the harmonies and background vocals. Once the song is ready, it enters postproduction for both the download version and the broadcast version simultaneously. It's a fast-paced and frantic process and one Adam couldn't oversee without his amazing crew. "Everybody working on my team is super talented; everything they bring to the party is top-notch," he says. "You really only get one shot when you're on this compressed a timetable. That's what I've been most proud of: how we've been able to pull off so much volume at such a high level."

Adam admits that the mash-ups Ryan asks him to make are by far the hardest. "Some of those songs do not belong together!" he jokes. But, somehow, he makes them work and now even has the confidence to suggest a song or two. Whatever Adam is doing, he needs to keep it up! Thanks to *Glee*, he's the first producer to ever have 18 hits on the iTunes Top 100 at the same time.

But *Glee*'s real magic happens on the set rather than in the studio. Making the songs work in the context of the show is a huge challenge, but Ryan Murphy pulls it off with three main strategies. First, there's something for everyone. If you're not digging the first song of the night, give it five minutes and something else will come your way. This eclectic but familiar soundtrack is a deliberate choice. "The key to the music is to do stuff for the most part that people know," Ryan reveals. "[This] is why I think so many people love *American Idol*, because it's musical comfort food in some way." Second, the singing and dancing on *Glee* doesn't come out of left field. Whereas traditional musicals require some suspension of disbelief (Does anyone think it's strange that people randomly burst into song and dance?), *Glee*'s musical numbers are grounded in reality. Ryan was very clear on this from the beginning, insisting, "Look, if they're going to sing, there's going to be three rules. It will be done [when] they're on stage rehearsing or performing, or [when] they're in the rehearsal room, or it will sort of be in that sort of fantasy that has been rooted on the stage, and you realize that they were performing it in their head or performing out to the auditorium the entire time." Third, the music fits the show stylistically and thematically. Each episode is centered on a major theme, and the songs are selected to reinforce them, adding depth and complexity to the show's narratives.

The *Glee* team knew they'd hit the right notes with their music formula when fans around the world started downloading the show's songs in record numbers. Fox shopped a record deal early, showing four-minute teaser trailers to all the major labels. Columbia believed in the project right away and knew it had potential to be huge. Rob Stringer, the Columbia/Epic Label Group chairman, orchestrated the record deal with Fox and *Glee*. "Everyone

Glee galore! The cast and Ryan Murphy celebrate their
2010 Golden Globe win for Best Comedy Series.

else said, 'Oh, this could do really well,' but Rob said, 'I don't think you know what you have,'" Ryan told *Billboard*. "He always had a plan and a passion." Rob, whose company now holds the exclusive deal for all of *Glee*'s music and the rights to option the cast members' recording contracts, is more modest. "We knew that once the show started rolling it would be great. But to be honest, I didn't think it would be this big this quickly. I thought it would take people a moment to catch up, but the reaction has been instant." Rob is not alone in his surprise. "In all the years that I've been in the business, I've never worked on anything quite like this," Geoff Bywater, head of music for Fox Television, says. "It's a real cultural phenomenon that you can just feel."

Once the tracks are chosen and laid down, it's time to get the cast grooving. Ryan and Adam may be the music minds, but it's Zach Woodlee who gets the dance party started. Born on April 27, 1977, in Mesquite, Texas, Zach has dancing in his blood. His parents owned a dance studio, and his mother was a Dallas Cowboys cheerleader. Zach and his three brothers caught the performing bug early and would rehearse at the Cowboys' stadium after football practice. He used to help his mom choreograph the

United Way halftime shows. He remembers, "We'd be in a parking lot, and she would give us all these time codes and color codes and we would all be line leaders. That's how I learned the pattern work and the way that you break it down."

After graduating high school, Zach studied at the University of North Texas and pursued a career planning recreation and entertainment in a retirement community. While he enjoyed his work, the drama of the dance world lured him away, and he moved to Los Angeles with a close friend. He slaved away at Starbucks in the mornings and spent every afternoon at the Performing Arts Center in Van Nuys. In 2004, his hard work paid off with a gig as a dancer on Madonna's Re-Invention Tour.

After he shot a LeAnn Rimes music video, he became intrigued by what happened behind the camera and decided to model his career after choreographer Anne Fletcher, who hired him as an assistant for the 2006 dance film *Step Up*. From there, he stepped up to do choreography for *Hairspray, 27 Dresses, Get Smart, Fired Up!* and *Eli Stone*. As Zach puts it, "one thing led to another" and he was hired to do the choreography for the *Glee* pilot. He was given only a day and a half to create all the numbers for the episode, but Zach was up for the challenge. After the pilot's success, he signed on to the show full-time and his role on *Glee* expanded. It's Zach who decides what stage the performance will be on, how many people will be in each number, how long each performance will be and if they need extra dancers. As a result, he now has a co-producer credit.

For Zach, the choreography and performance must add to the overall narrative of the show. "I think the number one thing is the storytelling. You've got to make the actors feel comfortable and feel good knowing that millions of people are going to see them dance."

Just as most of the glee clubbers needed a crash course in dance from Mr. Schuester in *Glee*'s pilot, most of the cast members weren't already triple threats when they were hired. Only Heather Morris (Brittany) and Harry Shum Jr. (Mike Chang) come from professional dance backgrounds, and everyone else in the cast is quick to admit that the dancing is the hardest part of being on *Glee*. Dance rehearsals begin almost every day at 7 a.m. and, depending on what needs work, can be as short as three hours or as long as twelve. Additionally, the team will sometimes juggle several dance numbers at a time. The cast goes through the steps with Zach without music first to learn the beat before giving it a shot with tracks the cast laid down earlier. When the entire performance is ready, it's filmed and seamlessly incorporated into the episode.

From the writing to the music to the dancing, *Glee*'s production process has to be as flawless as a Vocal Adrenaline number. With so much happening, the cast and crew are often working on several episodes at once. They may have dance rehearsal for one episode in the morning, spend the afternoon filming another episode, then spend the evening laying down vocal tracks for yet another episode. Yet when finished episodes reach viewers everywhere, there's no trace of these marathon workdays, and nothing can stop the cast and crew's natural glee from shining through.

you're the one that i want: principal players

matthew morrison (will schuester)

Birth date: October 30, 1978
AKA: Matty Fresh, Triple Threat
Audition song: "Rocket Man" by Elton John, "On the Street Where You Live" from *My Fair Lady* and "Over the Rainbow" from *The Wizard of Oz* (with ukulele)

Matthew Morrison is *Glee*'s resident showbiz veteran. An only child born on an army base to a registered nurse mother and a midwife father in Fort Ord, California, Matthew caught the acting bug at theater camp when he was ten years old. This passion stayed with him, and he enrolled in the Orange County High School of the Arts to nurture it, where he excelled. "I had the best time," he admitted to *Parade*. "I guess I was one of the popular kids. I played soccer, I was class president — I even dated the homecoming queen." Matthew struggled with the pull between the performing arts and sports and even had aspirations to play on the under-17 national soccer team. Fortunately, his drama and music teachers persuaded him to stick with the arts, as there was greater long-term potential in theater for the budding triple threat.

After high school, he enrolled at New York University's Tisch School of the Arts. The demanding school bans students from auditioning during the first two years they study there. Eager to launch his career, Matthew ignored that rule. He got himself an agent and scored roles in the Broadway versions of *Footloose* and *The Rocky Horror Picture Show*. In 2001, he had a real-life Acafellas moment when he was recruited for the boy band LMNT (pronounced "element"), consisting of Matthew and a few rejects from the 2000 ABC reality show *Making the Band*. His good looks and many talents made him perfect for the exploding boy band trend, but the match wasn't meant to be. Matthew hated the experience and left the group before they released their first album.

His big break came when he won the role of Link Larkin in the original 2002 Broadway production of *Hairspray*. This role earned him credibility in the theater community, and in 2005 he was nominated for a Tony for his role in *The Light in the Piazza*. After leaving the production later that year, Matthew tried to break into TV and film, shooting five television pilots in as many seasons. The actor worked hard and scored small roles in shows like *Sex and the City*, *CSI: Miami*, *Numb3rs*, *Law & Order: Criminal Intent* and *As the World Turns* and films such as *Dan in Real Life*, *Primary Colors*, *Music & Lyrics*, *Once Upon a Mattress* and *Marci X* before the role that would define his career came along.

While Will Schuester seems more comfortable singing '90s rap songs, Matthew's Broadway bravado impressed Ryan Murphy. It helped that *Glee* needed a song-and-dance man who not only would pass as a small-town high school teacher but would also be at ease with the "Thong Song," "Endless Love" and everything in between. Apparently this kind of actor is difficult to find. "You'd think there must be a lot of good-looking 30-year-old guys who can sing, dance and act, but there really aren't," Brad Falchuk admits.

Luckily Matthew was perfect for the role of Mr. Schuester. "I'd love to say that this is a huge acting stretch for me, [but] this is kind of me," he says. He even shared the same professional aspirations as his character. "I probably shouldn't say that because I'm discrediting myself as an actor, but I feel like if I hadn't gone to New York, I would have gone to Chico State in Northern

California, and I probably would have done theater, come back to Southern California and taught at a performing arts high school."

There are drawbacks to success, though, and Matthew admits he's not a fan of the fame the show brings him. He considers himself a loner, but he's taking it in stride. "This is certainly the most recognized I've ever been in my life. I kind of like my anonymity. More people saw the pilot of *Glee* than saw me in my entire ten-year career on Broadway. But people feel more of a connection to you because they see you in their living rooms." Matthew loves golf, running, boxing, skydiving and cycling and uses these solitary sports to escape the demands of Hollywood.

Despite his desire to keep his personal life out of the spotlight, Matthew's happy to keep his professional life there. "There's something for everyone in theater, but also I think it just brings so much joy to people. You can only throw a football for so long. You can always sing. You can always dance," he told *After Elton*. "It's an amazing gift and I'm just so proud to be a part of it."

lea michele (rachel berry)

Birth date: August 29, 1986
AKA: Child Star
Audition song: "On My Own" from *Les Misérables*

Born Lea Michele Sarfati in The Bronx, New York, Lea is half Italian and half Spanish, half Catholic and half Jewish, and 100% pure performer. The budding star grew up in Tenafly, New Jersey, with her nurse mother and deli-owner father, and began showing off her skills on the Broadway stage when she was only nine years old. Starting as a replacement in the role of Young Cosette in the original New York production of *Les Misérables*, Lea moved on to roles in the 1998 original Broadway production of *Ragtime* and the 2004 Broadway revival of *Fiddler on the Roof*. Just like Rachel, Lea's classmates at Tenafly High School saw her simply as the "musical theater girl" and never truly understood her. As a child she was also teased about her last name, Sarfati, and thus she gave it up early on in her career.

After high school Lea was accepted to the Tisch School of the Arts at New York University (where co-star Matthew Morrison had attended), but she chose not to accept the position. Instead, she continued her work on the stage. Ultimately, Lea made the right decision, as it led her to her big break, originating the role of Wendla Bergmann, the lead character in the 2006 Broadway production of *Spring Awakening*.

It was because of this role, in fact, that Ryan Murphy wrote the part of Rachel Berry with Lea in mind. Ryan had seen Lea's performance after he worked with her *Spring Awakening* co-star Jonathan Groff on the *Pretty Handsome* pilot. "When I sold the *Glee* pilot and started to write down the part, I said there's only one girl who can play this," Ryan told *E! Online*. "But no one would give her a deal, because she had never done anything other than Broadway, so I told her, 'I want you for this, but you're going to have to go through the whole cattle-call audition process,' and she was just great. . . . She opened her mouth [and sang] and all the guys were crying, and they hired her, literally on the spot, in the room."

Though she is grateful for the part, Lea admits that her transition to TV has taken some getting used to. "Waking up at 6 a.m. is something that is different for me. I really do miss the excitement of being in front of a live audience and feeding off the energy. Every day, we go to work on one scene, we work on it really hard, and then you say goodbye to that scene and you go on to the next one. Whereas, in theater, you're telling the same story every night, which is great and so interesting to bring new life to the same story and how to keep it alive and real." Not only is Lea now waking up before the sun rises, but she's playing the perkiest go-getter on TV when she does it! Lea claims that the combo of lots of rest, morning coffee and a vegan diet help her be at her bubbliest and give her "a lot of energy to play spunky Rachel Berry."

The budding star knew she wanted to perform from a very young age, and jumped at every chance she got to put on a show. She told the *Los Angeles Times*, "I always wanted to perform. Every Christmas video is me standing in front of my family singing 'Santa Baby' and putting on a mini-concert for my whole family." It's no wonder that she's already got Golden Globe and Emmy nominations for best actress in a comedy series under her belt. And like her perky alter ego, Lea lists Barbra Streisand as one of her idols and *Funny Girl* as her favorite movie — two things that definitely helped her rock her character's performance of "Don't Rain on My Parade" in "Sectionals." "The fact that Ryan Murphy trusted me and gave me that opportunity is so incredible," Lea told the *Wall Street Journal*.

Lea knows that it's not just Rachel's endless energy that makes her a challenging character to play — it's also her hard-core determination. Fortunately, in this regard, Lea sees a lot of herself in Rachel. "I was never like anybody in my high school; I didn't care about the things they cared about. I basically knew who I wanted to be, what I wanted to do, since I was a kid. In that way, I really relate to my character. If you ask my cast, they'll say I'm very much like Rachel." However, this is a comparison Lea is proud of, as she sees a lot of admirable qualities in her on-screen alter-ego. "I respect her so much: her confidence, who she is, and, I know it sounds cheesy, but I think she's such an incredible role model for young girls. She doesn't let what people think is cool get in the way of being who she is."

cory monteith (finn hudson)

Birth date: May 11, 1982
AKA: Frankenteen
Audition song: "Honesty" by Billy Joel

Cory Allan Monteith is Canadian and proud of it. Born in Calgary, Alberta, Cory moved to Victoria, British Columbia, at a young age and, just like Finn, was raised by a single mom. The high school drop-out didn't have big dreams. He struggled in school and wasn't interested in learning. It didn't help that he never found where he belonged. Cory admits, "I was an outsider, actually. I didn't groove with any one particular group of folks." After dropping out in grade nine, he figured a blue-collar job back home would be enough for him to build a cozy little life.

But fate had bigger things in store for Cory. After gigs as a Walmart greeter, telemarketer, roofer and taxi driver, he figured he might as well give acting a shot. "I was working as a roofer and taxi driver in some backwater town and I was at loose ends and somebody said, 'You should be an actor!'" he said to *E! Online*. "I was like, 'Sure! I need to pay my rent.'" He signed up for some free acting classes and moved to Vancouver to give acting a shot. His coach saw potential in him and pushed Cory to audition for roles and pursue acting as a career. He scored small gigs in movies like *Final Destination 3* and television shows like *Kyle XY* before getting his big break on *Glee*.

Cory's not much of a singer, so he substituted the singing requirement for some impromptu drumming with Tupperware, glasses and cutlery to prove he had musical talent in his audition video. "I needed to do whatever I could to show that I had a musical side," he explains. It wasn't what the casting team wanted, but they were intrigued. Too many people audition- ing for the role of Finn were polished professionals with extensive voice and dance training. They needed a wholesome football player with raw talent, not a slick teen heartthrob. "It was important that Finn be a very good singer, but he also had to be a guy's guy, a strapping football star, or the character wouldn't work," casting director Rob Ulrich explains. Cory seemed to fit the part and was offered a callback. He drove from Vancouver to L.A. with the *Rent* soundtrack and a Billy Joel CD and prepared to read — and sing — for Ryan Murphy. Cory's original song choice was from *Rent*, but Brad Ellis, the show's piano man, convinced him to switch to Billy Joel's "Honesty" instead. It was a smart choice, since the classic rocker's tune was better suited for Finn's character. A few more callbacks, and Cory got the job that would transform his career.

Since he had no singing and dancing experience before being on *Glee*, it's been a huge learning curve for the humble Canadian. Just ask *Glee*'s music producer, Adam Anders, who told *Mix* magazine, "The first time we recorded, he didn't know how to breathe and sing at the same time; he almost passed out. To see where he is now is like night and day; he's come so far."

Cory relates to Finn but claims he's nothing like the dumb-but-lovable jock. "Finn is almost as smart as rocks. I like playing that. To prepare [to play] Finn before a scene, I just stop thinking (kidding . . . kind of)," he jokes. "Well, I'm not 17 or from Ohio or play on the football team or date cheerleaders, etc. . . . But Finn and I share a certain kind of vulnerability. And virtue." Cory appreciates his lack of a full high school experience, because he feels it lets him really get into his character and prevents his portrayal of Finn from being influenced by personal experiences.

Cory is a laid-back guy who's grateful for his *Glee* gig and hasn't gotten hooked on a celebrity lifestyle. He doesn't drink and prefers chilling out and playing video games with his pals to a hard night on the town. Showing remarkable perspective, Cory stays focused on the show rather than on his new-found celebrity status. "I'm not in it to be famous. I'm in it to make a television show," he says. The modest actor is also eternally grateful and baffled by his success: "I still can't wrap my head around the fact that people are paying me to do this."

dianna agron (quinn fabray)

Birth date: April 30, 1986
AKA: Di, Lady Di, Little Lamb
Audition song: "Fly Me to the Moon" by Frank Sinatra

The gal who makes *Glee*'s head-cheerleader-turned-social-pariah vulnerable and, well, likable, is the sweet Dianna Agron. Dianna was born in Savannah, Georgia, to Ron and Mary (hence the nickname "little lamb") but grew up in San Francisco, California. She was raised in the San Francisco Hyatt Hotel, where her dad was the manager. Life in the hotel introduced her to a wide variety of people, and she draws on that for her art. "I got to see many walks of life — politicians, athletes, Tony Robbins," she recalls. "It was the ultimate fishbowl."

Dianna's been singing and dancing ever since she enrolled in ballet lessons at the age of three, and she started acting in the fifth grade, when she starred as Dorothy in a school production of *The Wizard of Oz*. "Finding out that I could incorporate acting, singing and dancing was novel to me as a kid. I did musical theater throughout school, and that paved the way," she told *Women's*

Health. She quickly found a role model who exemplified what she wanted to do: "I loved Lucille Ball growing up and wanted nothing more than to be like her." With the role of Quinn, Dianna knew she had a chance to follow in the footsteps of the true triple threat and beloved comedienne. To make her dreams come true, Dianna taught dance to fund a move to L.A., which she made at 18. She enrolled in acting classes and has been working ever since, with small roles on *Drake & Josh, Numb3rs, Shark, Close to Home* and *CSI: NY* and two recurring gigs on *Veronica Mars* and *Heroes.*

Dianna almost missed her shot at the role that would give her more exposure than all of her previous parts put together. The night before *Glee*'s pilot was supposed to start shooting, the role of Quinn still hadn't been cast. Dianna, who had been out of work for a year and was extremely nervous, went in for her audition, but the producers still weren't sure. "They told me to come back with straight hair and to dress sexier." She rushed to a Starbucks bathroom, transformed herself, and the role was hers.

While celibacy-club prez Quinn Fabray only pretends religion is important to her life, for Dianna, it actually is. Dianna and her brother were raised Jewish since their mother converted in order to marry their Jewish father. Their parents felt it was important for Dianna to receive a well-rounded religious education. "I went to Sunday school, Hebrew school and a Jewish [day school] through third grade. My brother and I loved everything about Hanukkah and Passover and all the food." Dianna feels a strong connection to her Jewish roots and loves celebrating Jewish traditions. She had a bat mitzvah at 13 and hopes to visit Israel one day.

A devoted vegetarian, Dianna frequently gives back to her community, participating in charity events like Youth Run for Haiti and hosting events for 826LA, a youth arts organization. Her dog, John Robie or Johnny, was adopted from the Amanda Foundation.

With her strong work ethic and winning personality, Dianna's future looks bright. She has several film projects in the works and even sold her first screenplay in 2008. Her positive outlook helps too. Dianna believes you can't dwell on rejection and you need to celebrate success, no matter how small. "With every job I've gotten, I've bought myself something. When *Glee* was picked up, I rented a piano for the year. For smaller victories, I'll go to dinner with a friend, or go for a walk and think about it all. It's important to say to yourself, 'Today was a good day.'"

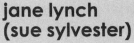

jane lynch
(sue sylvester)

Birth date: July 14, 1960
AKA: Lynch Mob

Jane Lynch may perfectly portray a megaphone-toting, insult machine, but trust us, she's no Sue Sylvester. Born and raised Irish Catholic to a housewife mother and banker father, Jane grew up in Dolton, Illinois, a place where the main pastimes were, as she explained to the *Guardian*, "beer, whiskey and storytelling." During her high school years Jane was a floater, never truly identifying with one core social group, although she did sing in her school's choir for four years. Rather than relating to the cheerleaders Sue coaches, Jane told Oprah.com that she most identifies with the character of Tina: "She's quiet. She stands in the back, and when you hear her sing, you're like, 'Oh my gosh. Where did she come from? She has talent.' I was kind of that person. I was kind of in the background, and then, every once in awhile, I'd pop in and people would be like, 'Where did you come from?'"

While Jane loved to sing, acting was her dream. Jane studied theater at Illinois State University before spending two years at a theater training program at Cornell. After completing the program, she returned to Chicago and spent the next ten years performing in the Steppenwolf Theatre Company and touring with improv comedy troupe The Second City.

It wasn't until she was 33 that Jane decided to try her hand at Hollywood. She moved to Los Angeles after being cast in *The Fugitive*, starring Harrison Ford. She immediately picked up work in theater, sitcoms, commercials and voiceovers. Unfortunately, the big break she was hoping for wasn't materializing. As she neared the big 4-0, Jane almost threw in the towel. She was 39 and still only snagging small roles, and she thought she had gone as far as she could go professionally. That is, until the comedian/actor/director Christopher Guest saw her in a Frosted Flakes commercial and cast her in his next three movies: *Best in Show*, *A Mighty Wind* and *For Your Consideration*.

"The man changed my life," Jane recalls. "He blew the doors open for me."

With over 130 film and television credits to her name, there are very few types of roles that this talented character actress hasn't played. The list of television shows on her résumé is impressive all on its own, including such hits as *Married . . . with Children, Frasier, Gilmore Girls, Dawson's Creek, The West Wing, The X-Files, Arrested Development* and *Friends*. In between TV appearances, Jane appeared in movies such as *Julie & Julia, Role Models* and *The 40-Year-Old Virgin*. Despite this diverse list, Jane does see connections between her varied roles. "There's definitely a common thread in all my characters — authoritarian, sarcastic, don't-give-people-the-benefit-of-the-doubt kind of characters. I think it's probably very good therapy, because I'm a much nicer person at home as I get it all out at work. That kind of contemptuous behavior is just below the surface for me, so it's nice I don't have to dig deep for it." As for her role on *Glee*, well, Sue definitely takes the contemptuous cake. "Sue Sylvester is the most scheming, unashamed person I've ever played, and I'm loving it."

Fortunately for Jane, the role of Sue Sylvester ended up being part of the main cast, even though that wasn't the original plan. Ryan Murphy explains, "The funny thing about that role was, it was a very, very small role when we did the pilot, and it was put in the pilot just to give Will a foil, like somebody to sort of butt against." "[She] leapt off the screen, I thought, and people loved her so much that we said to her, 'Would you like to enlarge the part and be a series regular?' and she loved that idea, so we did." Even though Jane was appearing in the Starz catering comedy *Party Down* at the time, she had actually shot the *Glee* pilot beforehand, and when it was time to choose a show, Jane traded in her cater-waiter bow tie for a tracksuit full-time.

Ryan isn't the only one who's noticed how fantastic Jane is as Coach Sylvester — the actress was nominated for her first Golden Globe award in 2009 for Best Supporting Actress on TV and snagged an Emmy nomination in 2010. She also found herself returning to voice acting in 2010 with a one-episode stint on *The Cleveland Show* in a character created specifically for her, and the fourth Shrek film, *Shrek Forever After*.

Things are also coming up roses for Jane in her personal life. The openly gay actress married her partner, Dr. Lara Embry, in May 2010. Not that it's always been easy for Jane, who didn't come out to her parents until she was 31. "I didn't want to be gay. . . . I wanted an easy life. And you know what? I am gay and I still have an easy life."

jayma mays
(emma pillsbury)

Birth date: July 16, 1979
AKA: Jaymazing
Audition song: "Touch-a, Touch-a, Touch Me" from *The Rocky Horror Picture Show*

Bambi, Annie . . . there are many pop culture references that can describe Jayma Suzette Mays' red-haired, doe-eyed beauty. Growing up the youngest of three in small town Grundy, Virginia, Jayma was fascinated with the clever orphan Annie. The two girls shared the same fiery red hair and active imagination. "The child wore a different costume every day," her mother Paulette Mays says. "I did nothing but make costumes for her the first 12 years of her life." The actress was born Jamia, named after her father James, but changed it to Jayma, as everyone pronounced Jamia wrong. Jayma loved small-town life but didn't come to appreciate it until she tried big-city living. "At the time, as a kid, I always kind of felt like I wanted to move out. I always felt attracted to big cities," she says. "But looking back on it now, I really feel like it was the right place for me to be growing up. I still feel like there's something so great about growing up in a small town and knowing everybody and having a community. It keeps you grounded."

Despite her love of playing pretend, Jayma didn't give acting a try until high school. "Performing is something I've always wanted to do, but I didn't think it was a viable option [for making a living]," she explains. She used high school as a place to try lots of different things. As a result, she didn't fit in anywhere but was never an outsider. "I don't think I necessarily fit into one particular group and to one clique. I was a cheerleader, so I was a part of that group. But also, I was a total nerd. I loved math. And I would do the little math competitions that we had at school." After enrolling at Southwest Virginia Community College, she debated a medical career. But the debate ended when she couldn't transfer her credits, and she ended up studying theater at Radford University.

After graduating, she moved to Los Angeles to put her degree to work. Her television debut came on NBC's *Friends* spin-off *Joey*, where she played Joey's quirky neighbor Molly. The show was canceled after two seasons, but Jayma quickly moved on to small roles in shows like *Entourage, House, How I Met Your Mother* and *The Comeback* and films like *Red Eye, Blind Dating* and *Smiley Face*. A starring turn in the surprise hit *Paul Blart: Mall Cop* and her recurring roles on *Heroes* and *Ugly Betty* made Jayma one to watch in Hollywood. The move to Los Angeles helped her personal life too. In 2007, she married British actor Adam Campbell, whom she met while filming *Epic Movie*.

Quirky, obsessive Emma Pillsbury may seem like a stretch for some actresses but not Jayma. She completely relates to Emma's craziness. "I absolutely love her, because she's so nutty," Jayma says. "She's off. And that seems more natural for me to do something that's a little quirky and offbeat." Jayma admits that some of her character's quirky habits are rubbing off on her. "I never really thought about [cleanliness] until I got this job and began to play Emma. But I will confess I am more aware now than I was before. Now I won't touch handrails, and I keep Purell in my pocketbook."

amber riley (mercedes jones)

Birth date: February 15, 1986
Audition song: "Sweet Thang" by Chaka Khan and "And I Am Telling You I'm Not Going" from *Dreamgirls*

When we refer to *Glee*'s sassy, confident fashionista with a voice that can bust your windows, we could easily be talking about Mercedes Jones or the girl who brings her to life, Amber Patrice Riley. Amber grew up singing in Long Beach, California. Her mother noticed her vocal talent when Amber was two years old and enrolled her in lessons. Her first public performance was two years later, when she sang in a local park. She was so determined to achieve stardom that she even made her own agency appointments — at eight years old! "I called this talent agency that I saw a commercial for and made my own appointment. I told my mom, 'Mom, I have an appointment at 10 a.m. on Wednesday, and you have to get me out of school.' My mom just started laughing, and her and my dad discussed it, and I actually got to go in."

Amber worked hard as a teen trying to break into both the acting and music industries by singing background and performing with the Los Angeles Opera in productions like *Alice in Wonderland, A Midsummer Night's Dream, Mystery on the Docks* and *Into the Woods*. She scored her first TV role in the 2002 Ryan Murphy project *St. Sass*, although it was never picked up. "I've always loved singing and acting equally and I was like, 'Well whichever one takes off first, I'm sure the other one will follow!'" she revealed. "It's cool because I get to do both and I love them both equally — I can't even pick one!"

Other than these few credits, Amber doesn't have a lot of professional experience. She auditioned for *American Idol* at 17 but got cut early; the rest of her television credits are pretty sparse. But she persevered and learned that she shouldn't take not getting a gig personally. "Rejection made me more resilient. I could then go out and audition for a role and [if I] didn't get it, it was like, whatever. I let it roll off my back." This professional attitude helped Amber learn that if she worked hard, her big break would be just around the corner.

She didn't know what she was getting into when she walked into the *Glee* audition. Her roommate pushed her into it after learning from the casting director that they still hadn't found their diva. "We couldn't find [Mercedes] anywhere," casting director Rob Ulrich told Emmys.com. "One day, a friend said, 'My roommate's friend sings.' This was very near the end, so I said, 'Have her come in.'" Amber thought she was auditioning for a background role and didn't stress. They asked her to sing "And I Am Telling You I'm Not Going" from *Dreamgirls*, even though Amber had never sung that song before. "I was completely mortified and terrified!" Despite her fears, the part was hers as soon as she started singing and blew everyone away.

Amber relates to Mercedes, who always seems to be around the drama but never part of it. "My high school was exactly like that," she admitted to the *Daily Voice*. "There was so much drama happening all the time. It's good to know that I'm not the only one who went to Melrose Place High School." That's not all Amber relates to. Like her character, she loves music and fashion.

It's not surprising, then, to learn that Amber has a big shoe fetish! She owns over 100 pairs (but considers her beat-up Chuck Taylors her favorite) and spent her first *Glee* paycheck on three pairs of sparkly Louboutins and, as she told Wendy Williams, "treats them like babies."

Despite her high-end footwear, Amber hasn't let success change her priorities, and her family and religion are still central in her life. "God is my greatest inspiration in life. And my family inspires and encourages me always. I'm really blessed." Amber also takes pride in being a role model. She participated in VH1's *Save the Music* and is vocal about arts education and having a positive body image. Since she loves fashion, she encourages girls to be proud of their bodies and wear what makes them happy. "Once I learned I am not my dress size and to never let anyone put me in a box, I was more content with being myself and letting the world see my light shine."

chris colfer (kurt hummel)

Birth date: May 27, 1990
Audition song: "Mr. Cellophane" from *Chicago*

Born in Fresno, California, and raised in nearby Clovis, Christopher Paul Colfer is quick to point out that he is not his character. While both Chris and Kurt grew up with a passion for performing (and both suffered socially for it), Chris actually wishes his high school experience could have been more like Kurt's. "I was definitely teased a lot in high school and I was definitely at the bottom of the food chain: total underdog, complete gleek," he told *The Advocate*. "I was never like Kurt at all; I wish I was now that I watch the show, but I was never fashionable. I wish I was like Kurt in high school!" Not that Chris completely shied away from controversy in his teen years. As a high school senior, Chris wrote, starred in and directed a spoof of *Sweeney Todd* called *Shirley Todd*, in which all of the roles were gender-reversed. But was he out in high school? "Oh, no. People are killed in my hometown for that."

Chris followed his spotlight dreams with the support of his family, especially his mother, who would accompany him on eight-hour treks to Los Angeles for auditions. After more than 30 auditions over the years, Chris ended up in front of the casting director for *Glee*. He originally auditioned for the role of Artie, and although he wasn't the right fit for that part, the casting team liked him. Chris was offered a callback with the show's producers for a new character they were writing, a character (surprise!) they wrote specifically for him. They called him Kurt because the actor once played Kurt Von Trapp in *The Sound of Music*, and Hummel because Ryan Murphy thought he looked liked the rosy-cheeked Hummel figurines. "He's never been formally trained and I just thought he was so talented and gifted and unusual," Ryan said to the *Los Angeles Times*. "I've never seen anyone who looks like him or acts like him or sounds like him. You'd think he'd been at Juilliard for six years, but he hasn't."

The role of Kurt may have been written for Chris, but the character was inspired by Ryan Murphy's own youth. Ryan grew up gay in Indiana and had a positive high school experience despite struggling with his identity, something that isn't often portrayed on television. Additionally, he thought that it was important to have a gay point of view in a musical about high school kids and self-expression. Coming from such a conservative town, however, Chris was nervous to play a character that was so confident in his sexuality, and Ryan took these concerns and Chris's own style into consideration. The actor explains, "In the original script, they were leaning on him being overly flamboyant and I didn't want to do that because it's so overdone. So I made him more internal and superior." The result? A touching portrayal of a likable but complicated young man struggling with high school.

Chris thinks the inclusion of Kurt on *Glee* was an important and bold move. He hopes that both Kurt's and Chris's stories will help kids who are different, whether they're gay, artistic or just plain unpopular. "I think coming from a small town after having grown up where I grew up, I definitely know on a personal level the type of kids that I'm affecting, because I was one of those kids," he explained to *After Elton*. "And I think whether it's the character or just my story in general coming straight from a small town to this roller coaster, to this role of *Glee*, I hope both stories are helping others out there."

jenna ushkowitz
(tina cohen-chang)

Birth date: April 28, 1986
Audition song: "Waiting for Life"
from *Once on This Island*

Jenna Noelle Ushkowitz is much more outgoing than Tina Cohen-Chang, likely thanks to her extensive perform-ing experience. Born in Seoul, South Korea, Jenna was adopted and raised in Long Island, New York, and entered show business at the tender age of three. "When I was little, my parents put me in modeling because I was one of those kids who wanted to be friends with everybody and talked to every-body at dinner in restaurants," Jenna explains. Jenna quickly landed spots in several commercials including one for Jell-O with Bill Cosby, as well as ads for Fisher-Price and Toys "R" Us. She even made an appearance on *Sesame Street*.

Her big break came in 1996 when she was cast in a Broadway revival of *The King and I*. Although she'd been doing acting work for years, it was this role that made Jenna truly realize her love for theater. "That's when it really clicked that this was something that I really loved to do. You find a community and a family." Jenna continued to pursue her passion by attend-ing a Catholic performing arts high school where she played roles in *Les Misérables, Honk!, The Baker's Wife, Into the Woods* and *The Laramie Project*, while also being a member of the show choir (making her the only member of New Directions who was in show choir in real life). She later went on to study acting in college, earning a B.A. with a major in drama and a minor in musical theater from Marymount Manhattan College in 2007. But Jenna hadn't lost the Broadway bug, so she returned to the stage, appearing in the original production of *Spring Awakening* (with *Glee* co-star Lea Michele, whom Jenna has known since she was eight years old) as the understudy for three different characters from December 2006 to January 2009.

Jenna lucked out in getting to audition for *Glee*, as one of the show's casting directors had also been a casting director for *Spring Awakening* and let most of the musical's cast try out. "I walked out of that audition and said, 'I didn't get that' and they called me back, and then they called me to L.A. and I went in for a day and I tested for network, and Tina just kinda happened from there," she explains.

Although Jenna feels very distinct from her character, she still sees some elements of herself in Tina. "I am much more bubbly and smiley but I definitely can relate to Tina's love for performing and her insecurities of fitting in, in high school. I am actually kind of shy in ways and Tina is very shy too." In addition to switching from happy to angsty and outgoing to shy, Jenna also faced a major challenge when filming the first nine episodes of *Glee* because unlike her stuttering character, Jenna has crystal clear diction. "It was really hard at the beginning. At first, it was a little more manipulated, and I had to kind of really think about it, but sometimes now I'll find myself stuttering off-set, too, just because I do it so much."

A vegetarian, Jenna cares about the environment and seeks to have a smaller carbon footprint, concerns that connect well with her lifelong desire to be a veterinarian. When asked what she would do if she wasn't acting, she replied, "I always wanted to work with animals. I really love dogs and dolphins." Jenna also hopes to return to the stage one day. "I am loving doing television, but theater is where my training is and I would love to come back."

kevin mchale (artie abrams)

Birth date: June 14, 1988
Audition song: "Let It Be" by The Beatles

Kevin Michael McHale might not have a lot of credits on his résumé, but it's safe to say he's not being typecast. He's gone from being a boy band babe to a wheelchair-bound show choir nerd. Born in Plano, Texas, Kevin was always a performer but never thought singing and acting could become a career. That all changed in the fourth grade. "My sister was an agent in Dallas," he says, "and I remember, in fourth grade, they were auditioning for some movie. I was like, 'Oh, I wanna do it!,' and she was like, 'No, you don't act. You can't.' But then, I forced her to let me audition, and I've been doing it ever since then."

Prior to his breakout role on *Glee*, Kevin's highlight reel included a bit part in an episode of *The Office*, a three-episode stint on *Zoey 101*, and a two-episode role on *True Blood*. But his biggest claim to fame was as a member of an American boy band called NLT (short for "Not Like Them"). The band was together from 2003 to 2009, but it wasn't until 2006 that producer Chris Stokes discovered the group and signed them to his label, TUG Entertainment. Although the group released four singles between March 2007 and April 2008, they never released a full album and disbanded in April 2009. But Kevin found another group that's "Not Like Them" in *Glee*'s cast of misfits and has ultimately found more success singing and dancing in a wheelchair on TV.

Not that he thought his first audition for *Glee* went particularly well. "I auditioned fairly early for Artie, and I thought I did awful. I sang 'Let It Be,' and I cut part of the song out 'cause I thought it was too boring, and then in the middle of the song, they're like, 'Okay, keep singing, don't stop!' I was like, 'I don't know any more words!' Everybody was laughing in the waiting room. But they asked me back, and then I had to wait six weeks to go test. I was a nervous wreck."

Fortunately Kevin's acting and singing prowess scored him the role of Artie, but he hadn't completely shed his boy band heartthrob look. "We actually had to give him what we call a make-under," Ryan Murphy explained to NPR, "because, you know, in this boy band stuff, he's in his tight little T-shirts and come-hither looks, and we sort of put him in these polyester, horror-show outfits."

The wheelchair was a whole other challenge. How would his smooth dance moves translate once he sat down? Kevin says that he knew about this aspect of the role from day one, but that it was the character he felt he would be best for. "And I never thought twice about it. That was it. I was like, 'Okay, I need to learn how to sit in a wheelchair and not move my legs. Each project and thing you go out for is different in some way, and I had never been out for anything in a wheelchair, but that's just what the part called for, so that's what I was going to do." Kevin didn't have a trainer to teach him how to dance in his wheelchair — he learned simply through practice. "It was just kind of in rehearsal me and Zach, the choreographer, just going over what I could do. The first number we ever learned was 'Sit Down You're Rocking the Boat' and that whole number was based around a wheelchair. So with those few days on the [pilot] I had kind of figured out what I could do." Playing a paraplegic wasn't just about learning new moves but also about stomping out old ones: "I instinctually want to start dancing and tapping my foot to the music. So I've been learning how to keep that under control."

But ride aside, Kevin relates to Artie, particularly in their joint love of performing and their disregard for what others think. "I'd have to say that I'm most like him in his passion for what he does, with the singing and the whole music thing. Everybody in the glee club all loves to do it and they do it, regardless of the entire school thinking they're complete freaks. Since fourth grade, I've always done singing, acting and dancing. I didn't care what anyone said. I was like, 'It's what I like to do. I'm sorry that you don't know what you like to do.' That's how I relate to him, in the biggest way."

mark salling (noah "puck" puckerman)

Birth date: August 17, 1982
AKA: Jericho

Mark Wayne Salling is a Texan transplant, growing up in Dallas in a Christian family with parents, John and Condy, and brother, Matthew. As a child, he had bit roles in a Heineken commercial, *Children of the Corn IV* and *Walker, Texas Ranger*, but music has always been his first love. The multi-talented musician started playing piano at age five, started writing songs at seven and eventually learned guitar, piano, bass and drums. "It was never a revelation I had, it was just what I did," he says. "Playing music was always a part of my life, I don't know anything else." Mark is athletic like Puck and participated in rugby and wrestling in high school, but he wasn't a bully. "I was mellow and kind of a hippie. I got along with everybody." After high school, Mark headed for California, enrolled in the Los Angeles Music Academy and had dreams of making it big as a rock star.

While in Los Angeles, Mark made a living with bit acting parts and teaching guitar lessons. He's got an ear for the studio as well and produced all the tracks on his debut album *Smoke Signals*, released under the name Jericho. After spending seven years living paycheck to paycheck, he thought he'd give acting one more try before heading home to Texas to launch a music career in Austin. "I enrolled in an acting class and sent out 100 packets with a head shot and résumé. I sent them to 50 different agents and 50 different managers, and one manager called me." That call led to a *Glee* audition. Mark was so intent on scoring the role of womanizer Puck that he lied about his age at the audition and was late for his regular job! He originally gave himself a Mohawk out of boredom and figured that standing out at his audition couldn't hurt. It worked and he got the gig (and so did the Mohawk).

As famous as Mark may get, he'll never forget his Texan roots, his blue heeler Hank or Tex-Mex food. A mama's boy at heart, this polite young man is grateful for his big break. "Hopefully I'll still be writing and recording music and I'll be on the show for as long as they'll have me," he says. "If I'm 35 and still in high school, so be it. I just want to keep growing as an artist."

jessalyn gilsig (terri schuester)

Birth date: November 30, 1971
AKA: Jess

From her role as Gina on *Nip/Tuck* to Terri on *Glee*, Canadian actress Jessalyn Gilsig knows how to bring the crazy. Growing up in Montreal, she attended high school at the Trafalgar School for Girls, where she dabbled in theater and art. "I was most comfortable in art class and in theater class, so that's when I felt most like myself. And then when those classes would end, and you go back out into the hall,

I was uncomfortable. I found high school kind of hard. When I was in the arts, that was when I felt like I could be myself and I was accepted and understood and I could feel a real connection with other people." She discovered acting when she was 12 years old and appeared in the National Film Board of Canada's 1984 production of *Masquerade* and their 1989 production of *The Journey Home*. That same year, she appeared in Robert DeNiro's *Jackknife*. Her parents, translator Clare and engineer Toby, were supportive but cautious. "I really, really wanted to be an actor and my parents kept saying, 'Wait until you are 18, then you can do whatever you want.' I just wasn't having it. I heard about an audition to do a voice-over and my parents said, 'If you can get there, you can go.' So, I took the bus and went to my first audition," she revealed to *South Beach*. "It just sort of never stopped. I always had the bug."

After graduating from McGill University with a degree in English, she studied at Harvard University's American Repertory Theater, where she starred in *The Cherry Orchard*, *Henry V*, *The Oresteia*, *Tartuffe* and *The Tempest*. These short years honed her acting skills, but she knew she wanted to try film and television again. Her big break came when she guest-starred on David E. Kelley's drama *The Practice*. Her role lasted a mere two episodes, but she impressed Kelley so much that he wrote the part of Lauren Davis on his next show, *Boston Public*, just for her. Jessalyn left the show after two seasons and scored another great gig — playing crazy sex addict Gina Russo on Ryan Murphy's *Nip/Tuck*. In 2008, Jessalyn had recurring roles on *Friday Night Lights* and *Heroes* and small roles in movies like *The Stepfather*, *Prom Night*, *The Horse Whisperer* and *XIII*.

Ryan wrote the role of Terri with Jessalyn in mind, and she was thrilled to take it. "[*Nip/Tuck*] was one of the best experiences as an actor I've ever had in my career. He really challenges you as an actor, and he really pushes you." Jessalyn admits that playing the most disliked person on *Glee* is difficult, but she loves the challenge. Gina Russo was another unlikable character and she stuck with her for five years. "I love playing characters like that and it's just so much fun, because you try to find the logic and you try to find the world in their head where all their choices are making sense to them, when on the outside it doesn't make any sense to anybody else. I think parts like that are challenging, but they're also really fun, because it's like a mind game."

Unlike her television marriage, Jessalyn's real one to film producer

Bobby Salomon is happy and successful. Their daughter Penelope was born on September 26, 2006. When she's not working, she enjoys spending time with her small family and letting her inner teenage art geek loose — she paints in her spare time and her artwork even appeared in the film *The Station Agent.*

iqbal theba
(principal figgins)

Birth date: December 20, 1963

You may not know his name, but you probably know his face. Iqbal Theba has over 70 television and film credits to his name, starting with a bit part in the 1993 movie *Indecent Proposal,* and moving on to guest spots on *Arrested Development* and *Friends* and recurring roles on shows like *Married . . . with Children, The George Carlin Show* and *ER.* However, it wasn't until his role as Principal Figgins in *Glee* that Iqbal finally became a full-fledged member of a television show cast.

Born in Karachi, Pakistan, Iqbal moved to the U.S. to attend college at the University of Oklahoma in 1981 and successfully earned a degree in construction engineering management — quite a far cry from acting! Fortunately for gleeks, Iqbal soon realized that his first career path wasn't the right choice for him, and he returned to his alma mater in 1986, this time to major in drama. After a few years back at school, however, Iqbal decided that his best chance for actually succeeding in acting was to, well, act. Iqbal left school in 1989 and spent a few years in New York City before he finally made the big move to Los Angeles in 1991 with only $37 in his pocket.

Like many starving artists, Iqbal waited tables to make some dough, taking whatever small roles he could get to beef up his résumé. During this time he played the most challenging role of his career: the confident aspiring actor. "From the summer of 1986 when I decided to become an actor till the end of 1994, for eight long years, every morning after I woke up, for the first five minutes I would be paralyzed with absolute fear. I could not move in my bed. All I could think was what *if* I am never able to make a living as an actor? What *if* I am 75 and still a waiter?! My whole body would get cold," he reveals. "Then I would finally find the strength to leave my bed. Once I left the bed I would be okay, ready to face the day."

Iqbal kept plugging away and discovered it was easier for him to get work in television. "Film is much more parochial; it's even difficult for women to find roles in film. . . . TV is much more open-minded. But you know, there's always been opportunity for me. If the role calls for a 40-something cabbie that doesn't speak English, I'll probably get a call, you know? But I get to make a living doing what I love, so it's great."

Even with Iqbal's easy-going attitude toward his tendency to be typecast, the actor must have been relieved when the *Glee* casting director was more open-minded. The role of Principal Figgins was written with no particular ethnicity in mind, and Iqbal was up against half-dozen or so Caucasian actors for the part. They were no match for him: he won the role of the penny-pinching principal on his first audition.

To make Principal Figgins come to life, Iqbal gets inside his head and creates a complicated backstory. "Figgins is somebody who wanted to be a CEO but is not for some reason, whatever it may be. I thought he's a guy who wanted to be somebody big but he's not and now he has to deal with it. He has to deal with all of these trivial things on a daily basis, like money, the students, the teachers and Sue; they come at him with the speed of light."

And as for whether or not we'll ever see New Directions' principal join in on the singing and dancing, if Iqbal and the show's choreographer, Zach Woodlee, have anything to say about it, we definitely will. "Our brilliant choreographer on the show saw me and said, 'We have to get you dancing!' I said, 'Sure, talk to Ryan.' I'd love it, though. I'll sing, dance, everything. It'd be a blast. You know, anything is possible on *Glee*."

patrick gallagher (ken tanaka)

Birth date: February 21, 1968

Sue Sylvester was right when she referred to Ken Tanaka's "melting pot of ethnicities." Patrick Gallagher, the actor who portrays him, was born in Chilliwack, British Columbia, has an American father and is of both Chinese and Irish descent. "Chirish," he calls it. "I'm kind of ethnically ambiguous," he said to the *Vancouver Sun*, "which is a really great opportunity."

Patrick maintains this generous and appreciative attitude toward his success in the acting world as well. After completing high school in his B.C. hometown, Patrick moved east and attended theater schools in both Toronto and Montreal in the early '90s. While he had a few small one-episode appearances in shows like *Dark Angel, Stargate SG-1* and *Smallville* in the first few years of the millennium, it wasn't until he snagged a recurring role as Detective Joe Finn on the popular Canadian drama *Da Vinci's Inquest* that Patrick started to really make a name for himself. He has since appeared as Attila the Hun in *Night at the Museum* and its sequel, and as a vampire for a four-episode stint on *True Blood*.

As for his role as Ken Tanaka, the football coach who hates football? Patrick says that although he doesn't see himself as much of a tough guy, there are more similarities between the two men than he'd like to admit. "I realized I was going for what I like to think as an older version of me from years ago. I think Ken is not happy with where he is in life. I think he's still got a good heart but there's this insecurity and bitterness piled on top of it. I think love is in Ken's head, and love for me is kind of an idealistic concept. But one thing I really respect about him is that he goes after something — he just doggedly pursues Emma. I wish I was more like that. In some ways, he's a little bit braver than I am. I mean — look at what he wears. That takes guts."

Interestingly, not all of Ken's uniform was created by *Glee*'s costume

45

designer, Lou Eyrich. The short shorts and tight T-shirts? Lou's idea. The trademark fanny pack? Patrick's idea! "The costume really helps, you just put it on and you can't help but feel a certain way. I think it's just an amalgam of my high school gym teachers and coaches in Chilliwack where I grew up."

Although Patrick's now a recurring cast member on a hit TV show, the fame isn't going to his head. He's just thrilled that he's a working actor and has been able to make a living at it for more than eight years. (His last non-acting job was as a bartender at a White Spot restaurant in Vancouver, the exact same restaurant co-star Cory Monteith worked at two years later!) Patrick hopes to continue coaching the McKinley High football team (no matter how lousy their record might be) for a few more years. Patrick loves the creative challenge *Glee* brings him, declaring that "the writing is so great that I think the real challenge is to find the balance between not trying to be too funny, not trying to make it funny, just letting it be funny, and just delivering the line and letting the writing do the work for you."

heather morris (brittany)

Birth date: February 1, 1987
AKA: HeMo

It takes a special person to make a character seem so dumb that you actually believe they think the square root of four is rainbows. Heather Morris is that person. The *New York Daily News* even called her "*Glee*'s secret weapon."

Heather's career began with dance; she took her first lesson when she was only one year old! Growing up in Arizona, she lived for dance, taking as many classes and attending as many competitions as she could. "I was a competition dancer. I did jazz, tap, contemporary dancing, everything," she says. After graduating high school, Heather decided to give a "regular" life a shot and enrolled in a local university. It didn't work. "I went to college and started living a normal life. All of a sudden, I was like, this isn't what I want to do, I want to move to L.A. and be a professional dancer." Heather felt compelled to follow her dreams because she knows how precious life is: her father passed away from cancer when she was just 14 years old. With her family's support, Heather made the risky move at 19 years old, rooming with actress Ashley Lendzion.

After a few years of dance classes and auditions, Heather thought she got her big break when she made it to the semi-final round of season 2 of the Fox dance hit *So You Think You Can Dance*. Heather auditioned with her close friend Ben Susak, but it wasn't meant to be. After a heartbreaking rejection, Heather threw herself into other projects. She was auditioning for a film when Beyoncé's choreographer spotted her. "Tina, the choreographer, called and said, 'You were dancing next to Beyoncé's old dancer and she doesn't want to be on tour. Would you like to come audition?'" Heather recalls. She worked nonstop at the auditions and caught up to Beyoncé's experienced dancers, appearing on *Saturday Night Live* and at the 2008 American Music Awards with the superstar. Dancing next to Beyoncé night after night on tour inspired Heather to push herself and follow her dreams. "She's one of the most inspiring and respectful people I've ever worked with," Heather told WKBW. "Every night she goes out there and dances her tush off."

Heather loves all aspects of performing, and, after the tour, she decided to give acting a shot, and scored small parts on *Swingtown, Fired Up!* and *Eli Stone*. Eventually, *Glee* called, wanting her to teach the "Single Ladies" dance to the cast. The show was also looking for a third Cheerio, and, before she even stepped on set, she had a cheerleader in *Glee* choreographer Zach Woodlee, who had worked with Heather on both *Fired Up!* and *Eli Stone*. Zach encouraged Heather to try out, telling her that if she came dressed for the part and ready to impress, the role could be hers. And that's exactly what happened. Heather was surprised by how easily she booked the part. "I thought I was going to have to read. I was prepared to do a read or sing but nope, I just kind of had to dance and be pretty."

Heather admits she's a lot like her character but promises she's not as dumb. However, she still has the occasional moment! "I have Brittany moments. I'm not a dumb girl but I can say some pretty stupid things sometimes. It makes the character me." She's always dreamed of having a career that showcases her different skills and *Glee* gives her that. "My favorite part about working on *Glee* is that I get to do what I love all day, everyday," she told the *Examiner*. "I get to do music, I get to dance and I get to act. It's amazing, and everybody's awesome."

naya rivera (santana lopez)

Birth date: January 12, 1987
Audition song: "Emotions" by The Bee Gees

Born and raised in Valencia, California, Naya Rivera is the woman behind McKinley High's bitchy cheerleader with a secret love for glee club. Half Puerto Rican, one-quarter German and one-quarter African American, Naya's been on the road to stardom since birth. Her mother had moved to the Los Angeles area to pursue modeling, and Naya followed her footsteps from a very young age. When Naya was eight or nine months old, her mother's talent agent began representing Naya as well, and the beautiful baby girl began working right away, appearing in Kmart commercials when she was still only crawling.

The child actress got her first real gig at the age of four, starring as Hillary Winston in the short-lived TV comedy *The Royal Family*, created by Eddie Murphy. From there she hopped in and out of guest spots on shows like *The Fresh Prince of Bel-Air, 8 Simple Rules . . . for Dating My Teenage Daughter* and *CSI: Miami*, while also snagging recurring roles on *Family Matters* and *The Bernie Mac Show*. But getting to combine her love of acting, singing and dancing in one role? Yep, *Glee* was definitely the right match for Naya. "My manager knows that I like to sing and dance so I was called in. I have always wanted to sing and dance in a TV show so she told me that this show would be perfect for me." Naya not only loves to sing, she also enjoys songwriting, a passion she heavily got into around the age of 15 as an outlet for her emotions. If she's not penning lyrics, Naya spends her free time eating sushi, shopping, hanging out with friends and reading, claiming that she's quite the bookworm when she has the time. Naya has also said in interviews that if she weren't acting, she would likely be a writer and still intends to pursue that career at some point.

What the multi-talented actress doesn't have any background in, however, is cheerleading! Her busy acting schedule kept her from pursuing that dream in high school. "I begged my parents to let me join the cheer squad my freshman year, but in the end, I was too busy acting for the time commitment it takes to be on a squad, and I didn't want to let the other girls down," Naya explained to *American Cheerleader*. "With that said, playing a cheerleader on the show gives me a chance to fulfill my abandoned high school dreams. I absolutely *love* playing a cheerleader. I get to wear a uniform for most of my scenes, and I've had the opportunity to learn some cheer moves. It's hard work!"

Although she loves her second chance at being on the squad, Naya doesn't think she has that much in common with Santana. "She loves to perform and so do I, but I am not an evil plotter. She is a really big follower just to stay popular, and I definitely did not do that in high school." On the contrary, Naya is passionate about boosting self-esteem in teens, a problem she once faced and still sometimes struggles with herself. "It takes a lot to accept yourself as you are and truly be happy with *you*. There are always going to be things you don't like about yourself or reasons to compare yourself to others, but once you realize that you only get one *you*, it's best to just love yourself."

harry shum jr. (mike chang)

Birth date: April 28, 1982
AKA: LXD, Jyve
Audition song: "L-O-V-E" by Nat King Cole

With successful gigs as an actor, dancer and choreographer already under his belt, this 27-year-old rising star is well on his way to being known as more than just "Other Asian." Born in Puerto Limon, Costa Rica, Harry, his parents and his two older sisters moved to the small town of Arroyo Grande, California, when he was five years old. Amazingly, this dancing superstar didn't discover his love for the stage until high school, when a friend dared him to join the school's dance team. As for how he actually became a good dancer, Harry thanks TV: "Training was music videos, watching music videos. I started going to different dance classes, but hip-hop wasn't really big in our little city. Hip-hop wasn't really known and guys dancing wasn't really happening much at all. I wanted to kind of change that with a couple of my friends and we did."

Harry's dancing career kicked off in 2002 when he was the only male dancer on BET's stand-up comedy show *ComicView*. Since then he's performed on tour with Beyoncé (alongside future *Glee* co-star Heather Morris), Jennifer Lopez, Mariah Carey and Jessica Simpson, danced as a silhouette in the now-iconic iPod commercials, and worked as both a dancer and choreographer for the Legion of Extraordinary Dancers. LXD is so hot that they performed on *So You Think You Can Dance* and at the 82nd Academy Awards, and their online web series premiered in 2010.

In terms of acting, Harry considers his role on *Glee* to be his big break. "Funny thing is, I didn't know how big it was. I didn't know what *Glee* was," he confesses. "I heard it was Ryan Murphy, there would be dancing and singing, it would be a really cool project. But I had no idea it would be this big. Also, I didn't know I was gonna be on the show that long. They said one episode, then it turned into two, three . . ."

Fortunately Harry's one, then two, then three episodes on *Glee* turned into him becoming a key member of McKinley High's New Directions, and Harry's not taking any of it for granted. "Man, to be able to get up in the morning and sing, dance and do what we love — you know, a lot of shows aren't able to do that," he explains. "There's a lot of shows that are comedy, but we have everything. You have comedy, drama, and you're able to sing and dance. So that's one of my favorite things, and I feel very lucky and blessed to be a part of it."

dijon talton
(matt rutherford)

Birth date: September 17, 1989
Hometown: Los Angeles, California
Audition song: A mystery,
like the man himself

Not much is known about the man who rarely speaks. It seems fitting considering how mysterious Dijon's character, Matt Rutherford, is. Dijon Hendra Talton was born under the Hollywood sign and started working at a young age, appearing in McDonald's commercials and a few children's shows. Other than that, his acting experience is limited to the little-seen 1998 film *L.A. Without a Map*. The devout Christian likes spending time on the *Glee* set with his fellow cast members. He thinks he, Heather, Naya and Harry bonded because their characters joined New Directions around the same time.

He's excited that New Directions is letting Matt find himself and his true talents and that he isn't subjected to the pressures of being cool so much anymore. "I think he's always wanted to, but living in a place like they do in such a small town where you're either a loser or you're a football player or basketball player, he chose to be a cool guy," Dijon speculates. "Finn's character made it kind of okay to be honest with yourself and be like, you know, I'd like to do something more than what's been put right in front of me and Matt jumped on board."

josh sussman
(jacob ben israel)

Birth date: December 30, 1983
Hometown: Teaneck, New Jersey

Josh Sussman, who plays the nerd with the Jewfro and a huge hankering for Rachel Berry, studied acting at the School for Film and Television in New York City before embarking on his career. Josh connects with his unpopular character and admits he was a lot like him growing up: "Well, I wasn't the most popular kid in high school." Instead, he was a member of the chess club and the drama club and loved playing Connect Four. After high school, he decided to pursue acting and scored small parts in *What About Brian* and the kiddie hits *Drake & Josh* and *The Suite Life of Zack & Cody*, along with a six-episode stint on *Wizards of Waverly Place* before landing the role of Jacob Ben Israel on *Glee*.

Josh originally auditioned for a one-episode stint as a jock in the celibacy club. He wasn't right for that part, but Ryan Murphy changed it to suit Josh and greatly expanded the role for him, turning him into Rachel Berry's biggest fan. "People say I'm creepy, but I like to think I'm endearing also," he told *Young Hollywood*. "It's like a creepy endearing."

Josh is the only cast member on *Glee* who can't sing and promises we'll never be subjected to hearing him try! He does, however, enjoy playing the role of the nerdy stalker. "I love creeping Rachel out!"

season one:
may 2009–june 2010

Recurring cast: Max Adler (Dave Karofsky), Jennifer Aspen (Kendra Giardi), Kent Avenido (Howard Bamboo), Kristin Chenoweth (April Rhodes), Kenneth Choi (Dr. Wu), Earlene Davis (Andrea Carmichael), James Earl II (Azimio), Eve (Grace Hitchens), Ethan Freedman (Giardi Triplet #1), Aidan Freedman (Giardi Triplet #2), Ben Freedman (Giardi Triplet #3), Josh Groban (Himself), Jonathan Groff (Jesse St. James), Michael Hitchcock (Dalton Rumba), Bill A. Jones (Rod Remington), Michael Loeffelholz (Phil Giardi), Idina Menzel (Shelby Corcoran), Olivia Newton-John (Herself), Mike O'Malley (Burt Hummel), Romy Rosemont (Carole Hudson), Molly Shannon (Brenda Castle), Stephen Tobolowsky (Sandy Ryerson)

♪♫♪

1.01 "pilot"
Original Air Date: May 19, 2009
Director's Cut Air Date: September 2, 2009
Written by: Ryan Murphy, Brad Falchuk and Ian Brennan
Directed by: Ryan Murphy

The Music: ★ ★ ★

The Drama: ★ ★ ✦
The Laughs: ★ ★ ✦

Rachel: Being a part of something special makes you special, right?

Will Schuester, William McKinley High School's Spanish teacher, takes over glee club (a group of "sub-basement" social misfits), recruits the football team's quarterback to his musical cause and remembers why he's a teacher in the first place.

Welcome to William McKinley High School in Lima, Ohio, where jocks and cheerleaders reign supreme and it's a good day for the school's social rejects if they don't get hit with a slushie facial. But this hierarchy is shaken up when Will Schuester takes over glee club and gets the golden-boy quarterback singing and dancing with the school's losers. Whether Will's new hobby is his shot to regain some former glory (as his wife Terri thinks) or an attempt to share something he loves with his students (as guidance counselor Emma Pillsbury believes) will become one of the ongoing questions of the show. This "new direction" isn't without problems — the school doesn't fund the program, there are only five interested students, and Will's wife's pregnancy is causing financial trouble in the Schuester household.

This episode introduces us to the social structure of McKinley High and the show's three main characters: Rachel Berry, the unpopular but determined self-described "stunning, young ingénue"; Finn Hudson, the well-meaning but dimwitted quarterback; and Will Schuester, the Spanish-teacher-cum-glee-club-director.

Rachel proves to be one of the most indomitable characters on television, getting former glee club director Sandy Ryerson fired to amp up her chance at stardom. Despite slushies in the face, derogatory comments on her MySpace page, and what she deems sub-par fellow glee club members, she marches on, planting gold stars after her signature until she can have one on her dressing room door and masking her loneliness with a picture-perfect smile and knee-high socks.

Popular quarterback Finn Hudson seems like a good guy — he lets Kurt remove his jacket before the football team puts him in the Dumpster, wants to make his mom proud and helps Artie out of a smelly predicament — but the social pressures of being a football player dictate many of his decisions. While originally forced into glee club by Mr. Schuester, Finn rediscovers the love for music he had as a boy and comes to care about the club. But with glee club being the uncoolest thing in school, how long can Finn toe the line between playing football and being footloose? Popularity is a fickle thing, and not even the quarterback is exempt from the ridicule glee club brings its members: Finn gets paintballed behind the school once his football pals find out what he's up to behind their back.

From this one episode, we can already see the clear parallels between the adult and teen characters on the show. Will and Finn, two good guys held down by their demanding partners, rediscover their childhood love for performing. Their partners, however, care more about currency (cold hard cash for Terri and social status for Finn's cheerleader girlfriend, Quinn Fabray) than they do their partners' happiness. Emma and Rachel, on the other hand, encourage their crushes to follow their dreams and do what they love. Their motivations may be selfish (Emma would miss having Will around and Rachel needs Finn as her male lead) but their deeds are good.

It also looks like family is going to play an important role on *Glee*. Rachel's two gay dads have been a huge influence on her life, putting her in singing and dancing lessons early and encouraging her dreams of stardom. Finn's mom raised him alone after his father died in the first Gulf War and, as a result, his desire to make his mom proud influences nearly every decision he makes. These family members may only be minor characters, but they could have major impact.

Glee has a large ensemble cast, but everyone except the three leads was background material in this episode. We meet the high-strung guidance counselor Emma Pillsbury and the aggressive cheerleading coach Sue Sylvester, who are both destined to become more central in future episodes. Emma's crush on Will threatens to cause tension as Will's family grows, and disdain from Sue and football coach Ken Tanaka toward the glee club will be problematic as the coaches fight over the school's limited resources and its students' time. Kurt, Mercedes, Tina and Artie bring diversity, depth and humor to New Directions and we're left wanting to know more about these so-called misfits. The Cheerios and other football players appear to be one-dimensional slaves to popularity, but it's only the first episode. Who knows what will happen in the halls of McKinley High?

High Note: Vocal Adrenaline's performance of Amy Winehouse's "Rehab" and New Directions' rendition of "Don't Stop Believin'" set the bar high for original show-stopping musical numbers.

The cast performing "Don't Stop Believin'," the song that started it all, at the 2010 White House Easter Egg Roll.

Low Note: Kurt, Tina, Artie and Mercedes all seem like really interesting characters, but we unfortunately don't get to see much of them in the pilot. Artie doesn't even get to sing a New Directions audition piece! Hopefully, we'll see more of them in future episodes.

Behind the Music:

"Where Is Love?" (Hank and Sandy)

Oliver! (1960)

Based on Charles Dickens' 1838 novel *Oliver Twist*, the musical *Oliver!* is the tale of a young orphan in England who is born into a workhouse, then sold into servitude before running away to join a gang of pickpockets in London. "Where is Love?," penned by Lionel Bart, is sung by Oliver after he's tossed into a cellar for fighting with another servant, and he sings the song while pining for his beloved mother that he never knew. After the twin trials of trying to save a floundering glee club and then being fired, Sandy, like Oliver, feels alone, unloved and unsupported.

"Respect" (Mercedes)

Aretha Franklin, *I Never Loved a Man the Way I Love You* (1967)

"Respect," Aretha Franklin's most famous song and #5 on *Rolling Stone*'s list

director's cut differences

Two versions of this episode were created: an extended-length director's cut and the hour-long episode that aired as the official pilot on May 19, 2009. Both versions eventually aired on Fox and the director's cut is the version available on the *Glee: Season 1* DVDs. If you didn't get a chance to watch the director's cut, here's what you missed on *Glee*:

- The show opens with the 1993 Glee National Invitational.
- In a voice-over, Will wonders how "glee fell so far so fast" and blames Sandy Ryerson and the rise of the Cheerios. Will also reveals he ran over Terri's dog on prom night and mentions rumors that Sue posed for *Penthouse* magazine and takes horse estrogen.
- The scenes where Rachel catches Sandy Ryerson, and Principal Figgins fires him are extended.
- Will forces the glee club to wear the hideous 1993 costumes. Thanks to Mercedes' insistence, everyone avoids wearing a polyester nightmare.
- When Will tries to talk to the football team, Puck farts in front of everyone.
- Ken calls Will out on "stealing" his quarterback and asks Emma to the Monster Truck "Truckasauraus" rally. Apparently, Ken asks Emma out (and is rejected) regularly.
- Will performs "Leaving on a Jet Plane," accompanied by a montage of him taking the accounting test and Emma doodling like a lovestruck teen on Will's yearbook page.

of the 500 Greatest Songs of All Time, was written and recorded by Otis Redding and covered by Aretha a few years later. Aretha's version became a feminist anthem and turned her into an R&B superstar, winning her Grammy Awards for Best Rhythm & Blues Recording and Best Rhythm & Blues Solo Vocal Performance, Female. Mercedes, who sings "Respect" for her New Directions audition, feels ignored and overshadowed by Rachel. She wants the recognition she deserves, both in glee club and outside of it.

"Mr. Cellophane" (Kurt)
Chicago (1975)
Set in Prohibition-era Chicago, *Chicago* is a satirical tale of corruption in the criminal justice system. Amos Hart, husband of murderous showgirl Roxy, sings "Mr. Cellophane" after he realizes he's irrelevant and invisible to his wife and everyone around him. Kurt, like Amos, feels invisible and

unappreciated. He's only noticed at McKinley High when the football team decides to torment him, and no doubt getting Dumpster-dumped is recognition Kurt (and his Marc Jacobs collection) could do without.

"I Kissed a Girl" (Tina)
Katy Perry, *One of the Boys* (2008)
Tina's audition song, a tale of bi-curiosity and ChapStick, was Katy Perry's breakout single, topping the Billboard Hot 100 chart and scoring a Grammy nomination for Best Female Pop Vocal Performance. This provocative song made Katy instantly edgy — a quality that outsider Tina has in spades. She doesn't get much screen time in this episode, but her punk rock look and provocative dance moves say it all.

"On My Own" (Rachel)
Les Misérables (1980)
"On My Own," a signature number from the "seminal Broadway classic" *Les Misérables*, is a heartbreaking song about unrequited love. Selecting such a famous and difficult piece proves Rachel means business and cements her status as New Directions' star, but it also underscores the facts she's a lonely, driven young girl whose quest for fame is all she really has. Her Broadway bravado hides her private pain.

"Sit Down, You're Rockin' the Boat" (New Directions)
Guys and Dolls (1950)
Frank Loesser wrote this song about petty criminals and professional gamblers in 1940s New York in 1950, and later that year, it made its way into the Broadway musical *Guys and Dolls*. "Sit Down, You're Rockin' the Boat" is sung to calm a crowd down after a big score. The McKinley High glee club boat was certainly rocked: Sandy is out, Will is in, and now he's changed the club's name and is actively recruiting members. Will needs to slow down and sit down if he's going to effectively steer this ship in a "new direction."

"Can't Fight This Feeling" (Finn)
REO Speedwagon, *Wheels Are Turnin'* (1984)
"Can't Fight This Feeling," a classic-rock power ballad penned by lead vocalist Kevin Cronin, became REO Speedwagon's second #1 hit. While the song

is about discovering romantic feelings for a long-time friend, it helps Finn discover his long-lost love of music and realize that he can't fight enjoying glee anymore.

"Lovin', Touchin', Squeezin'" (Darren and Young Finn)
Journey, *Evolution* (1979)
"Lovin', Touchin', Squeezin'," which tells the heartbreaking tale of a woman leaving her man for someone else, featured lyrics from gospel and R&B singer Sam Cooke's 1962 hit "Nothing Can Change This Love." Emerald Dreams employee Darren dated Finn's mom but left her for a hot blonde. The teen-aged Finn is dating his own hot blonde, but since Quinn is president of the celibacy club, lovin', touchin' and squeezin' is exactly what he won't be doing.

"You're the One That I Want" (New Directions)
Grease (motion picture version, 1978)
Danny and Sandy, two kids from different worlds, declare their love for each other in *Grease*'s "You're the One That I Want." Although the song wasn't in the original 1972 stage production of the musical, it became a huge hit when the soundtrack was released prior to the film, resulting in a *Glee*-esque phenomenon where the music buoyed the success of the movie. What Rachel wants is a male lead that can help make her a star. When Finn comes along, Rachel wants him (in more ways than one), while Finn wants to stay in glee club, even if it means a regular schedule of slushie facials.

"Rehab" (Vocal Adrenaline)
Amy Winehouse, *Back to Black* (2006)
Amy Winehouse's self-penned bluesy hit about not wanting help for her alcoholism won Grammys for Record of the Year, Song of the Year and Best Female Pop Vocal Performance, a feat even more impressive than Vocal Adrenaline's show-stopping performance. New Directions was getting cocky after Finn joined, but after seeing Vocal Adrenaline perform, they realize they need to go to glee club rehab if they're ever going to compete on Vocal Adrenaline's level.

"Leaving on a Jet Plane" (Will)
Peter, Paul and Mary, *Album 1700* (1967)
Originally titled "Oh Babe, I Hate to Go," John Denver's folk song about reluctantly leaving a loved one behind became Peter, Paul and Mary's only #1

hit, even though the band was one of the biggest and most influential acts of the 1960s. Will may not be leaving on a jet plane, but in the director's cut of the pilot he uses this song to say a bittersweet goodbye to McKinley High.

"Don't Stop Believin'" (New Directions)
Journey, *Escape* (1981)
Journey's iconic recording about following your dreams and never giving up could be *Glee*'s theme song. New Directions has several obstacles to overcome: they have only six members, they have no money or support from the school, they are not popular, and Sue Sylvester is out to get them. Yet, as long as they don't stop believin', they can, and will, succeed. New Directions can look to the song itself for inspiration: while it was never a #1 hit, over 20 years later it's one of the most popular song downloads of all time.

Give My Regards to Broadway: Based on the 1862 novel of the same name by Victor Hugo, *Les Misérables* follows many characters living in 19th-century France who are connected in unexpected ways as they seek love, redemption and personal and political change. *Les Mis* was originally a French production, until *Cats* producer Cameron Mackintosh agreed to bring it to an English stage and it opened in London's West End in 1985. Critics were convinced the complicated plots and heavy subject matter would turn audiences away, but the show became a huge success. It premiered on Broadway on March 12, 1987, and was nominated for 12 Tony Awards, winning four, including Best Musical. It closed on May 18, 2003, after 6,680 performances, making it the third longest-running Broadway show in history, after *The Phantom of the Opera* and *Cats*. A film adaptation of the stage musical has been in the works for years, but nothing concrete has developed.

That's Pretty *Popular*: On *Popular*, star quarterback Josh Ford auditions for the school musical — and scores the lead role — against the wishes of his father, coach, girlfriend and teammates. Josh's girlfriend is popular blonde virginal cheerleader Brooke McQueen. Her nemesis? Unpopular brunette go-getter Sam McPherson, who'll stop at nothing to become an award-winning journalist. The faculty looks familiar as well, with an eager young teacher looking to make a difference and a hardened veteran out to make the kids' lives miserable. "I wanted her to be the meanest teacher alive and totally androgynous," Ryan Murphy told Television Without Pity about Roberta Glass, the villainous biology teacher in *Popular*. That same description fits cheerleading coach Sue Sylvester as well as her wardrobe of androgynous tracksuits.

Slushie Facials:
- Kurt is dumped in a trash bin.
- Rachel gets a red slushie in her face.
- Rachel gets the following messages on MySpace:
  - Sky Splits: If I were your parents, I would send you back.
  - Hi Ho Cheerio: I'm going to scratch out my eyes.
  - The Cheerios: Please get sterilized.
- Offscreen, the football team shaved off a teammate's eyebrows for watching *Grey's Anatomy*.
- Finn is pelted with paintballs by the football team.
- The football team nearly toppled Artie in a Porta-Potty.
- We hear that Finn threw eggs at Rachel, pee balloons at Kurt and the football team nailed Kurt's lawn furniture to the roof.
- The football team signed up Gaylord Weiner, Butt Lunch and Penis for New Directions.

Off-Key:
- What happened to the former glee club members, aside from Rachel? If numbers were already low, why did Mr. Schue feel the need to have people audition again?
- On the New Directions audition sheet, Tina signs her name like she says it, TTTTTTina C. But after Rachel signs the sheet, the name above reads Tina C.
- Also on the sign-up sheet, Artie's name is spelled Arty.
- When Finn is singing in the shower, you can see Cory Monteith's armband tattoo on his right upper arm. His tattoo is usually covered by shirtsleeves or makeup to make Finn seem younger and more innocent.

Behind the Scenes:
- Finn's shower song, "Can't Fight This Feeling," was not Cory Monteith's audition song, as rumored. He received the pilot script (which already included this number) before sending in his tape. Cory sang that song

the evolution of *glee*: script differences

Like all good TV shows, *Glee* went through many drafts and many changes before its pilot script turned into what we see on screen. We were lucky enough to get our hands on a draft of the pilot episode from July 2008 and some of the differences are shocking! Here are a few of the bigger changes:

- Sue Sylvester? Not in the picture! The coach everyone loves to hate didn't even exist when this draft was written.
- Finn's girlfriend and president of the Celibacy Club was Liz Fabray and there's no mention of her being a cheerleader. She also doesn't have any dialogue!
- The kids of New Directions attended Harrison High School, not McKinley, in this version.
- There is an extensive Rachel flashback scene in which we see her being born via her surrogate mother with her two gay dads present, as well as a flashback scene of her auditioning for *American Idol* and being told by Simon Cowell, "Rachel, you strike me as a girl who people don't like very much."
- Since the role of Kurt was written specifically for Chris Colfer, Kurt wasn't in this draft. Instead, an Indian character named Rajeesh was the one the jocks threw into the Dumpster. There were also hints at a potential relationship between Rajeesh and Mercedes.
- Several songs changed between this draft and the final version. For her MySpace page Rachel sings "Look at Me, I'm Sandra Dee" from *Grease* instead of "On My Own" from *Les Misérables*; in Finn's first glee club rehearsal the group practices "Summer Lovin'" from *Grease* instead of "You're the One That I Want" from the same movie; and Vocal Adrenaline performs Robbie Williams' "Let Me Entertain You" instead of Amy Winehouse's "Rehab" at their invitational.
- Will actually accepted the job at H.W. Menken and spent a few days working there before he met with Emma and she convinced him that this wasn't the right career path for him.

for his audition package, but to this day is uncertain as to whether that tape actually made it to Fox. For his Los Angeles callbacks, he sang Billy Joel's "Honesty."

- Rachel's audition song, "On My Own," was Lea Michele's audition song. The original script called for "Look at Me, I'm Sandra Dee," but the song was changed after Lea impressed the producers with her version of the *Les Mis* classic.
- Kurt's New Directions audition song "Mr. Cellophane" was Chris Colfer's *Glee* audition song.

- The pilot was shot mostly at Cabrillo High School in Long Beach, California, over 17 days. Once the show was picked up, sets were built on the Paramount Studios lot in Hollywood. The new sets were closely based on Cabrillo to keep the same look and feel. However, the onstage performance numbers are still shot in Cabrillo's theater.
- "You think that's hard?" was actually a line improvised by Jane Lynch. Ryan Murphy liked it so much that he began to use variations of it throughout the show as a running gag.
- Lauren Gottlieb, a season 3 *So You Think You Can Dance* finalist, shows off her skills as a dancer for Vocal Adrenaline.
- Jayma Mays eats peanut butter every single day. Emma may not eat it every day, but she shares a PB&J sandwich with Will at Vocal Adrenaline's performance!
- Finn craves Sour Patch Kids before Vocal Adrenaline's performance. Could this be a nod to *Kyle XY*? Cory Monteith was on the ABC Family show in the 2006–07 season. Sour Patch Kids were the show's official sponsor and were referenced in almost every episode.
- Getting clearance for "Don't Stop Believin'" was difficult because Steve Perry, Journey's former frontman, was worried about his song being overexposed. After much persuading, he eventually agreed.

Center Stage:

- Puck says, "It's Hammertime." Rapper MC Hammer said this in the 1990 hit "U Can't Touch This" from his album *Please Hammer, Don't Hurt 'Em*. It became Hammer's catchphrase and *Hammertime* became the name of his A&E reality show that premiered in 2009.
- William McKinley High School was also the name of the school in NBC's *Freaks and Geeks*, another show about teenaged misfits.
- Will's former glee club director Lillian Adler shares a last name with two major music minds: Broadway actor Luther Adler, who performed in *Awake and Sing!*, *Alien Corn*, *Paradise Lost*, *Johnny Johnson* and *Golden Boy* in the 1930s, and record producer Lou Adler who worked with acts like Sam Cooke, The Mamas & The Papas, Carole King and Cheech and Chong.
- Kelly Rowland is a member of Beyoncé's original group, Destiny's Child. Kelly, like Beyoncé, is now a solo artist. She also earned several TV and film credits and hosted Bravo's reality show *The Fashion Show* in 2009.

- Will applies for a job at H.W. Menken. Alan Menken is a renowned musical theater and film composer who won eight Academy Awards for his work on films like *Aladdin, Beauty and the Beast, The Little Mermaid* and *Pocahontas.*
- Quinn calls Rachel "RuPaul." RuPaul is the world's most famous drag queen, a former talk show host and a successful recording artist. Currently she is the host of the reality TV competition *RuPaul's Drag Race.*

Jazz Hands:
- Sue's Cheerios were on Fox Sports Net last year. Fox Sports Net is an affiliate channel of Fox, the channel airing *Glee* in the U.S.
- When Will is accusing Finn of marijuana possession, the poster behind him says, "Priority #1: Help the Kids."
- Vocal Adrenaline's adorable polka-dotted blue and black dresses were designed by Betsey Johnson.

The Buckeye State: Lima, Ohio, is a real town in northwestern Ohio, with approximately 38,000 residents. Founded in 1831, it is best known for its oil production and railroads. Al Jardine of The Beach Boys, actress Phyllis Diller and professional wrestler Al Snow all hail from Lima. However, William McKinley Jr., the 25th president of the United States (who served from March 4, 1897, until he was assassinated on September 14, 1901) didn't, even though this (fictional) Lima school is named after him. He was born in Niles, Ohio, 200 miles east of Lima. Ryan Murphy chose to set *Glee* in Lima because it was similar to the small town Indiana he was familiar with from his childhood. Even though anywhere in Middle America could have worked, Ryan remembered Lima from his childhood because of the major tornadoes that had hit it one year, making it a major news story.

How Sue Cs It: "Your resentment is delicious."

♪♫♪

1.02 "showmance"

Original Air Date: September 9, 2009
Written by: Ryan Murphy, Brad Falchuk and Ian Brennan
Directed by: Ryan Murphy

The Music: ★ ★ ♪
The Drama: ★ ★ ★
The Laughs: ★ ★ ♪

Will (to Sue): I know you're used to being the cock of the walk around here, but it looks like your cheerleaders are going to have some competition.

Mr. Schuester needs more kids if he wants the glee club to succeed and plans a school assembly to attract new recruits. In an effort to not embarrass the few members the club currently has, Rachel turns to the one thing she knows will get everyone's attention: sex.

With Mr. Schue at the helm and their minds focused on Regionals, the New Directions kids are getting more comfortable with their sub-basement social status. But it wouldn't be high school (or TV teen drama) if there weren't still Frankenteen-sized hurdles constantly getting in the way of their happiness and self-acceptance.

Hurdle numero uno is the glee club kids' constant struggle for popularity. Needing 12 members to perform at Regionals, Mr. Schue signs them up to perform at a school pep rally, hoping the performance will garner some new recruits. But with their fearless leader stuck in 1993 and dead-set on re-reviving disco, rotten fruit seems more likely than rousing applause. (Sure, these kids endure daily slushie facials, but at least those taste good when they're thrown at you!) It's hard to say what's more frustrating: being embarrassed in front of the whole school or having a teacher that doesn't listen to your concerns. Will may mean well, but a little understanding could go a long way to helping the members of New Directions come into their own.

Then there's hurdle number two: love. Pat Benatar is right: love is a battlefield. Emma and Rachel's yearning for the strong, simple-minded types isn't reciprocated, but when their love interests tease them with gentle touches (Will to the nose, Finn to the lip) and make matching clothing choices (periwinkle for Will and Emma, maroon for Finn and Rachel), how can they

famous people who were in glee clubs

Rachel was right: Being in glee club can make you a star! Here are just ten big names that once sang and danced in a show choir:

1. **Woodrow Wilson, 28th President of the United States:** In 1879, Woodrow Wilson attended law school at the University of Virginia, and although he never graduated, the future president was a prominent member of the Virginia Glee Club during that year.
2. **Cole Porter, composer and songwriter:** While at Yale University from 1909 to 1913, Cole Porter sang in both the Yale Glee Club and the school's a cappella group, the Yale Whiffenpoofs. He wrote an astonishing 300 songs while at Yale, including several of the school's football fight anthems.
3. **Ashton Kutcher, actor:** Mr. Demi Moore was both a football stud and a glee heartthrob at Clear Creek-Amana High School, which he attended from 1992 to 1996. He could teach Finn a thing or two about balancing sports and singing!
4. **Blake Lively, actor:** While Ashton might be an early version of Finn, it seems that Quinn might be channeling Blake Lively, best known as Serena van der Woodsen on *Gossip Girl*. She attended Burbank High School from 2001 to 2005, where she was part of the school's show choir and cheerleading team.
5. **Theodore Roosevelt, 26th President of the United States:** The president stayed very busy while attending Harvard College (part of Harvard University) from 1876 to 1880: he was active in rowing, boxing, the Delta Kappa Epsilon fraternity and the Harvard Glee Club.
6. **Franklin D. Roosevelt, 32nd President of the United States:** Not only did FDR follow in his cousin's footsteps by becoming president, but he also sang in the Harvard Glee Club during his time at Harvard College from 1900 to 1904.
7. **Bob McGrath, actor and singer:** Best known in his role as Bob on *Sesame Street*, Bob attended the University of Michigan from 1950 to 1954 and was a member of the University of Michigan's Men's Glee Club.
8. **Lance Bass, singer:** Before joining 'N Sync, Lance was a member of the national award-winning Attaché Show Choir at Clinton High School which he attended from 1993 to 1997.
9. **Glenn Close, actor:** For several years in the mid-to-late 1960s, Glenn performed in Up with People, a motivational organization and musical performance group known as one of the first creators of the show choir concept.
10. **Marc Cherry, writer and producer:** Before he became the creator of *Desperate Housewives*, Marc toured with Young Americans, another one of the show choirs credited with starting the craze in the 1960s.

resist? Both Will and Finn need to stop playing with fire when it comes to these poor girls' hearts.

Things aren't much better for Will's wife or Finn's girlfriend. Thanks to their partner's flirtations, Terri and Quinn feel threatened and aren't being honest with their partners. Terri lies about her pregnancy, but she's doing it to save her marriage. And Quinn's newfound interest in glee club isn't just about spying for Sue Sylvester: she's trying to save her own relationship as well.

Quinn wins round one in the battle over Finn's heart. Rachel may end the episode singing about her broken heart, but her confidence was sky high earlier on, as it seems for the first time what she'd hoped is coming true — she's finally being respected, and accepted, for her talents. Standing up for her own beliefs about teenage sexuality and using the "sex sells" concept to attract new students to the glee club takes guts. Will she rediscover this confidence and learn that Finn's just scared and confused?

As for Will and Terri, their problems are a bit more complicated. Terri wants a bigger house for her bun in the oven, budget be damned! Always the supportive husband (well, except for when he's flirting with Emma), Will takes on a part-time gig as a school janitor to help make ends meet, while Terri continues to hide the fact that her pregnancy is of the hysterical variety. Between Will's not-so-innocent flirtation and Terri's lies, there's going to be trouble ahead for these high school sweethearts if they don't start being more honest with each other soon.

While "showmance" usually refers to onstage love continuing after the curtain, it also refers to romantic relationships concocted for the sake of cameras and television. While the first meaning is evident in this episode in Rachel and Finn, the more sinister side of the episode's title could apply to its other troubled pairings. When it comes to Finn and Quinn, and Will and Terri, is it possible their relationships are just for show? And will the eyes of their imagined audience eventually become less important than maintaining their acts to each other?

High Note: Everything from the kneepads to Kurt slapping Finn's butt during "Push It" is amazingly inappropriate. Emma's awkward dancing, Principal Figgins' oblivious swaying and Sue's and Will's looks of horror only enhance the performance.

Low Note: Wow, Finn and Rachel move fast! Not only do Finn's feelings for

Rachel come out of nowhere, but he has a girlfriend! What's up with all the infidelity around McKinley High?

Behind the Music:

"Le Freak" (New Directions)
Chic, *C'est Chic* (1978)
When Chic members Nile and Bernard were denied entry into Studio 54, the most famous club of the 1970s, they were inspired to write their #1 hit "Le Freak" as retaliation. They didn't need Studio 54 to have fun and New Directions doesn't need "Le Freak" to embarrass them. While Mr. Schue is set on reliving his glee club glory days, New Directions is worried that performing this song will prove their peers right in calling them "freaks."

"Gold Digger" (Will with New Directions)
Kanye West featuring Jamie Foxx, *Late Registration* (2005)
Kanye's smash single (it spent nine weeks at #1) tells the story of a wealthy, hardworking man being conned for his money by the women in his life. Jamie Foxx (channeling his role as Ray Charles from the 2004 film *Ray*) adds the soulful interpolation. The song was originally written in 2004, from a female viewpoint, but was changed after rapper Shawnna turned it down. Like Kanye, Will and Finn are dealing with a couple of gold diggers: Terri wants a dream house that is way beyond Will's budget, while Quinn demands Finn drop any activity that might rob him of some of the ultimate high school currency — popularity.

"All by Myself" (Emma)
Eric Carmen, *Eric Carmen* (1975)
Guidance counselor Emma Pillsbury is lonely and her romantic prospects look bleak. It's no wonder she connects with Eric Carmen's power ballad about being lonely and unlucky in love. Several artists, like Céline Dion and Frank Sinatra, have since covered this heart-wrenching hit. Eric's original version featured a seven-minute piano solo and borrowed from the Raspberries' "Let's Pretend" and from Sergei Rachmaninoff's Piano Concerto No. 2 in C minor, Opus 18.

"Push It" (New Directions)
Salt-n-Pepa, *Hot, Cool & Vicious* (1986)
"Push It" allowed Salt-n-Pepa and rap music to break into the mainstream

q&a: jennifer aspen as kendra giardi

As Kendra, Terri's loony sister, Jennifer Aspen performs the miraculous feat of making Terri occasionally look sane. Born October 6, 1976, in Richmond, Virginia, Jennifer has been a star since high school. After scoring the lead in her high school production of *How to Succeed in Business Without Really Trying*, she went on to study theater at UCLA's School of Theater, Film and Television. Since then, Jennifer has been working steadily in theater, film and television, starring in *Party of Five, Bob Patterson, Rodney, Vanilla Sky, Mr. Woodcock* and *A Very Brady Sequel*. A practicing Scientologist, Jennifer lives in Los Angeles with her husband. She won the role of Kendra on *Glee* after auditioning for the role of Terri. She lost that part, but Ryan Murphy liked her so much that he wrote the character of Kendra specifically for her.

We contacted Jennifer, and the gracious actress (who is nothing like her crazy character!) took a few minutes to give us a little extra insight into playing the role of Kendra:

How do you see Kendra?
I love being Kendra. She's crazy, but she totally knows it. With her, I completely become her. Once I get into the wardrobe, it's like I flip a switch and I'm a nut. Her wardrobe is insane, so il makes for a great gateway. It's incredibly fun and there's a lot of freedom with a character like Kendra. You can say anything and it works. It's so easy to riff off the character and improvise.

Do you see any good intentions behind Kendra's actions?
The thing that is good about her is that she is like a rock for Terri. She'll do anything for Terri. Even if she has to fake a pregnancy and steal someone's baby, she's going to make it happen for Terri. I definitely play for that when I'm being Kendra. It's a strong quality for someone to have, even if her actions are crazy. There's nothing she wouldn't do for Terri. *(Continued on next page.)*

market in the late '80s and '90s. The line "This dance ain't for everybody, only the sexy people" was a shout-out to funk band The Time's signature song "The Bird." Rachel decides to give her peers a taste of the sex they're craving, but she's not the only one pushing buttons: Finn is pushing social boundaries by performing with New Directions in front of the entire school.

"I Say a Little Prayer" (Quinn with Santana and Brittany)
Dionne Warwick, *The Windows of the World* (1967)
Dionne Warwick's ode to American soliders fighting in the Vietnam War was her only 1960s song to reach the one million sales mark, despite the fact it was never meant to be released a single. Quinn may be religious and say her

If Kendra were to sing a song, what song would she sing?
I begged to have a song in the Madonna episode, but it didn't happen. I wasn't hired for my voice or to sing, but I can carry a tune. I did start out in musical theater and think it's the most miraculous thing. I'm not like Lea or Matthew, but I want to sing so bad. I think Kendra should sing a song in Will's nightmare. He's having a nightmare about, like, selecting a song list for Regionals or is worrying about the competition or something and Kendra shows up singing "Umbrella" [by Rihanna].

What's the best part about being on *Glee*?
I definitely looked for a long time for something special and different. When I first read the script, I knew that's what it was and that's what I was looking for. I'm going to shoot this pilot, it's going to be a huge hit, and it's going to win every award. I knew it was going to be something different. When I watch the show, I get moments where I tear up, moments where I laugh, moments where I'm completely moved. *Glee* is more than everyday television; it's incredible and it's really special.

prayers regularly, but this time she does more than pray: she takes action and joins glee club herself.

"Take a Bow" (Rachel with Tina and Mercedes)
Rihanna, *Good Girl Gone Bad* (2007)
Rihanna's #1 hit tells her boyfriend to leave or "take a bow" because she's through with his cheating and lying, even though the break-up is breaking her heart. Rachel can relate, as Finn appears to have taken advantage of her and then lied about it — an offense serious enough to sap the sparkle from Rachel's permasmile.

That's Pretty *Popular*: Both Sam and Rachel have a thing for singing jocks with girlfriends who don't put out. Both schools have cheerleader-run abstinence clubs and Glamazon Poppy Fresh is the president at Kennedy High. Budgets are tight at both schools, but it looks like Kennedy High's janitorial union is stronger. Instead of getting canned when cash runs low, their janitors go on strike in "Wild, Wild Mess" to fight for better wages and working conditions.

Slushie Facials:
- Kurt is thrown in the Dumpster by the football team.
- Rachel gets a double dose of blue slushie.

Off-Key:
- The gag reflex line seemed so out of character for the prim and proper Emma.

Behind the Scenes:
- This is the first episode with Heather Morris (Brittany) and Josh Sussman (Jacob).
- "Take a Bow" was the first song to be offered to *Glee* at a reduced licensing rate (something that occurred regularly in future episodes).
- The Dumpster Kurt is tossed in may contain garbage bags filled with pillows, but that doesn't mean it's not dangerous! Chris Colfer sprained his toe on one of the many takes it took to get this right.
- The porcelain dog on top of the bookshelf in the choir room used to belong to one of Matthew Morrison's favorite high school English teachers.

Center Stage:
- Sue refers to New Directions as an "Island of Misfit Toys," the destination of Rudolph, Hermey (a misfit elf) and Yukon Cornelius (a treasure hunter) in the 1964 Christmas special *Rudolph the Red-Nosed Reindeer*.
- Quinn calls Rachel "Manhands," a term coined on the sitcom *Seinfeld*. In "The Bizarro Jerry," Jerry dated a beautiful woman he couldn't find attractive because of her giant masculine hands.
- Will instructs New Directions to use "John Travolta hands." John Travolta is not only an actor but an amazing dancer who tore up the dance floor in the 1977 dance movie *Saturday Night Fever*. His hand movements in this film are iconic and have since been copied (and parodied) thousands of times over.
- When asked to choose between the sun nook and the grand foyer, Terri calls it her own "Sophie's choice." *Sophie's Choice* was a 1979 novel by William Styron (and 1982 film starring Meryl Streep) about a Polish-Catholic Holocaust survivor who had to choose which one of her children would live and which one would die in a WWII concentration camp.
- Kurt wears a T-shirt that reads, "Sing Your Life." "Sing Your Life" was a 1991

single released by British singer-songwriter Morrissey from his *Kill Uncle* album. Morrissey fronted the 1980s band The Smiths and has had a successful solo career since they broke up in 1987. Morrissey is also known for giving conflicting and ambiguous answers when asked about his sexuality.

- The artists who "got their start in glee" on Rachel's New Directions poster were Justin Timberlake, *American Idol* alum Kelly Clarkson and Robin Thicke. Rachel helpfully identifies Robin Thicke, an American R&B singer-songwriter who has written songs for Christina Aguilera, Mya, Brandy, Marc Anthony and Jordan Knight.

- New Directions' "Push It" performance was the most offensive thing Sue Sylvester had seen since an elementary school performance of the musical *Hair*. *Hair* is a rock musical about the hippie counter-culture and sexual revolution in the 1960s — material not so appropriate for kids who do their only swinging at the playground.

- Principal Figgins says he hasn't seen the student body get that excited since Tiffany performed at the local mall. Tiffany was a 1980s pop star who did an extensive mall tour known as "The Beautiful You: Celebrating the Good Life Shopping Mall Tour '87." Tiffany was the first major artist to tour in malls and it has been a pop music staple ever since. The *Glee* cast did a mall tour of their own in 2009, visiting Hot Topic stores in ten American cities to promote the show's fall premiere.

- When Will shows Rachel the list of approved song choices, she asks what a luftballoon is. "99 Luftballoons" was a fiery political Cold War protest song that became an '80s pop hit sung in German by Nena.

Jazz Hands:

- Mr. Schue's license plate changed from "RP8 9624" to "glee."
- Kendra doesn't want Terri to go "Susan Smith" on her baby. Susan Smith drove her car into a lake and drowned her two young sons in 1993 in order to have a relationship with a wealthy man who didn't want children.
- Mr. Schuester is wearing a T-shirt that reads "Ditch Plains." Ditch Plains is in Montauk, New York, and has the best surf break on the Eastern seaboard, which is an odd choice for a teacher in small-town Middle America.
- Emma's collection of pamphlets is "Ouch! That Stings," "Divorce: Why Your Parents Stopped Loving You," "I Can't Stop Touching Myself," "Radon: The Silent Killer," "My Mom's Bipolar and She Won't Stop Yelling," "Wow! There's a Hair Down There!" and "So You Like Throwing Up."

- Mercedes calls Rachel "Eva Perón." Eva was the second wife of Argentinean president Juan Domingo Perón and the country's first lady from 1946 until her death in 1952 from cancer at the age of 33. Originally an actress, Eva fought for labor rights, women's rights and health rights and was nominated to run for vice-president of Argentina. She was the subject of the 1976 musical *Evita*, which was turned into a movie starring Madonna in 1996.

How Sue Cs It: Sue: Iron tablet? Keeps your strength up while you're menstruating.

Will: I don't menstruate.

Sue: Yeah? Neither do I.

♪♫♪

1.03 "acafellas"
Original Air Date: September 16, 2009
Written by: Ryan Murphy
Directed by: John Scott

The Music: ★ ★ ★
The Drama: ★ ★ ✦
The Laughs: ★ ★ ★

Rachel: We're going to win because we're different. And that's what makes us special.

When Rachel questions Mr. Schue's leadership ability, he forms an a cappella group to boost his confidence. New Directions tries to move on by hiring sadistic choreographer Dakota Stanley.

"Acafellas" is all about confidence — either you have it or you don't. Characters both major and minor struggle with feelings of self-doubt and learn the importance of believing in their own abilities. And while this message is delivered with a somewhat heavy hand, it's hard to take it all too seriously when there's a large dose of a cappella rapping thrown into the mix.

Mr. Schue's the first to suffer a blow to his ego, when Rachel (as directed by the double-agent Cheerios) suggests his choreography skills aren't up to snuff. Feeling shunned, Will goes off in search of his own little piece of glory, needing to prove (not just to New Directions, but to himself as well) that he has what it takes to lead them to Regionals. He ends up forming Acafellas, an a cappella group featuring himself and three other sad-sacks: Terri's Sheets 'N Things co-worker Howard Bamboo, thumbless woodshop teacher Henri St. Pierre and football coach Ken Tanaka. Singing and dancing puts the spring back in their step as this foursome begins to see their group as talented and successful. Sadly, their 15 minutes are over far too soon, with a heavy lesson learned: you can't dance around big problems — you need to face them head on, whether it's finding confidence, realizing friends don't file restraining orders or fighting a cough syrup addiction.

At the same time, the glee club kids are battling their own confidence issues when they hire famed choreographer Dakota Stanley. New Directions thinks that a successful dance instructor will help boost their self-esteem by giving them a new competitive edge, but the result is quite the opposite. The problem, of course, is what we've known since the first episode: New Directions isn't like other glee clubs. Vocal Adrenaline is all glitz and glamour, while the McKinley High crew is all about the music. They don't have fancy costumes or dance moves, and that's what makes them unique. Like Acafellas, New Directions needs to find inner confidence and believe in their own natural talents and individuality, something nine-plus hours of rehearsals every day and tear-induced dehydration can't give them.

The confidence theme also emerges with Will's dad, Kurt and Finn. It

josh groban

Josh Groban is a man who knows how to have fun. A talented singer-songwriter with four multi-platinum albums to his name, Josh got his start when he attended the Los Angeles County High School for the Arts as a theater major. He was accepted to Carnegie Mellon University, but dropped out after four months to pursue a career in music. Things took off for Josh at age 17 when he met Grammy-winning producer David Foster. David introduced him to the right people and it wasn't long before Josh had a record deal with Warner Bros. His unique spin on adult contemporary music has seen him perform with Charlotte Church, Andrea Bocelli, Sarah Brightman and others. At first, the Glee producers were unsure how far to push Josh's character, but when the singer came on set, he was game. Ian Brennan recalls, "He was like 'Yeah, that's hilarious. Can I be creepier?'"

whit hertford as dakota stanley

Remember that weird kid Stephanie and her friends called "Duckface" on *Full House*? That kid was played by Whit Hertford, who would also bring Dakota Stanley to the small screen. Born November 2, 1978, Whit is an American actor whose credits include *Jurassic Park*, *A Nightmare on Elm Street 5*, *Tiny Toon Adventures* and *Star Wars: The Clone Wars*. After graduating with a BFA from University of Utah's Actor Training Program conservatory, he studied improv and sketch comedy with the Upright Citizens Brigade Theatre and co-founded the sketch group THE ATTACK! Despite standing only 5'1", Whit's Dakota makes up for his lack of height with pure intimidation.

makes sense that while Will's dad feels inspired to finally make a gutsy move, Kurt and Finn are still struggling to find the courage to take control of their own desires. These boys are high schoolers through and through, and neither one of their situations is easy for someone their age to handle. Maybe there would be less emotional drama in New Directions if the club got a lesson about expressing their feelings through song? (Ahem, "Ballad," ahem.)

High Note: The songs are thoughtfully selected and well performed. Acafellas fits the cheesy boy bands of the '80s and '90s to a tight white tee, and Mercedes finally showcases her pipes with "Bust Your Windows."

Low Note: Why is Will so quick to turn his back on New Directions? Rachel, who has demanded the best from the beginning, was just trying to provide some constructive criticism. It's hard to believe Will when he says "I'm a teacher. A good one," if he turns his back on his students the second they question him.

Behind the Music:

"For He's a Jolly Good Fellow" (Will, Sandy, Howard and Ken)
(1709)
Traditionally sung to celebrate a great achievement, the guys sing "For He's a Jolly Good Fellow" to distract Henri from his bad luck. Supposedly written after the Battle of Malpaquet in the War of Spanish Sucession fought between several European powers over the unification of France and Spain under the Bourbon monarchy, this song is the second most popular song in the English language, bested only by "Happy Birthday."

victor garber as will's father

Sing, teach, practice law, spy, design the *Titanic*: what can't Victor Garber do? Born in London, Ontario, Canada, on March 16, 1949, Victor began studying acting at the University of Toronto at 16. His first major role was as Jesus for the Canadian production of *Godspell*. This perennial bridesmaid has been nominated for four Tonys and three Emmys. His credits include *Deathtrap*, *Sweeney Todd* and *Noises Off* on Broadway, films such as *Sleepless in Seattle*, *Legally Blonde*, *Annie* and *Tuck Everlasting*, and TV shows including *Alias* and *Eli Stone*. He officiated his *Alias* co-star Jennifer Garner's 2005 wedding to Ben Affleck and the two remain close. Victor is openly gay and is currently dating Canadian artist and model Rainer Andreesen.

"This Is How We Do It" (Acafellas)

Montell Jordan, *This Is How We Do It* (1995)

Acafellas shows us how a cappella is done with Montell Jordan's R&B jam about letting loose and having a great time. Montell became the first male solo artist to have a #1 debut single with this song, which held the top spot for six weeks. Montell acts as an authority on how to party and have a good time in this song, while Will uses the number to prove his authority status as a confident and talented leader who can bring success to Acafellas as well as New Directions.

"Poison" (Acafellas)

Bell Biv DeVoe, *Poison* (1990)

Bell Biv DeVoe, a spin-off group from the boy band New Edition, scored their first hit with this New Jack Swing–style song warning of the dangers of love. It warns certain girls should not be trusted, since they're poisonous to the men who date them. And who can be trusted in Lima, Ohio? Everyone, teachers and students alike, is interfering with someone else's relationship, plotting against someone or trying to change someone.

"Mercy" (Vocal Adrenaline)

Duffy, *Rockferry* (2008)

Soulful Welsh singer Duffy begs for mercy in her critically acclaimed Grammy-winning single. She loves someone, but they're wrong for her and she needs to break free and move on. Vocal Adrenaline should be begging for mercy too: they practice every day from 2:30 p.m. until midnight without breaks, water or excuses. Duffy's biggest problem may be break-ups, but Vocal Adrenaline has to worry about breakdowns!

"Bust Your Windows" (Mercedes)
Jazmine Sullivan, *Fearless* (2008)
Jazmine Sullivan's he-did-me-wrong anthem impressed both fans and critics, with *Slant Magazine* calling Jazmine the R&B answer to Carrie Underwood. Jazmine may sing about busting her cheating boyfriend's car windows, but Mercedes follows through and actually does it, breaking the windows of Kurt's car after he breaks her heart.

"I Wanna Sex You Up" (Acafellas)
Color Me Badd, *C.M.B.* (1991)
Will was upset with New Directions for singing "Push It" at a school assembly, but "I Wanna Sex You Up" at a PTA meeting is just as inappropriate. The title of this song says it all: nothing beats seducing and sleeping with a woman. Color Me Badd's first #1 hit received mixed reviews; VH1 named it one of the greatest songs of the '90s, but it made *Blender's* Worst Songs Ever list. It samples both Doug E. Fresh's "La Di Da Di" ("to the tick tock ya don't stop") and Betty Wright's "Tonight Is the Night" ("I know you not gonna sing that song!"). While it wasn't the best song choice for Acafellas to make, it certainly reminded viewers what was on everyone's minds. From Puck seducing MILFs to Kurt pining for Finn, everyone wants a little lovin'.

The Sound of Music: A cappella is the performance of music without any words. Either band members replace instruments by making accompanying sounds with their voice or groups harmonize to make instruments unnecessary. A cappella originated in the Italian Renaissance as religious music. In the 20th century, interest in the genre was revived, but it was reinterpreted to mean any music without instruments, including barbershop, doo-wop and more. A cappella is very popular in colleges, with groups like Yale's Whiffenpoofs and Tufts' Beezlebubs recording professionally and competing on the amateur level.

Give My Regards to Broadway: *The Sound of Music*, Rodgers and Hammerstein's beloved musical, was never intended to be a musical. Based on a set of Austrian films, 1956's *The Trapp Family* and its 1958 sequel *The*

debra monk as will's mother

Tony- and Emmy-winning actress Debra Monk was born on February 27, 1949, in Middleton, Ohio, but attended high school in Silver Spring, Maryland. She co-wrote her big break, the musical *Pump Boys and Dinettes*, based on her experiences as a waitress. The play eventually made it to Broadway and was nominated for the Tony for Best Musical in 1982. Her other stage credits include *Red Curtain*, *Steel Pier*, *Chicago* and *Curtains*. She's appeared in several films and television shows including *Fearless*, *For Love or Money*, *Quiz Show*, *Extreme Measures* and *NYPD Blue*.

Trapp Family in America, and on Maria von Trapp's memoir *The Story of the Trapp Family Singers*, *The Sound of Music* was originally envisioned as a non-musical retelling of the Von Trapp family's amazing-yet-true story of a widowed man falling in love with the nun-cum-nanny-cum-wife-and-mother and their eventual escape from the Nazis during World War II. While several names and characters were changed and events were dramatized, the essence of the story remained the same. Since the family was a musical one, a few songs were added . . . then another . . . then another . . . until the show became the classic we all know and love today. The show opened on Broadway on November 16, 1959, and ran for a successful 1,443 performances, winning four Tonys, including Best Musical (an honor it shared with *Fiorello!*). While the Broadway show was considered a success, the 1965 film was a phenomenon. Starring Julie Andrews and Christopher Plummer, the film sits third on the list of all-time inflation-adjusted box office hits and won five Academy Awards, including Best Picture.

That's Pretty *Popular*: Cheerleaders can be mean. Nicole, Mary Cherry and Poppy Fresh trick Carmen into believing she's a chicken in "Slumber Party Massacre." Their cheerleading budget is so large that they have a Prada allowance, which, frankly, sounds better than European dry cleaning. Henri, McKinley High's shop teacher, struggles with not having thumbs while the shop teacher at Kennedy High struggles with his gender and decides to become a woman in "Ch-Ch-Changes." Everyone at Kennedy High is subjected to a grueling boot camp in "Booty Camp," not unlike Dakota Stanley's rehearsals in this episode. The teachers at McKinley may hit the cough syrup

john lloyd young as henri st. pierre

John Lloyd Young played a Jersey boy on stage, but he's a West Coast boy at heart. Born in Sacramento, California, on July 4, 1975, John scored big as Frankie Valli in *Jersey Boys*, his first-ever Broadway role. Before he hit the big time, John attended Brown University and majored in theater arts. He's the only American actor to ever receive a Tony, Drama Desk, Theatre World and Outer Critics Circle award for a Broadway debut in a lead role. His *Jersey Boys* run ended in 2007. It's rumored that he once dated his *Glee* co-star Lea Michele. The twosome co-starred in the Hollywood Bowl's production of *Les Misérables*. Ryan Murphy wrote the role of Henri St. Pierre specifically for him.

bottle pretty hard, but at Kennedy High, it's the students. After a student dies of a cough syrup overdose in "Style and Substance Abuse," the student body undergoes random drug tests and the issue divides the school.

Slushie Facials:

- The Cheerios conspire to convince Mercedes that Kurt has a crush on her and to persuade New Directions to hire Dakota Stanley.
- When Kurt reveals he likes someone else, Mercedes bashes the window of his car.

Off-Key:

- Wouldn't being in a band with two teenagers violate Sandy's parole?
- Artie was the only New Directions member to agree with Finn when Finn protested hiring Dakota Stanley, and he didn't go on the field trip to recruit Dakota. Did they not have a wheelchair-accessible vehicle? Or did Artie not attend because he, like Finn, didn't want to hire Dakota?

Behind the Scenes:

- The role of Dakota Stanley was written for Broadway star Cheyenne Jackson, who had to drop out after getting the flu. Whit Hertford stepped in as a last-minute replacement. Dakota's name plays on Jackson's first name, as both are geographical places. (Cheyenne is the capital of Wyoming.)
- This is the second episode in which *So You Think You Can Dance* season 3 finalist Lauren Gottlieb appeared. Both she and Ben Susak (*SYTYCD* season 2) are in Vocal Adrenaline. Ben is friends with Heather Morris

and they auditioned for *SYTYCD* together. They even had a catchphrase: "Ben and Heather together forever." Ben made the top 20 but was cut in the third week.

- Ryan Murphy wrote "Bust Your Windows" into the script after hearing Amber sing it between takes.
- Dakota Stanley calls Finn "Frankenteen," which is Cory Monteith's Twitter handle (@frankenteen). Ryan Murphy coined the nickname because Cory is much taller and more awkward than everyone else.
- While Will's father never had the guts to go to law school, the actor who plays him, Victor Garber, has played several lawyers on-screen, including Jordan Wethersby in *Eli Stone* and Thomas Callahan in *Legally Blonde*.
- Victor Garber and Debra Monk, who play Will's mom and dad, have known each other for years. Debra was even staying at Victor's house when she got the call to appear on *Glee*. They also worked together in *Jeffrey*, *The First Wives Club* and *The Music Man*.
- Shoshandra from Vocal Adrenaline is played by Shelby Rabara, the real-life girlfriend of Harry Shum Jr. (who hasn't made an appearance yet).

Center Stage:

- John Stamos proved it "takes more certainty than talent to be a star" after he shot to fame as Uncle Jesse on *Full House*. Since that show, Stamos hasn't had a hit film or television show but is constantly working, despite never being heralded for his acting abilities.
- When Sandy demands to join Acafellas, he says he's "ready for [his] close up, Mr. De Mille," a line from the 1950 film *Sunset Boulevard*. In this film, Norma Desmond, a former silent screen actress who's never accepted that Hollywood no longer wants her, is so delusional that when the police arrive at the end of the film, she mistakes their presence for a film crew. Considering how Sandy won't accept that he's no longer needed at glee (or that Josh Groban might not actually be attracted to him), he may be as delusional as Norma!
- Emma encourages Will by reminding him about Van Halen and David Lee Roth. Van Halen was a 1970s rock band and Roth was their lead singer. He quit in 1985 over personal and creative differences. Instead of disbanding, the remaining members of Van Halen hired Sammy Hagar and went on to produce four multi-platinum albums.
- Dakota Stanley calls Mercedes "Effie," the singer in the Broadway musical *Dreamgirls* (played by Jennifer Hudson in the 2006 film) who was kicked out of the group, The Dreams, for not being thin.
- Dakota Stanley calls Rachel "Yentl," referencing Barbra Streisand's 1983 film *Yentl*, which Barbra directed, co-wrote, co-produced and starred in. Barbra played Yentl Mendel, a young Jewish girl living in Poland who pursued the study of Jewish Talmudic law disguised as a boy, because it was forbidden for women.
- Curtis Mayfield was an R&B and soul singer, songwriter and producer best known for his work on the *Superfly* soundtrack. He is considered one of the pioneers of funk and of music for the civil rights movement.
- Run DMC, one of the most successful hip hop groups of all time, was inducted into the Rock & Roll Hall of Fame in 2009, but it was Eminem who presented them with this honor, not Josh Groban.

Jazz Hands:

- Will's dad spent six months in the "Hanoi Hilton," a prison used by French colonists in the Vietnam War, where American prisoners were often tortured and beaten in an attempt to extract information.

81

- There's a "What You Need to Know About Staph Infections" sign in the staff room.
- Sue says she was part of the 1989 invasion of Panama (a.k.a. Operation Just Cause), which caused dictator and general Manuel Noriega to be deposed when President George H.W. Bush attacked to regain control of the Panama Canal. Sue's not quite telling the truth here, though, because women don't serve in combat positions with the U.S. Army.
- Howard is wearing his Sheets 'N Things nametag during the Acafellas' performance of "Poison."
- This is the first episode with a Puck voice-over.
- Jim Abbott played professional baseball from 1989 to 1999. He was born without a right hand (he wasn't missing a whole arm, as Finn stated) and threw his no-hitter against the Cleveland Indians in 1993.

The Buckeye State: Josh Groban says he was in Ohio to visit the Rock and Roll Hall of Fame in Cleveland. Since Cleveland is 180 miles from Lima, it seems unlikely Josh would simply "stop by" a PTA meeting. But it might be worth the trip to deliver a restraining order.

How Sue Cs It: "I'm going to ask you to smell your armpits. That's the smell of failure and it's stinking up my office."

♪♫♪

1.04 "preggers"
Original Air Date: September 23, 2009
Written by: Brad Falchuk
Directed by: Brad Falchuk

The Music: ★♪
The Drama: ★★★★
The Laughs: ★★♪

Kurt (to his dad): I'm glad that you're proud of me, but I don't want to lie anymore. Being a part of glee club and football has really shown me that I can be anything.

All eyes are on Kurt when he tries out for the football team. Meanwhile, Sue and Sandy work together to bring down New Directions, and Finn and Quinn's relationship is rocked by the news that she's pregnant.

Big secrets are revealed, an important game is played, a big star quits the glee club and a bunch of jocks dance to "Single Ladies" at a crucial point in a football game. How could this hour of television not be amazing?

Kurt takes center stage when he decides to join the McKinley High football team. Although the whole plot stems from Kurt being caught in a lie, it's the perfect way for him to try to be the man he thinks his dad wants him to be. He may disobey his father by wearing "form-fitting sweaters that stop at the knee," but Kurt still desperately wants to make his father proud. Kurt and his dad don't relate to each other very well, having little in common, and while Kurt sometimes mistakes that for lack of love, that's not the case. They may not express it well, but it's clear how much this father/son duo loves and respects each other. Kurt is almost as excited when his dad comes to the football game as his dad is proud when Kurt wins the game for the team. And thanks to their newfound football-inspired closeness, Kurt finds the courage to come out to his surprisingly supportive dad, making us cheer harder than when McKinley won the game. Kurt can only hope that one day he'll find the same acceptance he got at home in the halls of McKinley High as well.

While Kurt opens up about his sexuality, Quinn contemplates how to hide the evidence of her sexual activity. The Quinn/Terri parallels get stronger in this episode when it's revealed that Quinn, too, is lying about a

mike o'malley as burt hummel

The former host of Nickelodeon's *Get the Picture* and *Nickelodeon GUTS* is now one of Hollywood's great character actors. Of Irish descent, Mike O'Malley was born on October 31, 1966, in Boston, Massachusetts and studied theater at the University of New Hampshire. After his stint with Nickelodeon, Mike appeared in *Deep Impact*, *Pushing Tin* and *28 Days* and had a starring role on CBS's *Yes, Dear*, and slowly emerged as a respected character actor. He's also an accomplished playwright, with two of his plays, *Three Years from Thirty* and *Diverting Devotion*, being produced off-Broadway. He married his wife, Lisa, in 1991 and they have three children, Fiona, Seamus and Declan. After working with Ryan Murphy on his pilot *Pretty Handsome*, Ryan offered Mike the part of Burt Hummel without asking him to audition, and he happily accepted.

pregnancy. The queen bee is terrified of losing her social status and her football stud boyfriend, just like Terri's frightened of losing her seemingly perfect marriage and her high school sweetheart husband. Quinn's situation is even more complicated because her pregnancy also means the loss of her "good girl" image. Is Quinn really a strict Christian who believes in prayer and the celibacy club, or is she using religion to mask her true self? It's hard to say if Quinn's beliefs are more than skin deep or not, but her pregnancy dilemma adds an interesting twist to a character that initially seemed like nothing more than a slave to popularity. Even though both women are acting out of desperation and fear, these potential baby mommas need to follow Kurt's lead and bravely come clean with the people who love them.

Rachel's diva-esque tendencies are also an issue again in this episode when Mr. Schue chooses Tina for a solo. Thinking that his decision is a purposeful slight against her, Rachel quits the club in favor of the school musical, but the dramatic effect of her storm-outs is waning due to the sheer number of times she threatens to ditch the group. Though she plays the confident leading lady, Rachel's many tantrums cover up an ego that's fragile underneath that abrasive exterior. We know Rachel thinks her singing is her key to being special, and being denied the spotlight damages the image she's carefully constructed for herself. Rachel's diva personality could be her greatest act so far — one so convincing she's even fooled herself. Rachel and New Directions need each other equally: Rachel won't achieve the success or gain the friendships she desires without the club, while the group will definitely struggle competitively without her vocal prowess as their female lead.

Sometimes we become our own worst critics by internalizing our struggles and expecting the most negative outcomes. In this episode, Kurt's experience is a perfect example of how scary situations can still end well, when his dad proves supportive of his sexuality. Both Quinn and Rachel should take a lesson in confidence from Kurt and finally put aside the harsh pressures they put on themselves to be perfect. The support they receive might surprise them.

High Note: How touching, sweet and surprising was Kurt's coming out?! And Kurt's dad handled the delicate situation with such honesty, love and compassion.

Low Note: Terri's half-baked adoption strategy seems like it is more complicated than Dakota Stanley choreography. There are so many obstacles: faking a

q&a: stephen tobolowsky as sandy ryerson

Born and raised in Dallas, Texas, Stephen Tobolowsky's earliest claim to fame was as a guitarist and back-up singer in Stevie Ray Vaughn's high school band. In college, Stephen turned his focus to acting and majored in theater at Southern Methodist University, where he studied alongside *Home Improvement*'s Patricia Richardson. Since graduating, Stephen has appeared in over 200 films and television projects, including *Groundhog Day*, *Radioland Murders* and *Memento*. Coincidentally, both his *Glee* and *Groundhog Day* characters have the same last name. Like his *Glee* character, Stephen has a passion for the stage and is active in the theater communities in New York and Los Angeles. In 2002, he was nominated for a Tony Award for Best Performance by a Featured Actor in a Play for the revival of *Morning's at Seven*. He's so dedicated to his craft that he even auditioned for *Glee* with a broken neck. His weekly podcast, *The Tobolowsky Files* (tobolowskyfiles.com), is thoughtful and hilarious. We strongly recommend you give it a listen!

We contacted Stephen who happily shared some of his ideas on Sandy Ryerson and what it's like to work on the set of *Glee*:

Tell us about how you see the character of Sandy Ryerson, beyond what we see on screen.
Any role I work on can be framed by two main questions: What is my character's greatest hope and what is his greatest fear. All behavior is to some degree influenced by these two things. For Sandy, his greatest hope was encapsulated in a line he had in the "Acafellas" episode: "This is my shot of getting back to the world of the normal." The line was cut in editing but the truth remains — Sandy is pained by feeling like he lives in the outskirts of acceptability. It is a lonely place . . . or as he says in "Preggers": "I'm living in a cocoon of horror!" So loneliness and being ostracized is what Sandy fears most.

How do you relate to a character like Sandy? Are there any similarities between the two of you?
It's interesting that one of the lines that was cut from the pilot was Sandy pleading with Principal Figgins that he doesn't understand what all the accusations are about because he's "not gay!" Let's take Sandy at his word — he is not gay or a pedophile. Does it make the material funnier or the situation richer? I say, "Yes." It makes Sandy not a borderline criminal who is lying to cover his tracks but — like all of us — he is someone who is out of touch with who he is or how he is perceived. That is more universal — and funnier — and yes, I plead guilty to that one!

If Sandy were to sing a song to express his emotions, what would he sing?
How about "I'm Stone in Love with You" by The Stylistics sung to Josh

Groban or "Put on a Happy Face" from the musical *Bye Bye Birdie* sung with Sue!

What is it like working with such a large ensemble cast as *Glee*'s? How is it different from working on a set with a smaller cast?
When you have a large cast you have several storylines moving together and an actor usually works within the bubble of his own group. I worked with Lea, Matt and Jane — but I had almost nothing to do with Amber, Cory and Jayma. That is the reality of a large cast — like *Deadwood* or *Heroes*. On smaller cast shows you all work together through one story idea per episode — or maybe two.

pregnancy, coordinating due dates, faking an adoption, faking a birth, faking a birth certificate and arranging the hospital transfer without Will (or anyone, for that matter) noticing. This plot seems ridiculous on so many levels.

Behind the Music:

"Single Ladies (Put a Ring on It)" (Danced to by Kurt, Tina and Brittany, and later by the McKinley High football team)
Beyoncé, *I Am . . . Sasha Fierce* (2008)
Respect and commitment are two huge thematic threads in this episode and Beyoncé's Grammy-winning #1 hit (and pop culture sensation) reinforces this. The music video, which showcased the previously little-known J-setting dance style, spawned thousands of parodies, fan imitations and knock-offs online and won Video of the Year at the 2009 MTV Music Video Awards. Whether it's Kurt coming to terms with his sexuality; Finn balancing New Directions and football, and Rachel and Quinn; Rachel trying to find herself without New Directions; Will trying to make his way as a father-to-be and a teacher; or Mercedes and Tina trying to find themselves outside Rachel's shadow, everyone at McKinley High wants to be respected for who they are and who they're trying to be.

"Taking Chances" (Rachel)
Céline Dion, *Taking Chances* (2007)
Kara DioGuardi (a songwriter and *American Idol* judge) and David Stewart (a songwriter and record producer to A-list pop stars) wrote this ballad about taking chances on love and this episode is all about taking chances in life: Rachel auditions for *Cabaret*, Will gives the shy and untested Tina a solo,

Sue gets Sandy involved in her mission to destroy the glee club, and Finn performs a socially unthinkable mash-up of football and glee club.

"Tonight" (Tina)
West Side Story (1956)
Leonard Bernstein and Stephen Sondheim wrote "Tonight" in 1956 and it made its way into *West Side Story* (see "Give My Regards" below). Thanks to being affiliated with rival gangs, lovebirds Tony and Maria seem doomed from the start. However, they believe their love can conquer all and their romance offers them a new beginning, away from the grudges and rivalries their friends and families hold. New beginnings abound at McKinley High, with Tina launching her career as a soloist, Kurt becoming football's newest star and Rachel headlining the school's production of *Cabaret*.

Give My Regards to Broadway: Envisioned as a modern adaptation of *Romeo and Juliet*, *West Side Story* tells the tale of two rival teenage gangs in 1950s New York City. Trouble starts between these groups when Tony, a Jet, falls in love with Maria, the younger sister of a Shark. The show's dark themes, sophisticated dance sequences and creative storytelling made it a hit with fans and critics. It premiered on Broadway on September 26, 1967, ran for 732 shows and was nominated for a Tony for Best Musical. Several successful revivals have been made and it's now considered a Broadway classic. The 1961 film adaptation, starring Natalie Wood and Richard Beymer, was an even bigger success than the stage show, winning ten Academy Awards, including Best Picture.

That's Pretty *Popular*: Like Kurt, Sam lost a parent (when she was 14) and she struggles to relate to her mom in her dad's absence, but the two share a close bond. Two *Popular* characters have pregnancy scares — Brooke in season 1 and Carmen in season 2 — but both tests come back negative. Ryan Murphy must looooove pregnancy storylines, as Sam's mom becomes pregnant in the second season as well.

Off-Key:
- If Brittany is a Cheerio trying to destroy New Directions, why is she making a "Single Ladies" video with Tina and Kurt? Even if this is just a hat tip to Heather Morris, who was originally brought to set to teach the "Single Ladies" dance, it still doesn't work within the context of the characters.

- What happened to the new song restrictions? Are "Tonight" and "Don't Stop Believin'" on Principal Figgins' approved list?
- It's surprising that McKinley High has enough musical students for a production of *Cabaret*, yet Mr. Schue has to pull teeth to get people to join New Directions.

Behind the Scenes:

- The scene of Kurt coming out to his father was based on Ryan Murphy's own coming out to his father at 15, with Burt and Kurt's conversation being a near-verbatim reenactment.
- The costume department originally wanted Kurt in a leotard and heels for "Single Ladies," just like Brittany and Tina. Chris put his foot down and worked with costume designer Lou Eyrich to come up with the full-body unitard and tie.
- Kendra asks whether Terri's baby is black. Jessalyn Gilsig's character gave birth to a black baby in *Nip/Tuck*. Before the baby was born, Gina believed the father was Dr. Christian Troy, a white plastic surgeon, but the father turned out to be a forgotten one-night stand.
- #77 on McKinley High's football team is Isaac Tualaulelei from the dance crew Heavy Impact. Heavy Impact competed on season 5 of *America's*

Best Dance Crew.

- Thanks to the constricting and heavy football padding, the "Single Ladies" choreography was one of the most difficult dances of the season. "You have to exaggerate all the movements," Harry Shum Jr. revealed to *Desert News.* "We're out there and the director is yelling, 'Make it bigger! Make it bigger!' And I'm like, 'I *am* making it bigger!'"

Center Stage:

- Kurt's dad watches *Deadliest Catch*, a Discovery Channel reality show that premiered in 2005 and follows a fishing fleet in the Bering Sea while they fish for Alaskan King crab and *Opilo* crab.
- Rachel's "special connection" with Natalie Wood as Maria in *West Side Story* is a stretch. Natalie Wood is not Jewish and her singing in the film was dubbed over by Marni Nixon, a professional singer who also did voice dubbing for *The King and I* and *My Fair Lady*.
- The background music in Principal Figgins' Mumbai Air ad is "Didi Tera Deewar Deewana" from the 1994 Bollywood hit *Hum Aapke Hain Koun . . . ! (Who Am I to You?)*, a film about the complicated relationship between two families.
- When Sue convinces Principal Figgins to support the musical, she references *Raise Your Voice* and *Stomp the Yard*. *Raise Your Voice* is a film starring Hilary Duff as a small town girl with a big voice who goes to a prestigious summer music program. *Stomp the Yard* is about college fraternities participating in stepping competitions.
- Finn read Walter Payton's autobiography, *Never Die Easy*. Walter Payton played for the Chicago Bears from 1975 to 1987 and is considered one of the greatest running backs of all time. He was inducted into the Football Hall of Fame in 1993 and was an accomplished dancer — he even placed second in a couples dance contest on *Soul Train* in 1975.
- The "Super Bowl Shuffle" was a rap song recorded by the 1985 Chicago Bears football team before Super Bowl XX. The song reached #41 on the Billboard Hot 100 and was nominated for a Grammy for Best Rhythm & Blues Vocal Performance — Duo or Group. That same year, the Bears went on to win their first NFL championship.
- When Will talks to the football players, he references Dick Butkus. Dick Butkus was a linebacker for the Chicago Bears from 1965 to 1973 and was inducted into the Pro Football Hall of Fame in 1979. After football, Butkus

found a second career in acting, appearing in films like *Gus*, *Cracking Up* and *Any Given Sunday* and television shows like *My Two Dads* and *Hang Time*.

- Finn tries to help Will out by suggesting O.J. Simpson, a successful NFL running back. O.J. played for the Buffalo Bills and San Francisco 49ers and was inducted into the Football Hall of Fame in 1985. He appeared in the 1977 television miniseries *Roots* and acted in films like *The Cassandra Crossing*, *The Towering Inferno* and the *Naked Gun* trilogy. However, O.J. is most famous for being accused of murdering his ex-wife, Nicole Brown, and her friend, Ronald Goldman, in 1994. O.J. was found not guilty in criminal court but convicted of wrongful death in civil court.

Jazz Hands:
- This is the first episode with Harry Shum Jr. and Dijon Talton.
- Brittany speaks for the first time when she tells Kurt's dad that his son is on the football team.
- In Sue's first "Sue's Corner" segment, she comes out in support of caning. Caning is a legal punishment in Singapore. Offenses that may be punished by caning include robbery, theft, vandalism, assault, rioting and drug use. Parents are also allowed to cane their children, albeit with a smaller cane.
- When Quinn is in the hot tub, she's wearing one of the Cheerio bikini tops seen during the car wash in "Showmance."
- You cannot get pregnant in a hot tub. We repeat: you cannot get pregnant in a hot tub. Unless, you know, you actually have sex in a hot tub.
- The Hindi in Principal Figgins' Mumbai Air commercial translates to "And keep in mind, Mumbai Airlines never crashes. Well, it crashes only a little."

The Buckeye State: The residents of Lima, Ohio, get two very special meanings for Lima Loser. Lima Losers are people who are "lost in Middle America" or losers who get stuck in Lima, Ohio. Ryan Murphy and *Glee* appear to have coined the second meaning themselves.

How Sue Cs It: "I got a satellite interview. That's lingo for an interview, via satellite."

♪♫♪

1.05 "the rhodes not taken"
Original Air Date: September 30, 2009
Written by: Ian Brennan
Directed by: John Scott

The Music: ★ ★ ★ ★
The Drama: ★ ★ ♪
The Laughs: ★ ★ ★

Will (to New Directions): I screwed up bringing her here. It was about me, and glee club is supposed to be about you guys. You don't need her to be great.

With New Directions still minus a leading lady, Will recruits former glee club member, April Rhodes, to help restore glory to the team.

"Two roads diverged in a yellow wood," begins Robert Frost's classic poem, from which this episode borrows heavily. Being at a crossroads, deciding what road to take and choosing the more difficult road, the one less traveled, are both central ideas in the aptly named "The Rhodes Not Taken."

Although he won't admit it to New Directions, Will's beginning to worry that the group can't take Regionals without Rachel and he's scared he might be starting down a losing road. As a result, he resorts to uncouth methods to ensure success at Sectionals. Plucking April from squatter squalor and reinstating her as the glee club's female lead is a short-term solution; Will needs to make more responsible choices if he's concerned about the long-term success of New Directions.

Like Will, Finn is also nervous about the club's potential success (and therefore his chance at a music scholarship) and needs to make responsible choices to help his future and his unborn child. However, deceit and trickery aren't exactly responsible actions and Finn loses when Rachel realizes what's going on and quits, again.

Both Will and Finn employ tacky techniques, as the two men are thinking only about the easiest road for themselves, rather than the best road for

New Directions as a whole. The parallel between the situations is reinforced during the bowling alley "dates" when April and Rachel both make promises they don't keep. Can you blame them? While the promises are well-meaning, the reasons the boys are asking for them are selfish. Despite their misguided solutions, the guys come through and prove they're still good underneath it all by coming clean about their true intentions and apologizing for them.

Rachel "It's Clear My Talent Is Too Big for an Ensemble" Berry continues her struggle with her diva side in this episode, when she stands by her decision to star in the school musical. However, our leading lady learns a difficult lesson when she has a chance to look at her possible future, and it looks a lot like April Rhodes. If Rachel sacrifices everything for fame and falls flat, that could be her, a drunken squatter trying to relive her high school glory days. Rachel takes the episode's title literally by telling April that she will stick with the "difficult road," but by the end she's right back where she belongs. Whether the driving force was her love for show choir, her dedication to New Directions, her crush on Finn or her fear of turning into the next April Rhodes, it looks like Rach learned her lesson . . . for now.

The crossroads motif holds strong as the baby drama heats up when New Directions finds out about Quinn's bun in the oven. Being honest means taking the harder path, which is a good idea in theory but not for the faint of heart or those, like Quinn, who have a carefully crafted image to maintain. Even Robert Frost's narrator, who "took the one less traveled," plays coy as to whether that road is always best, noting only that his choice "has made all the difference."

High Note: The music is the strongest it's been since the "Don't Stop Believin'" performance, thanks to Kristin Chenoweth's appearance and to New Directions, which finally gels as a group. Everyone radiates joy and confidence during "Somebody to Love" and they never sounded better.

Low Note: Rachel quits and Will gives three solos to April? Doesn't this completely contradict what he told Rachel just last episode about how everyone needs to share the spotlight in order for the group to succeed?

Behind the Music:

"Don't Stop Believin'" (New Directions)
Journey, *Escape* (1981)

kristin chenoweth as april rhodes

The Emmy- and Tony-winning Kristin Chenoweth, born July 24, 1968, in Broken Arrow, Oklahoma, has made a name for herself as a pint-sized powerhouse, with roles in *Pushing Daisies; The West Wing; You're a Good Man, Charlie Brown; Bewitched; The Pink Panther* and Ryan Murphy's *Running With Scissors*. Adopted at birth, Kristi Dawn changed her name to Kristin under the advice of a voice instructor, who felt Kristin was a more appropriate name for a budding opera singer. After receiving degrees in musical theater and opera performance from Oklahoma City University, the devout Christian won a scholarship from the Metropolitan Opera National Council. The classically trained coloratura soprano turned it down after winning the role of Arabella Rittenhouse in the Paper Mill Playhouse production of *Animal Crackers*. She made her Broadway debut in 1997, starring in *Steel Pier*, and made her Broadway breakthrough in 2003, when she was cast as Glinda the Good Witch in *Wicked*. Ryan isn't the only member of the *Glee* gang Kristin's worked with before. She appeared in the 2006 movie *Deck the Halls* with Cory Monteith and was in the *Ugly Betty* episode "East Side Story" and the *Pushing Daisies* episode "Pigeon" with Jayma Mays. Maybe that's why April felt so at home in the halls of McKinley High!

"Don't Stop Believin'," sung for the second time this season, reinforces the series' main theme of pursuing your passion and never giving up. By the end of the episode, April, Rachel, Will and the rest of New Directions have all had a refresher course on this valuable lesson.

"Maybe This Time" (Rachel and April)
Cabaret (1972)
Sally Bowles, the lounge singer in Cabaret (see "Give My Regards" below), is looking for a second chance, just like *Glee*'s April Rhodes and Rachel Berry. The Kit Kat Klub, New Directions, *Cabaret*: maybe this time these song-stresses will get the stardom they crave. The actual song did, after all. Orignally penned for the unproduced musical *Golden Gate*, the song about second chances got its own second chance when film director Bob Fosse added it to the film version of *Cabaret* to showcase Liza Minnelli's amazing voice.

"(Life Is a) Cabaret" (Rachel)
Cabaret (1972)
A cabaret features comedy, song, dance and drama, a combination which describes *Glee* to a tee. Life is a wild and crazy ride and it's better to enjoy

it than sit back and be a wallflower. That's what Sally Bowles did, and what April, Rachel and everyone else at McKinley High should do too.

"Alone" (Will and April)
Heart, *Bad Animals* (1987)
Heart's #1 hit explores what it's like to fall in love for the first time. April was Will's first big crush and he spent most of freshman year wanting to get her alone. It's a nostalgic song choice, as both Will and April would have been in junior high when "Alone" was on top of the charts. While the song is about romantic feelings, its title reinforces the loneliness April, Will and Rachel are all feeling.

"Last Name" (April with New Directions)
Carrie Underwood, *Carnival Ride* (2007)
This Grammy-winning song (Best Female Country Vocal Performance) offers an important life lesson: if you drink too much and party too hard, you could end up hitched to someone you don't even know. Partying hard is something that April Rhodes knows too well. From the classroom to the bowling alley, she's always drinking, lying and shirking responsibilities, and, as a result, disappointing people.

"Somebody to Love" (New Directions)
Queen, *A Day at the Races* (1976)
Freddie Mercury wrote this complex song about searching for love, finding yourself and having faith, and it became one of Queen's greatest hits. The song's arrangement is based on traditional gospel choirs, making it a challenging but appropriate choice for New Directions. It certainly helps that people at McKinley High can relate to the song's message: everyone — the students, the teachers, April Rhodes — is looking for that special someone to love them for who they are and who they're trying to be.

Give My Regards to Broadway: Based on the 1951 play *I Am a Camera* by John Van Druten, *Cabaret* examines life in the Kit Kat Klub, a seedy nightclub in 1930s Berlin, focusing on the club's star, young songstress Sally Bowles. Sally becomes romantically involved as she deals with the club's politics, all set to the backdrop of the Nazis' increasing power and prominence in Germany. *Cabaret* premiered on Broadway on November 20,

> ## gleek speak: amanda kind
> ## (co-director of k-w glee, a show choir inspired
> ## by *glee* from waterloo, ontario, canada)
>
> **What are some of the similarities and differences between K-W Glee and what we see on the show? What are the hard parts of being a show choir that we don't see in *Glee*?**
> I think it's a bit of a learning curve for everybody because what they see on the show is that the kids get handed out the music and they instantly are good at it. We don't see the rehearsal process for all of those actors, so for them to get handed a piece of music and then have to spend that rehearsal time developing the harmony parts and learning how to blend and get all the words right, it's certainly a learning curve for everybody. I think the stereotyping that's on the show certainly to some extent fits what we have in our group. We have a lot of the drama kids, we have a lot of the really artistic kids and we don't particularly have a lot of the sports-oriented kids. Although we did have this one boy come in who plays basketball and hasn't really sung that much, and I turned right over to my colleague and said, "There is our Finn." He's blond, he's 15, he's adorable, he has a great voice, but he's kind of shy, and he's never really done anything like this before, so it's quite humorous to see the parallels on the show with our group. He comes into rehearsal and literally I'm sure that all thirty girls did a double-take.

1966, and it ran for 1,165 shows and won seven Tony Awards, including Best Musical. There were several changes between the original stage production and the 1972 film adaptation directed by Bob Fosse, including rewriting Sally Bowles as an American for Liza Minnelli, and dramatically changing the score. The musical's music and lyrics team Kander and Ebb wrote several songs, including "Mein Heir" and "Money, Money," exclusively for the film version, and "Maybe This Time" was added, having been originally written for another production. These songs are now included in contemporary stage revivals. The film won Best Director and Best Actress at the 1972 Academy Awards but lost Best Picture to *The Godfather*.

That's Pretty *Popular*: Why wouldn't Sandy want nudity in a high school play? It goes perfectly fine at Kennedy High in "Are You There, God? It's Me, Ann-Margaret" when Josh and Lily perform sans clothing for their school production.

Off-Key:
- When Finn and Rachel are kissing in the bowling alley, sometimes her hands are around his neck and sometimes they aren't, depending on the camera angle.
- Why did everyone ask who Quinn's baby's father is, like it's a big surprise? She and Finn have been exclusive for a while now and no one knows about the Puck incident. Who else could it be?

Behind the Scenes:
- The voice that gives you the lowdown on what happened last week on *Glee* is none other than executive producer Ian Brennan.
- Kurt's tears when April belts one for the first time? Those are real. Chris Colfer is a huge Kristin Chenoweth fan and was overcome on set after hearing her sing. The producers liked it so much they kept it in the show.
- Kristin Chenoweth had never sung "Maybe This Time" before appearing on *Glee,* but enjoyed singing it so much that she includes it in her current performances.
- In "Somebody to Love," Finn sings the line "Got no feel, I got no rhythm. I just keep losing my beat." Cory Monteith admits in the *Glee: Season 1* DVD extras that he's one of the worst dancers on the show and frequently loses his beat!

Center Stage:
- Terri claims she regularly does "Linda Blair" impressions at work. Linda Blair played the demon-possesed, vomit- and curse-spewing Regan in the 1973 film *The Exorcist.*
- Sandy Ryerson wants to perform *Equus.* Written in 1973 by Peter Shaffer, *Equus* is about a young man who has a sexual fascination with horses and features highly sexual content and full-frontal male nudity. (In 2007, Daniel Radcliffe caused a stir by tackling the role at age 17 for the play's West End revival, even though he'd have to bare everything — Hogwarts and all.)
- When Emma brings Will April's high school record, he says he's not on *This Is Your Life,* a documentary-style game show that ran from 1952 to 1961 on NBC. In every episode, the host would surprise a celebrity and then introduce them to people from their past.

- April Rhodes is reminiscent of the character Jerri Blank, a 46-year-old former alcoholic and drug addict who returns to high school in the Comedy Central show *Strangers with Candy*, which aired from 1999 to 2000.
- Kurt says he cried when the hunters shot Bambi's mom. *Bambi*, the iconic Disney film about a family of deer, was originally released in 1942 and has been rolled out in several formats regularly ever since.
- Bert and Ernie are roommates and best friends who have appeared in almost every episode of *Sesame Street* since the 1969 pilot. Despite Puck's insinuations, Sesame Workshop denies that they are gay.

Jazz Hands:

- New Directions has as much of a chance to succeed as the Jamaican bobsled team, who first competed in the 1988 Winter Olympics in Calgary. The team became a crowd favorite but was a long shot to medal. They crashed during one of their qualifying runs and did not advance. The team returned to the Olympics in 1992 and 1994 and was fictionalized on the silver screen in the 1993 comedy *Cool Runnings*.
- When Emma dipped back into her past and started an online flirtation with her high school boyfriend Andy, she says she paid for ending that revived romance when Versace died. Gianni Versace was a famous Italian fashion designer who was murdered on July 15, 1997, by Andrew Cunanan, a young man who went on a killing spree before committing suicide. Clearly Emma's ex-flame knew how to make revenge fashionable.
- April mentions that her high school sweetheart was named Vinny and that the current love of her life is vino. Very clever, Ian Brennan.
- April asked for "Maybe This Time" in the same key, B-flat, that Rachel asked for an episode earlier.
- Emma refers to her decontamination showers as the "full Silkwood." Karen Silkwood was a chemical technician who became severely contaminated with plutonium while at work, having ingested 400 times the legal limit. Despite several decontamination attempts, Silkwood could not rid her body of the plutonium. She was planning to go to the *New York Times* with her documented health records when she died in a mysterious car accident. The film about Karen's battle, *Silkwood* (1983), starred Meryl Streep and received five Academy Award nominations.
- Branson, where April is thinking of heading after leaving New Directions, is a town in Missouri with a substantial theater district. It's considered

the Broadway of the Midwest. Several well-known entertainers have performed in Branson, including Gladys Knight, the Osmond Family, Johnny Cash and June Carter Cash.

The Buckeye State: April's last name is Rhodes, which is the inspiration for this episode's title "The Rhodes Not Taken." There is a community college in Lima named James A. Rhodes State College.

How Sue Cs It: "When Sandy said that he wanted to write himself in as Cleopatra, I was aroused, then furious."

♪♫♪

1.06 "vitamin d"
Original Air Date: October 7, 2009
Written by: Ryan Murphy
Directed by: Elodie Keene

The Music: ★ ★ ★
The Drama: ★ ★ ♪
The Laughs: ★ ★ ★

Sue: Glee club. Every time I try to destroy that clutch of scab-eating mouth-breathers, it only comes back stronger, like some sexually ambiguous horror movie villain.

Will challenges New Directions to a boys versus girls mash-up competition to help pump up their energy for Sectionals, while Terri takes on a job as the school nurse to keep an eye on Will and Emma.

"Vitamin D" is all about pushing: pushing people to be the best they can be, pushing things too far, and, well, pushing drugs. Fresh off their crowd-pleasing school performance, New Directions is feeling cocky, but Will's determined not to let them become complacent. In an effort to push them toward success, he concocts a boys versus girls mash-up showdown to inject the kids with a healthy dose of competition . . . at the same time as Terri is injecting them with a not-so-healthy dose of pseudoephedrine. Hugs not drugs, Terri, hugs not drugs! We're terrified of your potential future parenting skills.

Terri enters Will's world in this episode for the same reason Quinn enters Finn's in "Showmance": she doesn't trust him. Both women are questioning the validity of their relationship and their self-worth, causing them to take desperate measures. Her uncertainty explains why Terri pushes things way too far when she convinces Ken to propose to that "doe-eyed little harlot" Emma, effectively taking her off the market (not that being married has stopped Will from flirting, but Terri's too crazed to consider that). From giving drugs to the students to forcing together a couple that's totally not ready for marriage, Terri's desperation has ventured into dark territory, and she sure isn't the perfect cheerleader queen bee anymore. Not that she's found it easy to give up that image, and we can see the strong parallels between her and Quinn here. Terri was once the teen queen with the hunky boyfriend just like Quinn is, and, well, we can see how well that worked out for her. Terri's a kind of cautionary tale for Quinn: trapping a man and freezing a high school romance in time is no guarantee of happiness.

Meanwhile, Will and Finn are so wrapped up in their own problems — Will with pushing New Directions to be the best and Finn pushing to succeed in his classes, football and glee club — that they don't notice the internal struggles that are prompting Terri's and Quinn's drastic deceptions. Maybe if they paid more attention to their relationships, they could preempt these potentially disasterous problems.

And then there's poor Emma, pushed into a relationship she's only settling for because she's scared to be alone. If Emma can't be with Will, it makes sense from her perspective to settle on a guy like Ken because she's smart enough to realize that she'd always have the upper hand in their relationship. By dating "beneath herself," Emma can stay in control without ruffling a ruffle. Just as Quinn tries to exert her power over Finn in their relationship because she thinks she's smarter than him, this concept of power imbalance applies in many of the adult relationships on the show as well, including Emma over Ken and Terri over Will. Sometimes the McKinley High staff room feels more like a schoolyard with all of its childish power struggles.

The New Directions gang was somewhat peripheral in "Vitamin D," acting more as accessories to the adult storylines, despite the fantastic mash-up numbers performed by each group.

High Note: More mash-ups, please! The drug-infused mash-up numbers were filled with energy and enthusiasm. Kudos to the actors who had to sing and dance and act like they were high, and to Dianna Agron in particular, who made Quinn slightly less energetic because Mrs. Schuester gave her prenatal vitamins instead.

Low Note: Why isn't Quinn being tougher on Terri? She's upset, scared and confused, but she has the power. She shouldn't let Terri push her around like that. Quinn is quick to use her power over Finn, Puck, Rachel and the other Cheerios, so why not an adult?

Behind the Music:

"It's My Life/Confessions Part II" (Finn, Puck, Kurt, Artie, Mike and Matt)
Bon Jovi, *Crush* (2000)
Usher, *Confessions* (2004)
Bon Jovi's rock anthem about living life to the fullest was an international hit and is credited with revitalizing the band's career. Usher's smooth #1 single tells the story of a man's mistress becoming pregnant — a dilemma Usher claims is not autobiographical. Finn, however, can relate, as he's "got one on the way" with Quinn and is struggling with these newfound responsibilities. Puck has confessions of his own he needs to make, as he is really the father of Quinn's baby. If Bon Jovi can overcome a declining career and Usher can overcome an unexpected pregnancy, Finn, Puck and the rest of New Directions can learn from their mistakes, discover who they are and stand up for themselves, despite these crazy curveballs.

"Halo/ Walking on Sunshine" (Rachel, Quinn, Mercedes, Tina, Santana and Brittany)
Beyoncé, *I Am . . . Sasha Fierce* (2008)
Katrina and the Waves, *Walking on Sunshine* (1983)
Beyoncé's love song about the importance of having a supportive and loving partner won her a Grammy for Best Female Pop Vocal Performance (which was handed to Beyoncé by Lea Michele). Katrina and the Waves' biggest hit celebrates the positivity and joy love brings. While both of these songs are about romantic love, romance at McKinley is more than a little complicated, and this jubilant mash-up celebrates a simpler love: the ladies' love of glee. Performing in New Directions makes everyone, despite their home problems, popularity problems and personal problems, happier. Which is a good

thing, because, if you look at the boys' mash-up, they seem to think that love is a messy and unnecessary nuisance. No matter what's happening in the kids' lives, they can come to glee club and find acceptance, solace and comfort.

That's Pretty *Popular*: When Kennedy High starts a trivia challenge team, they slack off once they learn their competition is John Ashcroft Private School for Special Needs Children in "The Brain Game."

Slushie Facials:
- Quinn drew pornographic pictures of Rachel on the bathroom walls.

Off-Key:
- There are two no-name Cheerios waiting to get decongestant tablets from Mrs. Schuester, a blonde and a brunette, at the very front of the line. Brittany is missing from this scene.
- Terri's pseudo-baby bump is really fake looking. Her waistband cuts into her stomach like she's wearing a pillow. How can Will not notice that?

Behind the Scenes:
- Lea Michele practiced speed talking for days in order to perfect her "sunshine, optimism and angels" speech. She wanted to make sure she had the perfect level of "mania."

Center Stage:
- According to Emma, Will has a "cute Kirk Douglas chin dimple." Kirk Douglas is an esteemed American actor and film producer known for his gravelly voice, cleft chin and tough-guy roles. Not only is he a legend, but his son, actor Michael Douglas, is one too.
- In a voice-over of his thoughts, Finn thinks about how hot Rachel is, even though she "kind of freaks him out in a *Swimfan* kind of way." *Swimfan* is a 2002 movie, considered a *Fatal Attraction* for a teen audience, about a girl who obsessively stalks her crush.
- Puck mentions the 2007 dance film *Stomp the Yard* when the boys are preparing for their mash-up. This is the second time that movie is referenced on *Glee*, the first being by Sue in "Preggers."
- Ken gets Emma a cubic zirconia engagement ring because *Blood Diamond*, the 2006 film starring Leonardo DiCaprio about a quest for

the evasive and rare pink diamond, affected her. Blood diamonds are mined in war zones and money made from the sale of those gemstones is used to finance wars.

- When Sue comes on board as New Directions' co-captain, she's excited about "puttin' on the ritz." "Puttin' on the Ritz" is a 1929 pop song written by Irving Berlin, which was included in the 1930 musical *Puttin' on the Ritz*. It's also slang for dressing fashionably, a term inspired by the Ritz Hotel in London.

Jazz Hands:
- One of the schools competing in Sectionals is the school for the deaf in Dayton. This is the same school for the deaf that beat the football team earlier this season, as mentioned by Ken in "Preggers."
- This is the first episode where Sue's journal makes an appearance.
- The *Hindenburg* was a German hydrogen-powered airship. In 1937, the LZ 129 Hindenburg, the largest in the Hindenburg fleet, caught on fire and exploded, killing 36 people.
- When Sue says that she was born in the Panama Canal and ran for office twice, it's a reference to Senator John McCain. McCain was born in the Panama Canal zone and ran for president in 2000 and again in 2008.
- Those yellow dresses the gals donned for their mash-up? Rachel wears Shoshanna, Quinn wears Calvin Klein, Tina wears Betsey Johnson, Brittany wears Kimchi Blue, Santana wears BCBG Max Azaria and Mercedes wears a custom-made creation. Tina's dress was originally white, and the costume department dyed it yellow for the performance.
- The jockstrap on the bench when Emma enters the locker room to accept Ken's proposal has "Scheu" written on it.
- When Rachel and Finn are tossing baseball metaphors for their drug use back and forth, Finn calls Rachel A-Rach, a nod to A-Rod, a nickname for New York Yankees star Alex Rodriguez who tested positive for steroid use.
- Rachel wears a grey one-shoulder sweatshirt when she tosses away her stash of pseudoephedrine. Is that a throwback to Jessie Spano in *Saved by the Bell*, who wore a similar sweatshirt when she threw her caffeine pills out? If so, costume designer Lou Eyrich deserves a round of applause.

The Buckeye State: Hickory Farms, the maker of the gift baskets Sue refers to when visiting Terri, is a specialty foods company based in Maumee,

show choirs versus glee clubs

The characters on *Glee* may use the terms "show choir" and "glee club" interchangeably, but the two are actually as different as night and day. Originating in the U.S. in the mid-1960s, a show choir is a group of people who combine singing with dancing, sometimes to relate a specific idea or to tell a story. A glee club, on the other hand, is traditionally a musical group that specializes in singing short songs called "glees," which are usually composed for three or four solo voices to sing together. Although they originated in London, England, in 1787 and were very popular in the early 1800s, by the mid-20th century, true glee clubs were no longer common. Nowadays when you hear the term "glee club," it's usually referring to a choir or, in the case of *Glee*, a show choir, even though New Directions is the only "glee club" we know of that dances!

Ohio. Founded in 1951 to sell cheese at local fairs, it now sells food gift baskets featuring summer sausage, cheese, fruit, nuts and sweets.

How Sue Cs It: "I always thought the desire to procreate showed deep personal weakness."

1.07 "throwdown"
Original Air Date: October 14, 2009
Written by: Brad Falchuk
Directed by: Ryan Murphy

The Music: ★ ★ ★
The Drama: ★ ★ ★
The Laughs: ★ ★ ✦

Will: I will destroy you.
Sue: I'm about to vomit down your back.

It's Will versus Sue. Who will come out on top?
What do you get when you take two supposedly responsible adults and

put them together to co-chair a glee club? Well, when they're two teachers who happen to be mortal enemies dead-set on destroying each other, you get one hell of a war zone. Little did Figgins know that when he appointed Sue as co-director of New Directions, he was actually aiding her bring-down-the-glee-club-from-the-inside mission. Acting on Quinn's spy tip that the glee club's "minority" students aren't being heard, Sue divides the group in two, calling out the recruits for her "elite" glee club, nicknaming most of them hilariously as she goes: Santana (the only one who gets called by her real name), Wheels (Artie), Gay Kid (Kurt), Asian (Tina), Other Asian (Mike), Aretha (Mercedes) and Shaft (Matt).

Sue's plan is to give these kids the opportunities that they don't usually have in glee club, and when you ignore her malicious intent for a moment, her main idea is both spot-on and necessary. Will continually favors both Rachel and Finn while preaching about how the glee club is open and inclusive to all. Sure, Sue's method may not be kosher, but Will, as demonstrated in previous episodes, is pretty stubborn in his ways when it comes to glee club. A harsh lesson, even one designed to destroy him, might be the only way to get through to him.

In the end, both Will and Sue lose this battle. Tired of hearing their teachers continually hurling insults at each other, the teens act like the adults in this situation and tell both directors to shut up and grow up. One of the best moments comes when Finn bluntly tells the two teachers that if the glee clubbers wanted to hear fighting, they'd stay home and listen to their parents. From Finn's and Kurt's single parents to Rachel's two gay dads, we've already seen how the home lives of the New Directions kids are anything but simple. Glee club is supposed to be the fun part of their day — a brief reprieve between the pressures of school and the struggles at home. Sue and Will's vicious vendetta isn't something the students have time for in their agendas.

While Sue and Will's rivalry may be the main focus of "Throwdown," the gleeks' growing friendship is a welcome antidote to the bitter venom between teachers. When Quinn's blossoming baby bump becomes the top story on Perez Hilton–wannabe Jacob's blog, Rachel steps up and shuts it down. In the previous episode, she says Quinn will need glee club and she already does. Let's face it, everyone in New Directions, from the social delinquents to the popular cheerleaders is, in some way, a card-carrying member of the Merry Misfit Minorities.

High Note: For someone so mentally thick, Finn is an emotional savant. It's great that he plans to be there for Quinn no matter what she decides to do and that he's mentally preparing himself just in case she decides to keep it. Finn isn't singularly devoted to Quinn anymore — if he was, he wouldn't be so into hanging out with Rachel — but he clearly cares about her. Helping her with her ob-gyn appointments and comforting her in the hallway is all very sweet.

Low Note: How dense is Will? He must know something is going on with Terri's pregnancy. That ob-gyn appointment is insane. It's possible that the New Directions and Sue drama is keeping him preoccupied, but he's *got* to catch on eventually.

Behind the Music:

"Hate on Me" (Mercedes, Tina, Kurt, Artie, Santana, Mike and Matt)
Jill Scott, *The Real Thing: Words and Sounds Vol. 3* (2007)
Haters hate on everyone, including R&B singer-songwriter Jill Scott and Sue's elite glee club, "Sue's Kids." The songstress was inspired to write her biggest hit after finding a group of people trashing her and her music online. Sue chooses this number (which was a creative departure for the usually soulful Jill) because Kurt, Santana, Matt, Mike, Tina, Artie and Mercedes face discrimination in their daily life but rise above it, both inside and outside of New Directions. Will may ignore their suggestions for more R&B music and some pop-and-lock dancing, but he can't break their spirits.

"Ride wit Me" (New Directions)
Nelly, *Country Grammar* (2001)
Deviant behavior abounds in Nelly's catchy summer hit and at McKinley High. But this time, it's the teachers, not the students, creating waves. Will and Sue are taking New Directions on a ride with their rivalry and no one knows the final destination. It's just too bad Will and Sue won't let their two groups ride together, as that's what the club would clearly prefer.

"No Air" (Rachel and Finn with Quinn, Puck and Brittany)
Jordin Sparks and Chris Brown, *Jordin Sparks* (2007)
American Idol winner Jordin Sparks sings about needing her partner as much as she needs airs to breathe in "No Air," her biggest hit to date. Rachel can relate. Her crush on Finn is so strong that she'll do anything for him, even if it means they can't be together. As for New Directions, they need both halves — Will's kids and Sue's kids — to be able to breathe (and succeed) as a group.

"You Keep Me Hangin' On" (Quinn)
The Supremes, *The Supremes Sing Holland-Dozier-Holland* (1967)
The Supremes' #1 hit about needing to move on from a failed relationship is classic Motown but stands out thanks to its spoken-word hook and its Morse code–inspired baseline. Now that Quinn's pregnant, both Finn and Sue keep her hanging on, so to speak. Her relationship with Finn isn't working anymore, but Quinn's pregnancy pushes it forward. As for Sue, Quinn is trapped by the fear of losing the status and security her Cheerios uniform (and thus, Sue) gives her.

"Keep Holding On" (New Directions)
Avril Lavigne, *The Best Damn Thing* (2007)
Avril Lavigne's pop rock ballad about being there for a friend and not giving up during hard times was originally recorded for the 2006 film *Eragon*. Quinn, despite what she may think, is not alone. Everyone in New Directions, from her frenemy Cheerios to her nemesis Rachel, is there to support her through these tough times. As long as Quinn continues to hold on, New Directions will be there for her.

That's Pretty Popular: Jacob Ben Israel is a lot like another creepy secondary character: *Popular*'s April Tuna. April Tuna is a bizarre outsider no one understands who has a huge crush on Carmen Ferrara, even starting a Carmen fan club. Both creepsters even go to great lengths to score underpants from their objects of affection.

Slushie Facials:
- Sue throws a kid's slushie on the ground.

Off-Key:
- Why is Will suddenly failing the Cheerios? Had he been giving them good grades because they were cheerleaders? Or has he never had a cheerleader in his class before?

Behind the Scenes:
- "Ride wit Me" is one of several songs that made it into the show because Ryan Murphy overheard the cast singing it. Mark Salling likes to break out his guitar between takes and everyone else challenges him to play something. One day, it was "Ride wit Me" and the entire cast sang along. The result impressed Ryan so much that he wrote it into this episode. The jam session vibe remains intact; it really just looks like 12 kids having fun.
- Watch Brittany's face when she and Puck are in Sue Sylvester's office. This is the moment Brittany goes from stereotypical mean cheerleader to a lovable dumb blonde. Ryan Murphy thought Heather Morris looked confused in this scene, found it hilarious and decided to change Brittany from a mean cheerleader to a dumb one to highlight this.

Center Stage:
- As Rachel Berry pointed out, New Directions is not a crunk club. Crunk is the fusion of hip hop and electronica that originated in the late 1990s. Originally it was not a type of music but dancing associated with large, out-of-control crowds. Lil John and the group Three 6 Mafia are credited with pioneering the musical genre inspired by this dancing.
- Finn is disappointed that the baby doesn't have any cool mutations. In the *X-Men* series, the mutants' variations are caused by genetic mutation known as the X-Gene, which humans lack. Those who carry this gene are known as *Homo sapiens superior* and are considered the next evolutionary step for the species.

gleek speak: RPing *glee*

There are several roleplayer groups online creating their own version of McKinley High. We chatted with one of the more prominent groups about what it's like running a (pretend) glee club on Twitter. Find and follow all of their accounts at tweepml.org/Glee-RPs/.

How did you choose which character to play? Is your RP character one of your favorites on the show, or was it just a character you thought you could relate to and play well?

Kylie (Tina Cohen-Chang): Picking who to be really took deep thought, because I wanted to be sure that I could play my character well. To choose, I tried to put myself in each female character's mind and see which came most naturally, and to me, that was Tina. And although as a player I need to detach myself from the character, it was the similarities between her and me which drew me to her. (I also have a speech impediment and confidence issues.)

Oscar (Finn Hudson): Finn is one of my favorite characters on the show, so I knew it would be a fun experience! I can't say I relate a lot to him on a personal level since I'm not a football jock who was cheated into thinking he was the father of his pregnant girlfriend's baby, but I love Finn so I went for it.

Sarah (Jacob Ben Israel/Ken Tanaka): For Jacob, I thought it would be fun to give him a bit more of a personality, seeing as on the show he hasn't been given a lot of screen time. Plus it would give him yet another medium to stalk Rachel!

Chance (Kurt Hummel): I chose Kurt Hummel because he is my favorite character on the show and he is easily relatable for me. We also share a lot of the same struggles because we're both openly gay. Chris Colfer's performance in the episode "Preggers" really meant a lot to me because I was depressed. I felt like I couldn't come out without being ridiculed for it, but seeing that episode gave me the courage to tell my family, who acted *exactly* like Kurt's dad did. *Glee* has really helped me.

Jack (Terri Schuester): I chose Terri, as she was my favorite of the characters left. She does cause a bit of ruckus, but she means well, I think. Terri's been getting a whole lot of smack-talk towards her, so I thought it was time for Terri to take on the haters one tweet at a time.

What struggles or challenges have you faced while trying to remain true to your character at all times?

Spencer (Rachel Berry): Rachel can be all about herself at times and sometimes it's really difficult to act rude to others because it's not like me at all in real life. Although, it can be really fun at the same time to act so boldly.

Josh (Matt Rutherford): I think the hardest thing for me is when you get comments that are just so random, so quirky and imaginative — you have not got a clue how to respond. Say someone asks you, "Hey, what is Matt's favorite sock color?" You just sit there at the screen with a blank look on your face.

Megan (Artie Abrams): I just want to make my Artie seem like the Artie everyone knows and loves from the show. I don't have his sense of humor or comedic timing, so that makes it a little bit harder.

Amber (Noah "Puck" Puckerman): Well, if you haven't figured it out because my name is Amber, I am not a dude. So playing a male has been pretty hard for me, and especially playing somebody like Noah. He always knows what to say to the ladies, although he can be and sometimes is a total jerk. And those are two things that I have the most trouble with because A: I do not hit on cougars, and B: I'm usually a pretty nice person.

Jordan (Santana Lopez): In the beginning especially, Santana wasn't shown a lot. When she was, she had some funny one-liner and then it was over. It's not easy to know how she would react to certain situations because of this. Honestly, one of the things that made it easier to play Santana was her line in "Sectionals" when she said that glee was the best part of her day. I felt I could combine the mean side they showed in earlier episodes with this admission of "No one is forcing me to be here."

Jazz Hands:

- This is the first episode Jayma Mays doesn't appear in, marking the first absence of a main cast member.
- Mike Chang speaks!
- Sue's refers to herself as Ajax. Ajax is a Greek hero prominent in the *Iliad*. He is the strongest Achaean and the most valuable warrior in Agamemnon's army. He is so heroic in battle that he is the only soldier who does not receive godly help.
- This is the first episode where *Glee* breaks the fourth wall, which is when a character breaks the division between the real world and the world that exists onstage or on television. In the voice-overs at the beginning, Will acknowledges his voice is a voice-over.
- Sue wears a blue and black Nike pullover in this episode, just when fans were beginning to think Adidas had her under an exclusive contract.
- When the couple buying Sue's house did her wrong, she salted the backyard so nothing could grow there for one hundred years. This is a ritual that originated in Western Asia and is mentioned in the Bible several times. The salt curses whoever inhabits the land next.
- According to Will, Sue's Cheerios have been pushed through since 1992.

Since Will won nationals at McKinley High in 1993, it's possible that Sue taught at the school while Will was a student there.

- It doesn't matter where he is, Finn's got football on the brain. He even dotted the "i" in "Drizzle" with one.
- The red light district in Amsterdam is famous for its brothels, legal prostitution and sex shops and is one of the city's largest tourist attractions.

How Sue Cs It: "I don't trust a man with curly hair. I can't help but picture little birds laying sulfurous eggs in there and I find it disgusting."

♪♫♪

1.08 "mash-up"
Original Air Date: October 21, 2009
Written by: Ian Brennan
Directed by: Elodie Keene

The Music: ★ ★ ★
The Drama: ★ ★ ♪
The Laughs: ★ ★ ★

Puck: It was a message from God — Rachel was a hot Jew and the good lord wanted me to get into her pants.

While Finn and Quinn deal with the loss of their social status, a flirtation between Rachel and Puck blossoms into a mash-up of their own.

"Welcome to the new world order," says hockey player Dave Karofsky to Finn and Quinn after throwing a slushie at Finn's face. New world order, indeed. Now that the whole school knows that Quinn's knocked up, Finn and Quinn being outcasts and the forecast doesn't look good. And as much as Quinn has grown (both in maturity and in waist size), she still has the same main priority, which she reiterates in Emma's office: social currency. This admission further emphasizes her similarities to Terri, while undermining some hard-won viewer sympathy. Like Terri, Quinn refuses to acknowledge that her problems are big ones; they can't be fixed by wearing a pregnancy pad or sunglasses indoors.

Finn has even more to deal with now that he's being forced to choose between football and glee club after a bitter Coach Tanaka schedules a new mandatory practice at the exact same time as rehearsals. His vindictive decision is yet another example that McKinley's teachers aren't above the petty rivalries of their students, and unfortunately the teens end up as pawns in their game. The football versus glee club issue isn't a new one. Finn battles with competing priorities time and again, and every time he achieves a comfortable equilibrium, someone upsets the balance. Finn may love glee club, but he also loves football and the popularity that comes along with it. We can question Finn's morals in his decision to pick being cool over being true to his heart, but ultimately the decision makes sense for him. The popular clique is all he's ever known and it's only natural for him to be afraid of the unknown. Fortunately, Mr. Schue saves the day with a classic motivational speech during a "father-son" bonding moment, reminding Finn that sometimes leaders need to make tough choices.

Finn can keep a foot in both worlds for a while longer, but because Sue responds to the pregnancy news by kicking the mom-to-be off the team, Quinn can't. At first, Sue shows some compassion for Quinn, so it's tough to tell whether this is Sue being Sue or whether she's genuinely hurt by Quinn's secret-keeping. This ambiguity might be thanks to the softer side of Sue, which comes out when she enters into a whirlwind romance with Rod, the local news anchor. Sue may act tough, but she's very much like every other character on this show: lonely and looking for love. However, it doesn't take long before Rod breaks Sue's heart and she's back to her old terrorizing self with just another axe to grind in her arsenal. Thank goodness lovey-dovey Sue doesn't last longer than a single episode because she's funnier when she's bitter!

Meanwhile, the show runners throw us a curve ball when Rachel and Puck start making out in her bedroom. But just like Emma settles for Ken when she can't be with Will, Rachel's settling for Puck because she can't be with Finn. As fun and as risqué as a Rachel/Puck relationship might seem, Rachel's Finn crush and Puck's Quinn crush makes this duo doomed from the start. This plot twist does give us a little more insight into what's going on beneath the Mohawk though, and Puck's attempt to be a good Jew reveals that this bad boy might be a momma's boy at heart. And if Puck really cares for his mom, does that mean he actually might be a good caretaker for the mother of his child?

Rachel and Puck's tryst isn't the only scandalous relationship development as Emma and Will's flirtation also enters into dangerous territory in

cast connections

Many of the *Glee* cast members have crossed paths before:

In 2007, Jayma Mays and Matthew Morrison both starred in an unaired pilot called *Nice Girls Don't Get the Corner Office*. Jayma played Angela, an ambitious employee with big corporate dreams. She's passed over for a big promotion because she's exactly what the title says — too nice for the job. Matt played Brody, the office's slacker bad boy. Even though the show never aired, you can find it on YouTube and see early signs of that now-famous Jayma/Matt chemistry!

Dianna Agron, Jessalyn Gilsig, Jayma Mays and Stephen Tobolowsky all had guest-starring gigs on the NBC hit show *Heroes*. Quinn's not the first character Dianna Agron carried pom poms for — she appeared in four episodes as bitchy cheerleader Debbie Marshall who gets suspended for drinking too much. Jessalyn appeared in ten episodes as Meredith Gordon, the biological mother of Claire Bennet, the indestructible cheerleader. Jayma appeared in five episodes as Charlie Andrews, the lost-in-time love interest of Hiro Nakamura. Stephen played hero Robert Bishop for 11 episodes. He had the power of alchemy before he was killed by superhuman villain Sylar.

Jenna Ushkowitz and Lea Michele, who have known each other since they were eight years old, both appeared in the Broadway production of *Spring Awakening* alongside *Glee* guest star Jonathan Groff. Lea and Jonathan originated the lead roles while Jenna was the understudy for three different characters.

Jayma Mays, Stephen Tobolowsky and Iqbal Theba all appeared in the 2006 film *Blind Dating*, a comedy about a blind American man who, after undergoing risky surgery to restore his eyesight, falls in love with an Indian woman whose marriage to someone else has already been arranged.

Iqbal Theba and Jane Lynch both had guest-starring roles in the critically acclaimed TV show *Arrested Development* in its first season. Iqbal played the role of an incredibly ugly *girl* for one episode and Jane appeared as an undercover agent in two episodes, one of which was the same episode as Iqbal's gig!

Both Kevin McHale and Patrick Gallagher had multi-episode arcs on the HBO vampire hit *True Blood*, but the two never crossed paths. Kevin played coroner assistant Neil Jones in two episodes in the first season, and Patrick played a vampire named Chow during his four-episode stint in the second season.

"Mash-Up," making us wonder if the title refers to the song mash-up Will tries to create for Ken and Emma, or if it's a tip of the hat to the many mashed-up couples this week. Romance hits the halls of McKinley High hard this week, and we can't help but wonder who will get bit by the love bug next.

High Note: The "Bust a Move" sequence is the perfect representation of New Directions' overall dynamics. Finn is reluctant to step up and take the lead and Puck is embarrassed to participate at all. Matt and Mike get down and dance right away, while Kurt is offended by the tacky dance moves. Quinn and the other Cheerios are wary of getting into the groove, but eventually warm up and have fun. Rachel, Mercedes, Tina and Artie are gung-ho from the get-go and Will is their fearless leader who loves the spotlight, selecting an uncool song but singing it with so much joy that you have to love him. Some are reluctant to join in on the song, just as they were the club, but you can't fight the rhythm forever.

Low Note: Why would Will go wedding dress shopping with Emma after promising to Ken that he wouldn't encourage Emma anymore? Are all bets off between Ken and Will because Ken refuses to cancel football practice? Even if things are rough between these two, it's uncool of Will to do something he knows is wrong.

Behind the Music:

"Bust a Move" (Will with New Directions)
Young MC, *Stone Cold Rhymin'* (1989)
What's better than dancing and picking up ladies? Nothing, according to Young MC's top ten hit. Mr. Schue agrees — with the dancing part at least! He wants New Directions to "bust a move," as everyone is too preoccupied with personal drama or social status to loosen up and have fun.

"Thong Song" (Will)
Sisqó, *Unleash the Dragon* (2000)
"Thong Song" is a ridiculous romp about the joys of the thong bikini. It's an insane choice for a wedding song but then, Ken and Emma getting married is an insane idea and the "Thong Song" only amplifies what a terrible romantic match they are. And while singing this song to someone as conservative as Emma is ridiculous, Will getting down with some risqué dance moves to this scandalous tune generates more than a little sexual tension between him and Emma.

"What a Girl Wants" (Rachel)
Christina Aguilera, *Christina Aguilera* (1999)
Sometimes a girl doesn't know what she wants, but having a supportive and intuitive boyfriend by your side can help you sort that out. Christina Aguilera sang about exactly that and scored a #1 hit and a Grammy nomination for Best Female Pop Vocal Performance with "What a Girl Wants." Rachel thinks she knows what she wants: Finn. She may only date Puck to make him jealous (and Puck may only date Rachel to be a better Jew) but he seems to know what she wants, even when she doesn't: someone who recognizes both her talent and her insecurities and treats her with respect.

"Sweet Caroline" (Puck)
Neil Diamond (1969)
Neil Diamond's karaoke, sport stadium and cover band staple may have been inspired by Caroline Kennedy, but its message about the joy love can bring is universal. Puck celebrates his and Rachel's brief romance with a public serenade of "Sweet Caroline," a song written and recorded by a Jew, and covered by a Jew to win over a Jew. Puck's mom wouldn't have it any other way.

"I Could Have Danced All Night" (Emma)
My Fair Lady (1956)

Eliza Doolittle (see "Give My Regards" below) sings "I Could Have Danced All Night" after an impromptu dance session with her crush-worthy tutor, Henry Higgins. Emma, like Eliza, is in complete bliss when she's dancing with Will, her dance tutor. To Emma, Will is a great partner, both on the dance floor and in life, and she'd dance all night with him if she had the chance.

The Sound of Music: Mash-ups, the blending of two or more songs together by seamlessly integrating vocals and music, are as old as music itself. Classical mash-ups are known as quodlibet, which can be traced back to the 15th century. Frank Zappa developed a mash-up technique he called xenochrony in the 1970s. Contemporary mash-ups became popular again in 2002, when 2 Many DJ's (a collaboration between Soulwax's Dewaele brothers) released an album titled *As Heard on Radio Soulwax Pt. 2*, featuring 45 different mash-ups. Other artists followed suit, and combined with the increased acceptance of synthesized music and DJs as legitimate artists, mash-ups have soared in popularity. There are many different kinds of mash-ups in popular music today, including version versus version, abstract mash-ups and remixes.

Give My Regards to Broadway: Inspired by George Bernard Shaw's 1913 play *Pygmalion*, *My Fair Lady* is the story of Eliza Doolittle, a working class girl who dreams of working in a flower shop. However, her thick Cockney accent discourages potential employers from hiring her. She turns to a speech professor, Henry Higgins, who agrees to teach Eliza on a bet, hoping to train her so well that people mistake her for a duchess. *My Fair Lady* debuted on March 15, 1956, and ran for 2,717 shows. The 1964 film stayed faithful to the original stage version with the exception of the ending. The casting of Audrey Hepburn was controversial, as Julie Andrews played Eliza Doolittle on Broadway and was considered perfect for the role. Audrey's singing in the film had to be dubbed, but the film still won eight Academy Awards, including Best Picture.

That's Pretty *Popular*: Drama teacher Mr. Vincent and Coach Peritti, the football coach, clash over Josh Ford's desire to be in the musical and on the football team. Mr. Vincent moves the musical's opening in "Under Siege" so it conflicts with football and forces Josh to choose.

Slushie Facials:

- Finn gets a slushie facial from hockey player Dave Karofsky.
- The entire football team slushies Finn and Quinn.
- Puck gets slushied in the hallway while walking with Rachel.
- Kurt slushies himself because Finn feels guilty about having to do it.
- Everyone in New Directions hits Mr. Schuester with a grape slushie.

Off-Key:

- During "Sweet Caroline," Brittany is sitting in front of Quinn. When the camera pans from Quinn to Rachel, Brittany's seat is empty, but when the camera returns to Puck, Brittany is in her seat again.
- As good as Puck's "Sweet Caroline" is, aren't they supposed to be working on a mash-up?

Behind the Scenes:

- Ryan Murphy wrote "Sweet Caroline" into *Glee* after hearing Mark play it on set in between takes.
- The slushies in the pilot and "Showmance" were real 100% cold slushies. "It felt like I was bitchslapped by an iceberg," Chris Colfer recalled. No one wants to feel that, so the prop department concocted a special warm corn syrup slushie recipe to lessen the pain.
- Mercedes was supposed to get slushied, but Amber suggested the "My weave!" line to get out of it. Ryan Murphy liked the idea and kept it in.
- Securing rights for "Sweet Caroline" was difficult. Neil Diamond originally said no, then yes. After the episode was recorded, he retracted his offer. Music producer P.J. Bloom had to convince him to change his mind, again, but it all worked out. Neil was so impressed with Puck's rendition of his song that he released other songs in his catalog for future use.

Center Stage:

- Emma is turned on by Will's "Gene Kelly charm." Gene Kelly was an American dancer, actor, singer, director, producer and choreographer who dominated musical films in post-war Hollywood. His most famous films were *An American in Paris* (1951) and *Singin' in the Rain* (1952). Kelly was renowned for being charming, attractive and likeable both on- and off-screen.

- Rachel teaches Puck about Tommy Tune, a true triple threat who impressed both onstage and behind the scenes during his time on Broadway. He won nine Tony awards in four different categories (Best Actor, Best Featured Actor, Best Choreographer and Best Direction) during his career. He's worked steadily since 1966, starring in productions like *The Best Little Whorehouse in Texas* and films like *Hello, Dolly!*
- Finn believes Thomas Jefferson and the kid from the *Terminator* movies imagined a better future. Thomas Jefferson was the third president of the United States, the principal author of the Declaration of Independence and one of America's most influential founding fathers. The kid from the *Terminator* films, John Connor, grows up to lead the human resistance against machines throughout the series.

Jazz Hands:

- The episode is titled "Mash-Up" but there isn't a single music mash-up in the episode. Perhaps the songs, like this week's couples, just aren't compatible?
- This is the first episode Jessalyn Gilsig doesn't appear in.
- Emma's practice wedding dress is like her relationship with Ken: bulky, restrictive and a poor fit. This dress was inspired by Princess Diana's 1981 wedding dress. Princess Diana's David and Elizabeth Emanuel–designed dress featured a 25-foot train and cost almost $15,000 (which today would be more like $35,000).
- Puck's family watches *Schindler's List* every year on Simchat Torah while they eat sweet and sour pork. Simchat Torah is the annual Jewish celebration that concludes the cycle of public Torah readings and marks the beginning of the new cycle. *Schindler's List* is the 1993 Academy Award–winning Steven Spielberg film that tells the story of Oskar Schindler, a man who saved the lives of thousands of Polish Jews from the Holocaust. Jews who keep kosher do *not* eat sweet and sour pork.
- Emma's second wedding dress channels Audrey Hepburn in *Sabrina*, when she wore a now-famous little black dress by Givenchy. Audrey portrayed Eliza Doolittle, the character who sings Emma's wedding song in *My Fair Lady*.

The Buckeye State: Puck has posters for Ohio State University on his wall. Ohio State University is considered the best public university in Ohio.

Its Columbus campus is America's second largest and OSU has subsidiary campuses throughout Ohio, including one in Lima.

How Sue Cs It: "I will go to the animal shelter and get you a kitty cat. I will let you fall in love with that kitty cat. And then on some dark cold night, I will steal away into your home and punch you in the face."

♪♫♪

1.09 "wheels"
Original Air Date: November 11, 2009
Written by: Ryan Murphy
Directed by: Paris Barclay

The Music: ★ ★ ★ ★
The Drama: ★ ★ ★ ★
The Laughs: ★ ★ ★

Burt: This is really getting you down, isn't it?
Kurt: I'm full of ennui.
Burt: So . . . it's really getting you down?

New Directions rallies together to raise money to rent a bus for Artie. Puck and Finn try to raise money for Quinn's doctor's bills and Kurt discovers family is more important than fame.

Artie gets his turn in the spotlight in "Wheels," an episode that focuses on his disability and Will's attempt to have the other glee club members better understand Artie's struggles. After the group is reluctant to run a bake sale to raise funds for a handicapable bus to take the whole club, Artie included, to Sectionals together, Mr. Schue takes action in the name of team camaraderie. New Directions will have a bake sale, and they'll also spend three hours per school day in a wheelchair and perform a wheelchair musical number. Call it a roll-playing challenge.

Artie finally gets some lovin' from Tina in this episode, but their romance fizzles quickly. Artie feels betrayed by Tina's lie, but considering that he gives a speech to her about how he doesn't purposely try to seclude himself from others, he shouldn't push her away so easily. Seeing Artie push back a little is a great touch as it balances out his story, which is sad enough that it could make him an object of pity, rather than a regular teen.

In "Throwdown" Sue questions Will's treatment of minorities and these issues come to the forefront again in "Wheels." Will is adamant that his students should support Artie and work to better understand his daily challenges, yet at the same time he dismisses Kurt's request to sing a solo traditionally sung by a girl. Will really needs to treat his students equally. From continually favoring Rachel and Finn to this unfair refusal of Kurt's request, he needs to better remember his claims that glee club is inclusive to all.

This episode proves that appearances can be deceiving: Kurt, the wannabe superstar reveals his family-first mentality; meanie Sue shows off her softer side with her disabled sister; Puck uses his bad-ass exterior to mask a caring and confused interior; and Artie displays his self-righteousness when he rejects Tina. "Wheels" may be about the internal struggles everyone, show choir geeks and cheerleading coaches alike, face, but it's also about how you can't judge a book — or a person — by its cover.

High Note: "Defying Gravity" is the first song Kurt seems truly excited by. Good for him for standing up to Rachel and Will and proving he has the confidence to be a star. Mercedes makes the occasional snarky comment, but this is the first time someone stands up and asks for a fair fight.

Low Note: Would two teenage boys really battle over who can take care of their future child and baby mama the best? *Glee* has some pretty out-there plot lines, but this one doesn't ring true, even with an extreme suspension of disbelief.

Behind the Music:

"Dancing with Myself" (Artie)
Billy Idol, *Don't Stop* (1981)
"Dancing with Myself" was originally written and recorded by Billy Idol's band with Tony James. Billy released his own version later that same year, which soared to #2 on the Billboard Hot 100 chart. There have been persistent rumors that the song is about pleasuring oneself, but Tony and Billy claim that watching their own carefree dancing in a mirror at a Japanese nightclub in the late 1970s was the inspiration. Artie may not be able to move his legs, but it doesn't mean he can't dance, both literally and metaphorically, and it's

lauren potter as becky jackson

Lauren Potter proved dreams can come true when she beat out 13 other hopefuls for the role of Becky Jackson on *Glee*. Lauren scored her primetime debut through the Down Syndrome Association of Los Angeles, after *Glee* producers contacted them about the role. Born May 10, 1990, Lauren attended Poly High School in Long Beach, California, where she tried out for the cheerleading squad but didn't make it. The tables turned when she was cast as Sue Sylvester's replacement Cheerio.

nice to know that thanks to New Directions, he doesn't have to do it on his own. But offstage Artie is always dancing with himself, facing daily obstacles able-bodied people don't, and it can get in the way of everything, even a budding romance with Tina.

"Defying Gravity" (Rachel and Kurt)
Wicked (2003)
In *Wicked* (see "Give My Regards" below), Glinda, the future good witch, and Elphaba, the future Wicked Witch of the West, sing "Defying Gravity" after Elphaba discovers that the Wizard of Oz is not a hero and decides she must do everything she can to stop him. Glinda does her best to discourage Elphaba, thinking she doesn't have a chance. Kurt, like Elphaba, is tired of being discounted and fights for his first solo, while Rachel is like Glinda, trying to stop his fight.

"Proud Mary" (New Directions)
Creedence Clearwater Revival, *Bayou Country* (1969)
Creedence Clearwater Revival's first top 10 hit pays homage to the riverboat culture of the South. However, the song is also about a community who comes together for their friends. New Directions may roll onstage in wheelchairs for this number, but they also come through for Artie and raise the money he needs to travel to Sectionals with them, just like those who live on the river would do.

Give My Regards to Broadway: In the tradition of turning a beloved story on its head and making the audience look at the characters in a new way, *Wicked* recasts two characters from *The Wizard of Oz*. Before they become the Good Witch of the North and the Wicked Witch of the West, Glinda (formerly Galinda) and Elphaba were college roommates. The radically different women were constantly butting heads, loved the same boy and reacted differently to the discovery of Oz's corrupt government. Elphaba, with her green skin and progressive views, has a very public falling out and becomes known as the Wicked Witch, though she is simply misunderstood. The musical, based on Gregory Maguire's 1995 novel of the same name, premiered in May 2003 in San Francisco and moved to Broadway on October 8, 2003. It received mixed critical reviews but was a hit with its audience, breaking box office records around the world. The production was nominated for ten Tony awards, including a Best Actress nod for Idina Menzel as Elphaba. Idina and Kristin Chenoweth, the original Broadway stars, both make multi-episode guest appearances in *Glee*'s first season.

That's Pretty *Popular*: In "Hard on the Outside, Soft in the Middle," Sam, Lily and Carmen are discriminated against for being brunettes. To see if blondes really do have more fun, the two groups swap hair color — the cheerleaders going brunette and Sam's group going blonde — and learn what it's like to live someone else's life, just like the students on *Glee* find out what it's like to be in a wheelchair.

wheelchair dancing: it's for real

Will Schuester seems pretty proud of himself for forcing New Directions to perform in wheelchairs, and to the team's credit, they had a blast and did a great job. But there's no way the kids in New Directions could keep up with the pros that participate in Wheelchair DanceSport, a competitive wheelchair dancing circuit for pairs. George Hart is credited with developing wheelchair dance in the early '70s. After an accident left the British dancer paralyzed, he refused to give up his passion and instead adapted his favorite dances for a wheelchair. A Dutch group formed a wheelchair dancing collective in 1977, and the pastime has only grown from there. Wheelchair DanceSport became an official competitive sport in 1977, when the first international competition took place. Each duo must have at least one wheelchair-bound member to be eligible to complete. Today, over 5,000 dancers in 40 countries take part in the competition, which features standard competitive dances like the waltz, tango, rumba, samba and foxtrot.

Off-Key:

- Artie's wheelchair does not consistently have the back support wheels. They disappear and reappear when Artie is singing and dancing to "Dancing with Myself."
- Rachel bakes secret-family-recipe apology cookies in "Acafellas" but can't bake anything for the bake sale?

Behind the Scenes:

- Kevin McHale had to record "Dancing with Myself" twice. Why? His original version was deemed "too sexy" by Ryan Murphy.
- Kurt wanting to sing "Defying Gravity" was written into the show because it actually happened to Chris Colfer in high school. "When I was in high school, every year we would have a talent show," Chris told *People*. "Every year I would beg the teachers to let me sing 'Defying Gravity' from *Wicked*. And every year they turned me down because I'm a boy and it was 'a girl's song.'" The script was originally written with Kurt singing the song by himself but was later changed to include Rachel because the producers loved Lea Michele's version too.
- Zach Woodlee called the wheelchair number the "scariest" sequence he ever had to choreograph. "It was like roller derby," he told the *New York Post*. "All of the actors would fall backwards and hit their heads —

123

gleek speak: adina herbert
(a social worker based in toronto, ontario)

As a social worker and disabilities rights activist, how do you feel about how *Glee* handles Artie's disability?

I think it's important that Artie and his disabilities are important to the show's plotline and inclusionary. This isn't a story about "regular kids" and Artie just happens to be there. He is a major part of the group and that concept does not ever seem to be compromised. It's easy to get sucked into prime-time drama and selling a show, and it seems they didn't feel they were compromising the "Hollywood-ness" of it by demonstrating real issues. There's an idea out there now that inclusiveness means inserting difference "into" the norm. But there is also the notion out there that true integration can also mean the opposite. That able-bodied people learn just as much and gain just as much by being included into a disabled environment. I think the fact that they demonstrated the effort by all the kids to be truly inclusive of Artie and his disability was truly refreshing and is certainly something you don't see often on TV.

particularly Lea Michele, who plays Rachel. You lose your balance really quick when you try to go up a ramp in a wheelchair. Amber Riley, who plays Mercedes, caught an edge going down a ramp and fell off completely."

- The rocking of the wheelchairs back and forth? That was an improvised move. The actors were goofing around and wanted to see what it would be like if they all rocked back and forth at the same time. Zach liked the effect and incorporated it into the choreography.

Center Stage:

- Kurt's dad listens exclusively to Mellencamp. John "Cougar" Mellencamp is an American rock musician known for his blue-collar music. His biggest hit, "Jack & Diane," is about two kids growing up in the Midwest, dreaming about getting out of their small town. His popularity was at its peak in the 1980s, and he was inducted into the Rock and Roll Hall of Fame in 2008.
- Kurt's dad assures Principal Figgins that Kurt sounds just like Ronnie Spector. Ronnie Spector was the lead singer of the 1960s girl group The Ronettes and was married to mega-producer Phil Spector. They had three huge hits that decade, "Be My Baby," "Baby, I Love You" and "Walking

in the Rain," but broke up in 1966. The Ronettes were inducted into the Rock and Roll Hall of Fame in 2007.

Jazz Hands:

- Neither Jayma Mays nor Jessalyn Gilsig appears in this episode, marking the second absence for each.
- Sue makes a passing reference to the Falkland Islands. This self-governing British territory in the South Pacific was invaded by Argentina in 1982. The United Nations Security Council called for Argentina to withdraw their troops. The British eventually sent over troops to reclaim the islands, resulting in the Falklands War. The Argentineans surrendered later that year.
- During their "Defying Gravity" diva-off, Rachel's outfit is mostly white and Kurt's outfit is mostly black. This is reminiscent of Glinda and Elphaba: Glinda wears a lot of white and Elphaba wears a lot of black. In the musical, Elphaba is the underdog who was picked on and teased all of her life, where Glinda was the popular princess who had things handed to her. By wearing similar colors, Kurt and Rachel are reinforcing who's who.
- In grade six, Tina avoided giving a speech on the Missouri Compromise, which was an 1820 agreement between pro-slavery and anti-slavery factions in the United States that regulated slavery in the western territories. It was the first major compromise between these two groups. The compromise outlawed slavery in the Louisiana Territory, except in certain areas of Missouri. However, the U.S. Senate refused to pass the measure.

How Sue Cs It: "If I have a pregnant girl doing a handspring into a double layout, the judges aren't going to be admiring her impeccable form, they're going to be wondering if the centrifugal force is going to make the baby's head start crowning."

♪♫♪

1.10 "ballad"

Original Air Date: November 18, 2009
Written by: Brad Falchuk
Directed by: Brad Falchuk

The Music: ★ ★ ★
The Drama: ★ ★ ★ ✦
The Laughs: ★ ★ ★

Rachel (to Will): It means I'm very young, and it's hard for you to stand close to me.

When Will and his New Directions crew express their feelings through song, some messages are received better than others.

What do you do when you can't tell someone how you feel? Why you put your feelings into a song, of course! It's rather convenient that Mr. Schue learns about a new requirement for Sectionals — the Rachel Berry–endorsed ballad — right when the show's drama and characters' hidden feelings are building in the episodes leading up to the fall finale. Because nothing puts your heart on a platter quite like singing a ballad. This isn't the first time we've seen songs used to express emotion (Rachel singing "Take a Bow" about her crush on Finn in "Showmance," and Mercedes singing "Bust Your Windows" about her frustration with Kurt in "Acafellas" are just two examples), but this time, it's definitely the focus.

Both Will and Finn try to use the power of song to say something important in this episode — Finn needs to tell Quinn's parents about the pregnancy and Will needs to tell Rachel to back off. Unfortunately, both ballads have adverse consequences: Rachel only falls more in love with Will, and Quinn suddenly finds herself homeless. Neither guy remembers a performer's golden rule: know your audience. Rachel's crush on Will stems from his amazing vocal talent, so by singing to her, no matter what the lyrics say, he only entices her further. Finn, on the other hand, forgets how strict and conservative Quinn's parents are. Expressing a difficult emotion through song might work onstage, but in real life even a bit of music can't ease the blow of such jarring news.

We also find out that this isn't the first time one of Will's students has been "hot for teacher," and you'd think with all his experience, he'd actually

brad ellis as brad, the piano man

New Directions' piano man is played by Brad Ellis. And in this episode, Rachel refers to him as . . . Brad. It's possible Lea Michele slipped up and Brad was supposed to be nameless forever, or maybe his character was finally given a name. Brad Ellis has worked on many off-Broadway productions including *Forbidden Broadway*, with future *Glee* guest stars Idina Menzel and Kristin Chenoweth. He composed the music for the 2009 Broadway musical *The Tin Pan Alley Rag* and arranged the world premiere of Billy Joel's *Waltz Variations No. 2 Op. 5* in 2006. Originally hired to accompany hopefuls during *Glee* auditions, Ryan casually mentioned that "when you're in the show," he'd accompany the singers as well. Brad thought it was a joke, but Ryan was serious. Watch Brad's facial expressions and wardrobe choices — they're often some of the episode's highlights. He even sat in a wheelchair during "Proud Mary" in "Wheels."

get better at dealing with this type of situation. However, after learning about the fiery consequences of his rejection of Suzy Pepper, viewers start to feel for Mr. Schue, especially since Rachel has previously demonstrated that she doesn't deal with rejection well either. Like April Rhodes, Suzy is another cautionary tale for Rachel, and thankfully she comes to her senses and gets her "mildly attractive groove back" by the end of the episode, because we really didn't need to add another complication to McKinley's already messy love triangles (and quadrangles).

The family drama heats up when both Finn's mom and Quinn's parents find out that Quinn's pregnant, and the contrast in their reactions is surprisingly telling. Finn's mom, while clearly disappointed with Finn, manages to put him first and anticipate his needs. They can have a conversation about responsible choices later, but right now, he just needs love and support. Quinn's parents, instead of discussing the pregnancy rationally with their daughter, kick her out. The family that seems troubled on the outside — Finn, the dimwitted jock with an uncertain future, and his depressed but hardworking single mom — is the family that stands by each other. Quinn's family, on the other hand, is picture-perfect — former beauty queen mom, proud father, two beautiful daughters on the cheerleading team and the honor roll — and it's the one that implodes the second trouble comes knocking.

Similarly, back at McKinley, the band of misfits that is New Directions seems like a dysfunctional family at the best of times, but when Finn and

Quinn need their support, the crew bands together. Music is what unites these 12 teens, and if their touching rendition of "Lean on Me" is any indication, it just might hold them together too.

High Note: Rachel is one smart cookie. Sure, her tunnel vision and insecurity get the better of her sometimes, but she's the most self-aware teenager ever. Everything from her acknowledgement that she's high maintenance in "Wheels" to her realization of why she's in love with Mr. Schuester shows maturity beyond her years.

Low Note: What's up with Finn and his hot and cold homophobia? He seems cool with Kurt and his beauty advice, but as soon as any sort of homosexuality touches him, he flips out. We understand he's a teenager struggling with his identity and popularity, but this reoccurring homophobia troubles us.

Behind the Music:

"Endless Love" (Will and Rachel)
Lionel Richie and Diana Ross, *Endless Love: Original Motion Picture Soundtrack* (1981)
How could Rachel not fall for Mr. Schue after singing one of the most romantic songs of all time with him? Lionel Richie and Diana Ross's declaration of love was written and recorded for the Brooke Shields film of the same name. The film bombed, but the song was the second most popular song of 1981 (after Olivia Newton-John's "Physical") and was nominated for an Academy Award for Best Original Song. Rachel's not the only one with romance on the mind. Declarations of love flourish in this episode, with Finn expressing his love for his unborn daughter, Suzy also pines over Mr. Schue and Kurt nearly spilling the beans about his crush on Finn.

"I'll Stand by You" (Finn)
The Pretenders, *Last of the Independents* (1994)
The Pretenders' most recent hit was originally conceived as a love song about standing by someone during good and bad times. However, its lyrics work equally well for a parent declaring their never-ending love for their child, just as Finn does to his unborn daughter. This message of endless love and support applies to other characters too: Puck is trying to prove to Quinn that

gregg henry as russell fabray

Gregg Henry's character-actor career demonstrates two things: he loves to sing and he's great at playing stern fathers. Born on May 6, 1952, in Lakewood, Colorado, Gregg now makes his home in sunny Los Angeles, where he has made a living guest starring on shows like *Firefly, 24, Airwolf, CSI, L.A. Law, Falcon Crest* and *Moonlighting*. Russell Fabray isn't the first time Gregg's had high expectations for his television offspring. He played Logan Huntzberger's demanding dad who disapproved of Logan's girlfriend Rory in *Gilmore Girls*. He's a busy guy, but still makes time for the theater, acting in several local productions in Los Angeles.

he'd stand by their family, Will will always put his family first, Finn's mom gives Finn and Quinn the parental support they need and Kurt puts Finn's needs ahead of his own crush.

"Don't Stand So Close to Me/Young Girl" (Will)
The Police, *Zenyattà Mondatta* (1980)
Gary Puckett & The Union Gap (1968)
Sting has denied that "Don't Stand So Close to Me," a tale about a school-girl crush on a teacher, is autobiographical, but it struck enough chords to win the Grammy for Best Rock Performance by a Duo or Group with Vocal. Will is nervous about Rachel's school-girl crush and wants her to back off before she gets hurt, so he combines this song with "Young Girl," a song about an inappropriate relationship with a much younger woman. To stress his point, Will changed the lines in "Young Girl" from "young girl, get out of my mind / My love for you is way out of line" to "young girl, you're out of your mind / Your love for me is way out of line."

"Crush" (Rachel)
Jennifer Paige, *Jennifer Paige* (1998)
One-hit-wonder Jennifer Paige may think that crushes aren't a big deal, but Mr. Schue sure does — especially when the crushes in question are the ones his students have on him. In "Crush," Jennifer tries to contextualize a crush someone has on her: they can give you an emotional high, but it doesn't necessarily means it's love. Unlike Jennifer, Rachel may be thinking about forever, but tries to use "Crush" to prove to Mr. Schuester that her feelings

aren't inappropriate and he shouldn't worry so much — she thinks she's old enough to handle a mature relationship, not just a brief infatuation.

"(You're) Having My Baby" (Finn)
Paul Anka and Odia Coates (1974)
CNN named "(You're) Having My Baby" the worst song of all time. Despite being panned by critics, this extremely literal ode to the mother of his child became Paul Anka's first hit in 15 years. Since Quinn is having Finn's baby, he wants to show her (and her parents) just how much he loves her and their unborn child. Right idea, Finn, wrong song choice.

"Lean on Me" (New Directions)
Bill Withers, *Still Bill* (1972)
"Lean on Me," the ultimate declaration of friendship, was Bill Withers' first and only #1 hit. Withers was inspired to write this song after moving to a tough area of Los Angeles from a small town in Virginia and found he was missing the close-knit and supportive community there. Just like with "Keep Holding On" in "Throwdown," New Directions uses music to reach out to Quinn (and Finn, this time). Despite love triangles and power struggles, they are truly a team now and will be there for each other, through good times and bad.

The Sound of Music: Ballads, like Mr. Schue explained, are stories set to music. Ballads originated in medieval England and Ireland before finding their way into mainstream music throughout Europe and North America. In the 1800s, ballads became synonymous with love songs, but any song with a story and a powerful emotional core is considered a ballad. Ballads can be classified into three groups: traditional, which are associated with minstrels

Dianna Agron and Cory Monteith celebrate their 2009 SAG Award for Outstanding Performance by an Ensemble in a Comedy Series.

and medieval times; broadside, which were popular in England in the 16th century and covered a variety of topics; and literary, which came out of the 18th century romantic movement and were inspired by poets like William Wordsworth and Samuel Taylor Coleridge.

That's Pretty *Popular*: Sam develops a crush on her journalism teacher Mr. Grant and asks him on a date in the first season episode "Mo' Menace, Mo' Problems," but it doesn't go as planned when Mr. Grant's girlfriend appears. Josh's WASP-y parents could be Quinn's parents BFFS. They're conservative traditionalists who believe in status and power. They constantly compare Josh to his successful football-playing older brothers and Josh's mom, a glamorous ex–beauty queen, is completely submissive to Josh's dad, catering to his every need.

q&a: sarah drew as suzy pepper

Sarah Drew has had her acting career take her to the popular side of high school and back. Her October 1, 1980, birthday means she's a Libra and is all about balance! After scoring a voice role as Stacy, secretary of the Fashion Club on MTV's *Daria*, Sarah guest-starred in several shows including *Wonderfalls*, *Cold Case*, *Law & Order: SVU*, *Medium*, *Private Practice* and *Mad Men*. Her musical theater background in high school in Boston, Massachusetts, prepared her well for playing McKinley High's craziest senior, Suzy Pepper.

We contacted the former musical theater geek and she gladly answered our questions about her guest turn on *Glee*:

How did you get your role on *Glee*?
The way you get most roles, you get the appointment sheet. I had just started seeing some of the promos for it but hadn't seen the pilot and was like "oh my gosh." I grew up doing musical theater. That was my life. Knowing there was a show about singing songs and dancing, I had to be a part of this.

If Suzy were to sing a song, what song would she sing?
Definitely "Every Breath You Take" by The Police. She'd have to sing something stalker-y and dark. We'd probably have to change the lyrics to with "every step you take, I'll be stalking you."

What was it like to play Suzy?
It was so much fun. It's really fun to get to play people who are off and twisty and psycho. We all have that in us but are not allowed to let it out. When I was playing Suzy, I just went there and let all my crazy out.

In the moments or characters where I'm allowed to let out the crazy, I get really excited. When I get full-on crazy, Brad [Falchuk] and I would rank the craziness for the scene. He'd be like, "Okay, you're a nine, dial it back to about a six." Or "you're a five, amp it up to an eight." There were a couple of scenes where Suzy is truly crazy that didn't make the episode. They're hilarious. There's one scene that I'm really sorry didn't make it in that was after Suzy ate the pepper. She's on the gurney completely convulsing and screaming, "It tastes like fire!" It was such a fun scene to do, and the end result was hilarious. I think that's so brilliant about the way they write the show that literally when you're in the bathroom scene you think Suzy's going to kill Rachel. There are layers to Suzy, and Brad wanted me to access them. Suzy's crazy, but she's also vulnerable. I like the ability to bring in the crazy with the vulnerable.

Which Glee cover is your favorite so far?
Actually, this is so funny. It's the Avril Lavigne song they're singing to Quinn a few episodes before mine. The reason why is because I saw the episode then went on set to shoot an episode of a new show, Miami Medical, and for my character I had to be very emotional. I'm literally listening to that song on repeat. That song touched a special place in my heart. I have such a strong nostalgic feeling about being in high school and singing. The place I felt most at home and alive was in my community of misfit theater geeks. The "It's going to be okay, I'm here for you!" brought me back to those days with those geeks as my rock when a lot of the crap going on at school was bringing me down.

Slushie Facials:

- According to Finn, Puck is still throwing Kurt in the Dumpster.

Off-Key:

- Rachel gets another romantic storyline? How is this even possible? Rachel sure gets a lot of romance for a supposedly unpopular gal.
- When Suzy Pepper eats the world's hottest pepper, she's chewing her hair. However, when she's shot from the side, her hair isn't in her mouth.
- When Kurt plays the piano for Finn's ballad, he's wearing brown leggings. On the close-up shots of the piano, the person playing it is wearing blue jeans.
- Kurt's in the locker room talking about shoulder pads? Is he still on the football team? If so, why isn't that an issue in "Mash-Up"?

Behind the Scenes:

- Brittany's explanation for what a ballad is ("a male duck") was a last-minute addition to the script. Ryan Murphy whispered the line to Heather Morris just before the scene was shot so that the reactions from the cast would be authentic.
- During rehearsals for "Lean on Me," Cory and Dianna weren't allowed to participate. Why? Ryan Murphy wanted their emotions to be as real as possible when they filmed the scene for the first time.

Center Stage:

- Quinn's parents are really excited to see Glenn Beck on television. Glenn Beck is a conservative radio and television host who hosts a self-titled news show on Fox, the same channel that airs *Glee* in the United States. He's well known for his controversial views including being anti–gun control and not believing humans are the main cause of global warming.
- "More Than Words," a 1990 ballad by rock band Extreme, is playing in the background while Suzy Pepper eats the hot pepper. The song is about wanting someone to show you how much they love you rather than just saying it.
- The film *How Stella Got Her Groove Back* launched the "groove back" catchphrase. The 1998 romance starred Angela Bassett as Stella, a hard-working single mom who never gives herself a break. A romantic vacation to Jamaica and an unexpected romance with Winston Shakespeare (Taye Diggs) shows Stella how to prioritize what's important and how to achieve happiness.
- "Sorry Seems to Be the Hardest Word," the apology song Rachel wanted to sing for Will, is a ballad about unrequited love written and performed by Elton John. It hit #6 on the Billboard Hot 100. It's one of the few songs Elton John wrote by himself and it appeared on his 1976 album *Blue Moves*.

Jazz Hands:

- Jane Lynch does not appear in this episode, her first absence.
- This is the first episode in which Quinn has a voice-over.
- Tina's rosacea is acting up because of the baby drama. Rosacea is the redness of the face, especially around the cheeks, nose and forehead.
- Will drinks Brockman Beer. Brockman is a fictional beer brand developed by Independent Studio Services to use as a prop on television and

in movies.

- Rachel serves Will venison for dinner. Venison is the culinary name for deer meat.

The Buckeye State: Finn has a poster for Ohio Stadium, as well as one for Dashboard Confessional, Thrice and The Get Up Kids in his room. Ohio Stadium is where Ohio State University's football team, the Buckeyes, play. Dashboard Confessional, Thrice and The Get Up Kids played the 2004 Honda Civic Tour together. The tour stopped at the Tower City Amphitheater in Cleveland and the Riverbend Music Center in Cincinnati. Will makes Rachel sit in the back seat because he says it's the law (again, trying to emphasize her youth). However, there isn't actually such a law in Ohio. Children under seven years old must sit in a booster seat, but it doesn't have to be in the back.

♪♫♪

1.11 "hairography"
Original Air Date: November 25, 2009
Written by: Ian Brennan
Directed by: Bill D'Elia

The Music: ★ ★ ★
The Drama: ★ ★ ★
The Laughs: ★ ★ ★

Quinn: I'm starting to realize that what I need right now, even more than looser pants, is acceptance.

After challenging rival schools to a scrimmage, Will worries about New Directions' chances at Sectionals. Finn and Quinn are both exploring romantic interests but not with each other.

Smoke and mirrors can take many forms, and this time it's called "hair-ography." This notion of misdirection runs throughout this episode. Let's focus on these distractions, shall we?

Hairography #1: Inspired by the girls at Jane Addams Academy, Mr.

Schue tries to add glitz and glam to New Directions' set list with more hair tossing than a shampoo ad. Hairography #2: Quinn decides to distract Finn with a Kurt-sponsored makeover for Rachel so Quinn can give Puck a daddy test-drive. Hairography #3: Will keeps trying to get it on with his wife, and so to distract him, Terri buys him an old car to spend all his free time fixing up. And in the end, what do we learn? Hairography always fails.

But despite hairography falling flatter than locks without product, this episode's distractions still had some positive outcomes. Even though New Directions' hairography-laced rehearsal bombs, it helps Will realize that New Directions doesn't need distractions to win. And even with Rachel's shamelessly sexy makeover, Finn still decides to stand by Quinn. Though Will loves his retro ride, he's determined to be a good dad so he buys a hideous but family-friendly wood-paneled van.

The similarities between Will and Finn continue in this episode, too. Although the guys get temporarily distracted from their problems, they come through in the end and want to work on them, not ignore them. This parallel is solidified when both Will and Finn tell their leading ladies "I love you" after confessing major secrets: Will sold the Blue Bomber for their family, and Finn turned down Rachel's advances to help his relationship with Quinn.

"Hairography" drove its theme home hard, distracting us from the tear-worthy musical numbers and Quinn's fantastic character development. When she tells Terri that what's most important is that her baby has a good father, we see that the fallen teen queen is growing up and can finally see that her social woes at McKinley are really just a distraction from what matters most.

High Note: The understated nature of the "True Colors" performance was perfect. From the different colored T-shirts to the simple stools, New Directions focused on their best asset with this song: their talent.

Low Note: The "Hair/Crazy in Love" mash-up is, by far, the worst performance we've seen on *Glee*. We know it's supposed to be terrible to prove how off-the-mark Will is, but it is still a huge step back for New Directions.

eve as grace hitchens

Eve Jihan Jeffers is a multi-talented, award-winning star. She began her career in music before expanding into acting and eventually fashion design. Growing up in Philadelphia, Eve always wanted to be a performer. She formed an all-girl group, EDGP, before going solo as Eve of Destruction. After moving to New York and a brief stint as a stripper, Eve met rapper Mase and her music career took off. Her first album, the 1999 *Let There Be Eve . . . Ruff Ryders' First Lady* became the second rap album by a woman to break into the Billboard 200, topping the charts. Her second album, *Scorpion*, established her as a bona fide artist. She won a Grammy for Best Rap/Sung Collaboration for "Let Me Blow Ya Mind," which she performed with Gwen Stefani. From there, she began to explore other interests and starred in films like *xXx*, *Barbershop*, *Barbershop 2: Back in Business*, *The Cookout* and *Whip It!* Her self-titled television show aired on UPN from 2003 to 2006 and she launched her clothing and accessories label, Fetish, in 2003.

Behind the Music:

"Bootylicious" (Jane Addams Show Choir)
Destiny's Child, *Survivor* (2001)

Destiny Child's fun and upbeat anthem for confident and curvy women was the band's fourth #1 hit. Beyoncé was inspired to write "Bootylicious" after hearing Stevie Nicks' sexy guitar riffs in her 1981 hit "Edge of Seventeen," as it reminded her of a confident, voluptuous woman. "Edge of Seventeen" is sampled in the song and Stevie Nicks even appeared in the "Bootylicious" music video. Beyoncé would be proud of Jane Addams Academy's club, who performs with tons of confidence. Their version of "Bootylicious" is risqué and filled with lots of booty, leaving Will wondering if New Directions will be ready for that jelly when they have to face it at Sectionals.

"Don't Make Me Over" (Mercedes)
Dionne Warwick (1962)

"Don't Make Me Over" was slang for "don't lie to me" and the song reminds listeners that good partners love you for who you are and don't lie to you, two things Finn reinforces when he tells Rachel he doesn't like her makeover and when he chooses to stand by Quinn. The song, which was Dionne Warwick's first single, was accidentally released under Dionne Warwick, not Dionne

Warrick, her real name. She kept the typo and recorded professionally under the name Dionne Warwick for the rest of her career.

"You're the One That I Want" (Rachel and Finn)
Grease (motion picture version, 1978)
This is the second time "You're the One that I Want" is sung on *Glee*, and most of the characters on the series are pursuing at least one other person romantically, whether it's Rachel and Kurt using extreme makeovers to win Finn, or Finn and Puck trying to prove to Quinn they deserve her love.

"Papa Don't Preach" (Quinn accompanied by Puck on guitar)
Madonna, *True Blue* (1986)
Composer Brian Elliot was inspired to write Madonna's fourth #1 hit after overhearing teen girls gossiping near his studio about pregnancies. The song is a cry for parental support during a tough time. Like Madonna (as portrayed in the music video), Quinn wants her dad's support in "Ballad," but, unlike Madonna, Quinn is kicked out of the house. It's the only song on *True Blue* that Madonna didn't co-write, although she did make minor lyrical contributions. The song was extremely controversial and several groups accused Madonna of endorsing teenage pregnancy.

"Hair/Crazy in Love" (New Directions)
Hair (1967)
Beyoncé featuring Jay-Z, *Dangerously in Love* (2003)
Will uses "Hair," the title song from the Broadway musical *Hair* (see "Give

michael hitchcock as dalton rumba

Michael Hitchcock plays a deaf choir director, but his hearing is perfectly fine. Born July 28, 1958, in Defiance, Ohio (less than an hour from Lima!), Michael moved to Chicago at a young age and pursued drama and band in high school. After graduating with a science degree from Northwestern University and an MFA from UCLA, Michael made a living writing comedy films before scoring a gig as a writer for *MadTV*, eventually working up to the role of producer. He made his name in Hollywood starring alongside *Glee*'s Jane Lynch in several Christopher Guest films, like *Best in Show*, *A Mighty Wind* and *For Your Consideration*.

My Regards" below), to encourage hairography when he forces everyone in New Directions to wear wigs. Beyoncé may be crazy in love, but New Directions is just crazy when they perform this number. This Grammy-winning #1 hit samples the infectious hook from the Chi-Lites' 1970 song "Are You My Woman? (Tell Me So)."

"Imagine" (Haverbrook School for the Deaf Show Choir)
John Lennon, *Imagine* (1971)
Lennon's call for a unified, peaceful world is his best-known and most influential post-Beatles song, and *Rolling Stone* declared it #3 on their 500 Greatest Songs of All Time list. "Imagine" was inspired by Yoko Ono's poetry about growing up in Japan during World War II and many of the song's lines are directly borrowed from her work. "Imagine" reinforces *Glee*'s main themes of believing in yourself and breaking boundaries. Haverbrook's beautiful and touching performance reminds Will (yet again) why he coaches New Directions, reminds everyone in the glee club why they come to practice every day and reminds viewers that beauty can come from unexpected places.

"True Colors" (New Directions)
Cyndi Lauper, *True Colors* (1986)
"True Colors" was a huge hit, topping the Billboard Hot 100 chart for two weeks. Originally intended to be a gospel-style song by the composer, Cyndi rearranged the number to come up with something truly original and very powerful. "True Colors" is a celebration of everyone's uniqueness, something Will loses sight of when Jane Addams Academy shows up. It takes Haverbrook School of the Deaf to bring it back.

Give My Regards to Broadway: *Hair* is a rock musical that was inspired by the bohemian culture and sexual revolution that dominated the 1960s, and it tells the story of a group of hippies living in New York and fighting the Vietnam draft. It opened on Broadway on April 29, 1968, and was an immediate success, running for 1,750 performances. A film adaptation was released in 1979. At the time, *Hair* was considered very daring and controversial because of its depicted drug use, treatment of sexuality and explicit musical numbers.

The *Glee* cast has just as much fun in the choir room as New Directions does!

That's Pretty *Popular*: The Glamazons attempt to makeover the un-makeover-able April Tuna to get her a date in "Hope in a Jar." As a result, April scores the hottest guy in school. Carmen struggles with who she truly is throughout *Popular* but finally accepts herself and rejects her role as cheerleading clown for the Glamazons in "The Trial of Emory Dick" because she realizes she's better than that. She doesn't need the distraction of a cheerleading uniform — she can be herself and be happy.

Off-Key:
• Is anyone else confused about what songs they're performing at Sectionals? What happened to "Defying Gravity"? Did that get cut?

Behind the Scenes:
• Heather Morris inspired the concept of this episode. One day, Ryan asked Heather about how she makes her hair move so in line with the rest of her body, and so she explained hairography (which is an actual dance concept) to him. Ryan wrote that conversation into the script and

based the entire episode around her explanation.

- *So You Think You Can Dance* contestants Katee Shean, Kherington Payne and Comfort Fedoke appear as Jane Addams Academy glee club members.
- Those wigs for the "Hair/Crazy in Love" mash-up are awful, but at least the cast had fun getting to pick their own.
- The cast and crew found the "Imagine" performance so moving that several of them got tattoos to commemorate the occasion.
- Getting clearance for "Imagine" was extremely difficult. The music producers had to convince John Lennon's widow, Yoko Ono, that the show was paying homage to John and not compromising his vision or creativity.
- The role of Grace Hitchens was originally offered to Whitney Houston, who turned it down. Eve was excited to appear on the show, as she had been a fan since seeing the pilot.
- All the actors in the Haverbrook choir are hearing-impaired.

Center Stage:

- This is the second time the musical *Hair* is referenced in *Glee*, the first being by Sue in "Showmance."
- Will feels like he's living a Springsteen song. Bruce "the Boss" Springsteen is known for his blue-collar anthems about Middle America and the pride one can find in honest hard work. His two most successful albums, *Born to Run* and *Born in the U.S.A.*, epitomize his status as an icon for the struggling American everyman. He's sold over 65 million albums in the U.S. and has won 20 Grammy awards, two Golden Globes and an Academy Award for his music.

Jazz Hands:

- This episode features Terri's first voice-over.
- Emma references the fable about Mohammed and the mountain. Mohammed is challenged to move a mountain using only his gaze. After being unable to do so, Mohammed declares that if he cannot move the mountain, he will go to it himself.
- Born in Illinois in 1860, Jane Addams was a social activist and the co-founder of Hull House in Chicago, a settlement house offering social, educational and artistic programs. Jane was awarded the Nobel Peace Prize in 1931 — the second woman ever to receive the honor.

q&a: heather morris as brittany

As Brittany, Heather Morris gets one-liners that are as jaw-dropping as her dance moves. We contacted Heather, and the dancer-turned-actress talked to us about what it's like playing Glee's dumbest blonde:

How do you see your character?
I see my character as everyone else sees her! She's doing EXACTLY what she loves and nothing else, but honestly has no clue what's going on ever, hahaha! She's the best. She just loves everyone and loves to perform!

What's it like playing both a Cheerio and a gleek? Which role do you most relate to personally?
I think it's the confusion of having something [new] that you truly love and that feels amazing to you, and then having something you've been doing forever that you know works for you and you just can't simply quit it. I think it's crazy that I have that connection with [both] dancing and acting. Dancing metaphorically is my role as a Cheerio [because] I know it's gotten me to where I am today, but I always passionately and secretly wanted to act, just like Brittany secretly and passionately wants to be a GLEEK!

What's it like to work with such a large ensemble cast as Glee's? Who do you have the most fun working with on the cast?
There's so many of us all the time and yet we work so well together; that's truly outstanding to me. We literally have fun 24/7 while filming so I cannot say I specifically have more fun with any particular person! It's honestly the best job in the world . . . from the cast AND to the crew, too . . . the crew is so wonderful to us and they're also having so much fun. It's all around a giant family!

Is there a character in particular you'd most like to see your character interact with? Or, alternatively, a cast member you'd like to work more with?
I know that Brittany loves everyone and everything under the sun so I don't think I have an opinion in the matter. The only actor that I'm so shamelessly honored to be even NEAR TO in a scene is the one and only Jane Lynch. Now that is a dream come true and I do look forward to hopefully getting to work with her more and more . . . she truly is the most wonderful and talented person on earth!

What's it like working with Ryan Murphy?
Also AMAZING. He likes to play just as much as us kids do but he also knows how to focus. He's gotten the balance of both down pretty well!

- Will's wallet is stolen by a girl named Aphasia, which is a disorder where someone's language ability is impaired.
- Kurt thinks that Rachel's room looks like Strawberry Shortcake and Holly Hobbie hooked up. Strawberry Shortcake is a cartoon character owned by American Greetings, which expanded the franchise to dolls and a television show in the 1980s. American Greetings also owns the rights to Holly Hobbie, a cat-loving American girl who became a popular book character.
- The deaf choir director's name is Dalton Rumba. Rumba means "party" in Spanish and is both a type of Cuban dancing and a formal ballroom dance, though the two dance styles are very different from each other.
- Quinn's "Papa Don't Preach" dance moves are directly lifted from Madonna's original 1986 music video.

How Sue Cs It: "Never let anything distract you from winning. *Ever.*"

♪♫♪

1.12 "mattress"
Original Air Date: December 2, 2009
Written by: Ryan Murphy
Directed by: Elodie Keene

The Music: ★ ★
The Drama: ★ ★ ★ ♪
The Laughs: ★ ★ ♪

Finn: We can't do this without you, Mr. Schue. Hell, we probably can't do it with you.

While the glee club struggles with yearbook photos and their quest for fame, Will and Terri's relationship suffers its biggest blow yet.

It's the week before Sectionals, but the number one thing on every glee clubber's mind is yearbook photos — and how they *don't* want one. As if daily slushie facials weren't enough, their yearly torture tends to be permanently memorialized in McKinley High's Thunderclap with markered graffiti. New Directions is more than happy to avoid this sadistic annual ritual. Well, everyone except for Miss Rachel Berry, who makes it a point of appearing in the yearbook more often than the school mascot. Though this appears to be just another side of Rachel's diva persona, her photo-mania likely stems from Rachel's desire to be remembered, and being the Waldo of the yearbook is just another way for her to pretend she fits in somewhere. It looks like New Directions will be spared a marker-mustachioed future when budget cuts and Sue Sylvester get in the way of the club's group photo. But still stuck in his own glee club glory days, Will decides he needs to play the hero yet again and fights for his students' inclusion at any cost.

While the group is worried about the future humiliation of the yearbook photo, Will and Finn are the first to deal with the issue and reassert their status as leading men. Will thinks he needs to step up and do whatever it takes to make sure the club gets their due in the yearbook, even if the result is embarrassing. Finn needs to step up and prove that New Directions is worth future ridicule by posing in the picture with Rachel. However, the difference in Will's and Finn's maturity is clear when Will comes through, even against Terri's wishes, and Finn does not, caving to peer pressure once again.

Terri's pregnancy charade finally comes crashing down when Will stumbles upon one of her fake baby bumps. It's easy to see Will's side of things in the World War III that follows, but not all of Terri's points of view are completely crazy. While we've been eagerly awaiting her exposure all along, her pleas and Will's rage allow us a little sympathy for the scheming shrew. Terri is, after all, trying to salvage their relationship. She still loves Will and blames the glee club for changing the way Will feels about her. Considering how many times Will has gone to great lengths for his students (with him stepping down as glee club director at the end of the episode being the biggest fall he's taken for them yet), it's understandable why Terri would feel like she's second best. And it isn't just the kids getting extra-special attention — even when Will thought his wife was pregnant, he was still flirting with Emma, sharing secrets with her and helping her pick out a wedding dress. As it turns out, a phantom baby may have been the only thing this ghost of a marriage is capable of creating. The explosion of this pregnancy storyline also offers some sinister foreshadowing and amps up the dramatic tension: since Will and Terri find their teen counterparts in

gleek speak: sarah erdman, music teacher

One of the biggest criticisms of the show is how overproduced the music is. It's unrealistic for kids in glee club practice, singing a song for the first time, to sound that perfect. Why do you think they chose to go this route?

I think the reason *Glee* has decided to make the music sound so produced is because it's what the audience expects to hear. I know there are many people who criticize the "perfect" sound they're hearing the first time, but there are also many people who would criticize it if the students sounded less than perfect. In the past 15 or 20 years sound production has made leaps and bounds and now the general public is accustomed to hearing perfection in the sense of tuning and blending of voices. The producers may have also chosen to go this route because there is a wide range of vocal abilities in the cast. Yes, there are some members who are professional singers and have been on Broadway stages, but there are also members who are actors that just happen to sing well. Those people, while they have nice voices, may not have the "technical chops" to know when a note goes out of tune or when they are singing too loud to blend with the group. The other thing to consider is that any sound that is recorded for a movie or television show has to be produced to a certain degree. The microphones used to pick up general dialogue in a scene are never strong enough to pick up the subtle changes that happen in music, so there always has to be a pre-recorded backup track at least. Also, if we compare a *Glee* taping to a recording session with a musician, musicians will often do 50 or more takes of a piece in order to get everything done right. So if a TV show was dependent on both a good picture and good sound, they would likely be running the same scene for days on end. Pre-recording the voices removes that element from filming day, which just makes life that much easier.

Finn and Quinn, will a revelation of Quinn's lies result in a violent confrontation like this one?

The glee club also learns not to do things behind Mr. Schue's back. After the "Push It" incident in "Showmance" and the pill-popping in "Vitamin D," you'd think they'd know better. But, then again, Rachel re-learns the importance of teamwork and Will learns to put his students first more than once. It looks like everyone at McKinley High needs to learn a lesson a few times before it sinks in.

When Sue throws the rulebook at Mr. Schuester, forcing him to step down as glee chair, our motley crew will have to stand on its own, and with Sectionals ahead, yearbook photo woes are the least of their problems.

High Note: Thank goodness Terri's fake pregnancy is out in the open. We weren't against it in the beginning, as it said a lot about Terri and Will's relationship, but it lasts far too long. However, it makes for a pivotal moment in their relationship and a very powerful scene. Terri hits the nail on the head when she says, "You love the girl you met when you were fifteen." Both Will and Terri have repeatedly shown that they don't want to let their high school glory days go. Even if their relationship doesn't work anymore, staying married reinforces — to everyone else, if not them — that they're still the golden couple.

Low Note: It feels unbelievable that Figgins would lay down such a harsh punishment for a single mattress but overlook all the special attention Sue and her Cheerios get.

Behind the Music:

"Smile" (Rachel and Finn)
Lily Allen, *Alright, Still* (2006)
Sometimes, after someone really does you wrong, it's fun to watch them suffer. That's exactly what Lily Allen is singing about in "Smile," a ska-infused tune, whose peppy beat masks the tale of a girl relishing her boyfriend's downfall after he cheats on her. Rachel and Finn may sing this to warm up for their yearbook photos, but the darker side of the song fits too. Rachel is enjoying sharing this moment with Finn, and is glad she got her way with the yearbook photo, even if it's going to cause a lot of social grief for everyone else.

"When You're Smiling" (Rachel)
Louis Armstrong (1929)
Louis Armstrong recorded this sweet reminder that when you smile, the world smiles with you, but when you cry, you cry alone, at least three times, in 1929, 1932 and 1956. Rachel reminds herself that it's how she presents herself to the world that matters, not how she feels inside. If she projects happiness and confidence, the world will be happy and confident with her.

"Jump" (New Directions)
Van Halen, *1984* (1984)
Van Halen's only #1 hit marked the band's move toward more synth-driven music. This transition eventually prompted lead singer David Lee Roth to quit the group. Van Halen took a lesson from their song and moved past

McKinley's former golden couple, back in their glory days. My, how the mighty have fallen.

Why the long face, Ms. Pillsbury? Are there GERMS on your desk?

MR + MRS SCHUE

MR. & MRS. SCHUE BRIEFLY SHARED TIME IN THE MCKINLEY HIGH STAFF ROOM, UNTIL MRS. SCHUE WENT BACK TO FOLDING SHEETS... AND THINGS.

KURT
knows a fierce pose makes even a football uniform look good.

Mercedes knows she's a Beyoncé, she ain't no Kelly Rowland.

mercedes

PREPPING FOR REGIONALS... GLEE CLUB IS GOING TO NEED ALL THE HELP THEY CAN GET!

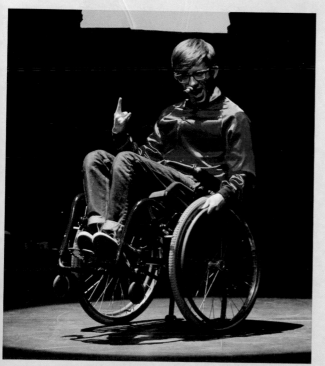

ARTIE KNOWS HOW TO ROCK AND ROLL.

When Puck
on the prou
not even a
slushie facia
will get in
his way.

PUCK

As Mr. Schue likes to say, "Glee club... it's about expressing yourself to yourself."

Roth's departure, hiring Sammy Hagar and continuing to release new music. No one quits New Directions this episode, as they're learning to "roll with the punches," take the bad with the good and just go for it, whether it's a yearbook photo or local commercial. Being able to perform without the attached social stigma glee brings them at school shows New Directions that they genuinely love performing and feeling like stars.

"Smile" (New Directions)
Modern Times (1936)
"Smile," the instrumental theme for Charlie Chaplin's film *Modern Times*, reminds listeners to cheer up, because there's always a brighter tomorrow. Without their coach and with an impending yearbook photo, New Directions is in a dark place. But they're facing these hardships together and have Sectionals to look forward to. As long as they focus on the future and keep on smiling, things will get better.

That's Pretty *Popular*: Like Quinn after getting pregnant and kicked off the Cheerios, popular cheerleader Nicole becomes lost and confused after discovering she's adopted. She tries to figure out who she is and where she belongs. While the glee kids appear in a mattress commercial, Sam gets a chance to star in a PowerGirl commercial in "All About Adam."

Slushie Facials:
- Every year the glee club photo gets defaced in McKinley High's yearbook, the Thunderclap.
- Brittany and Santana deface the Thunderclap.
- Kurt mentions that everyone in glee club regularly gets swirlies, patriotic wedgies and slushie facials.
- Artie got a patriotic wedgie off-screen.
- Brittany promises Rachel that she's going to ruin the glee club picture — even if she's in it.
- Hockey players deface the new glee club yearbook photo.

Off-Key:
- Puck's name in the glee club yearbook photo is Nathan, even though his first name is Noah.
- Brittany doesn't have a last name in the yearbook photo. This could be

intentional, as her last name has never been mentioned.

- When Mr. Schue drops the mattress on the floor, you can see the red X where he's supposed to drop it.
- If every teacher and club gets a full page in the Thunderclap, the yearbook would be more like 8,000 pages long.

Behind the Scenes:

- The working title of this episode was "Once Upon a Mattress." Matthew Morrison starred in the 2005 ABC television version of the play *Once Upon a Mattress*, which reinvents the classic fairy tale *The Princess and the Pea*. Matthew played Sir Harry, a knight who discovers his girlfriend is pregnant and must find a way around the queen's law that no one can be married until her son, Prince Dauntless, has wed.
- Rachel refuses to do nudity and exploit animals to achieve fame. Interestingly, Lea Michele appeared nude and performed in a very graphic sex scene in *Spring Awakening*.
- Those mattresses New Directions jump on? Not real mattresses! Zach Woodlee originally tried the choreography on real mattresses, but it wasn't working. Production had to design a trampoline that looked like a mattress so the cast could do the flips and spins that make this number so fun.

Center Stage:

- Terri thinks a pocket square would make Will look like Ted Knight, an American actor best known for portraying Ted Baxter on *The Mary Tyler Moore Show*, Henry Rush on *Too Close for Comfort* and Judge Smails in *Caddyshack*.

Jazz Hands:

- Rachel's two gay dads are very involved with their local ACLU, the American Civil Liberties Union, a partnership between two non-profit organizations to promote individual rights in the United States, through litigation, communication and legislative lobbying.
- Rachel is in the Speech Club, the Mock United Nations Club, the Renaissance Club, the Muslim Students Club and the Black Student Union.
- Mercedes uses Kwanzaa as an excuse to get out of glee club captainship.

Kwanzaa is a celebration held from December 26 to January 1 every year to celebrate African heritage and culture. Participants mark the celebration by lighting a kinara, and the festivities end with a feast and gift giving. Kwanzaa was created by activist, academic and author Ron Karenga and was first celebrated in 1966.

- The locker room's sign reads "Those Who Stay Will Be Champions," a not-so-subtle message to those who quit football to stay in the glee club.
- New Directions don matching PJS by Cambridge Pajamas for their Mattress Land commercial.

The Buckeye State: As a Cheerio, Quinn scored season passes to Cedar Point. Cedar Point is an amusement park in Sandusky, Ohio, and holds the world record for most roller coasters, of which there are 17. One of these is Top Thrill Dragster, the second tallest and second fastest coaster in the world.

How Sue Cs It: "What if I were to innocently murder you, Will? I'd still have to go to trial. I'd still probably get off for justifiable homicide."

♪♫♪

1.13 "sectionals"
Original Air Date: December 9, 2009
Written by: Brad Falchuk
Directed by: Brad Falchuk

The Music: ★★★★
The Drama: ★★★★
The Laughs: ★★★★

Will (to Finn): Sometimes being special sucks.

New Directions arrive at Sectionals sans both Mr. Schue and Finn, only to find that their set list has been leaked and their competitors have stolen their performances. Will New Directions be able to come out on top when it matters the most?

"Sectionals" had a lot of hype to live up to, and it exceeds even the greatest expectations with big songs and even bigger drama.

While she ultimately takes the lead diva role with her Barbra ballad at Sectionals, Rachel finally embraces the importance of being a team player by supporting Mercedes in taking on the all-important ballad and accepting Santana's confession without doubt or ridicule. That's not to say that she's not still putting her own desires first at times. She does, after all, reveal Quinn's baby daddy secret to Finn under the guise of looking out for what's best for the team. Let's face it, it's obvious that this revelation is just another attempt to break up the golden couple and become the new girl on Finn's arm. She even admits as much. Still, our star is slowly but surely realizing that it's not *always* all about her.

Finn faces a struggle even greater than leading the football team to victory. Who can blame him for wanting to ditch everything to do with Quinn and Puck, glee club included, after finding out the truth? But Will's right — New Directions needs him. He's their leader, the one that they all trust and believe in, and he can't say that about the football team anymore. And they know that New Directions can't win Sectionals without him. After shirking his leadership role in "Mattress," Finn is finally strong enough to take the lead when it matters. With some fatherly prompting from Mr. Schue, our glee stud valiantly puts aside his personal issues and returns to lead the club to victory, but tension remains between him and Puck that may play out in the future.

The big revelation of Quinn's secret is reminisicent of the revelation of Terri's secret only an episode ago: the truth comes out through means other than the gal's intentions, and both boys react with extreme and unprecedented anger. The fact that Will shows better restraint than Finn by not resorting to physical violence (even though it looked like he was considering it when he pinned Terri against the cupboards) is only a testament to his maturity. Quinn, like Terri, is upset but relieved the secret is out. But while the revelation may be similar, it will be more interesting to see if the effect on the relationship is different.

Another charade comes to an end with Emma's wedding day. After Emma opts to push her wedding back to give Will a helping hand, Ken finally grows a pair and dumps her. As a result Emma finally confesses her true feelings to Will. What Will can't express in words, however, he gets across in one fiery episode-ending lip lock. It's a turning point for Emma who's opening herself up to someone (and their germs) and for Will, who obviously hasn't given up on love. It'll also be interesting to see what kind

intermission

In the United States, "Sectionals" was considered a fall finale for *Glee*, with new episodes not returning until April 13, 2010. Fox chose to do this for a number reasons. First, their initial episode order was only 13, and all 13 episodes were completed before the show ever aired. Producing the show is so time consuming, it would have interfered with marketing and promotion. The break gave the production team time to write, create and produce the final nine episodes. Second, the XXI Winter Olympics aired from February 12-28, 2010, on NBC, which affects television programming on every network. Third, *American Idol* takes up three nights a week on Fox during the early part of the season, meaning there's no prime-time room for *Glee* even if they wanted it to run at the same time. Fourth, having the show air in April meant Fox could pair it with the single-hour *American Idol* on Tuesday nights, making it two hours of powerhouse music television. Fifth, airing the show in April means it will be on during May sweeps, a very important time for television networks. The viewership in May determines their advertising rates for the fall television season. The network made sure *Glee*'s popularity didn't wane by producing *Gleewinds* on YouTube, airing reruns of the show, releasing online-only looks at the cast, launching a nationwide casting call for season 2, airing charity screenings of "Hello" and hosting a "Biggest Gleek" contest.

of partner Mr. Schue will be to someone who isn't crazy . . . or is at least less crazy.

It's not all passionate kisses for Will, though. It's painfully sad to see him proudly listening to his glee club perform over the phone, and he suffers the most vicious attack from Sue yet when she leaks their Sectionals set list to Jane Addams and Haverbrook. Fortunately good wins out over evil this round, and Figgins simultaneously suspends Sue as the Cheerios' coach and reinstates Will as the glee club director. It might seem that the tides are turning for Coach Sue, but we all know that the Sue Sylvester Express (Destination: Horror!) will be arriving back at McKinley High station very soon. Though the curtain may have dropped, it's only intermission.

High Note: Everything. The performances at Sectionals are the best we've seen so far and many storylines take a dramatic turn. Everyone handles the big revelation scene beautifully and Emma turning down Will was as classy as it is heartbreaking. And that kiss? This episode has it all.

Low Note: Mercedes gives Puck a big speech about backing off and letting Quinn make the decision that is right for her, then goes and tells the entire club? Including the Cheerios? How did that happen? Mercedes is super chatty, true, but spilling the beans to the whole club seems a bit extreme.

Behind the Music:
"And I Am Telling You I'm Not Going" (Mercedes)
Dreamgirls (1982)
Effie, one of the original members of the supergroup The Dreams (see "Give My Regards" below), refuses to give up on her relationship with the group's manager, even though he's trying to end it. While Mercedes's version lacks the romantic message, she's standing up for herself like never before with this song. She's tired of being pushed to the background, and by singing a belter that showcases how talented she is, she's proving that she's here to stay.

my life would suck without these dance moves

The "My Life Would Suck Without You" dance sequence includes dance steps from tons of New Directions' past performances. Here's the complete list. Try them for yourself at home!

- Turning from back to front ("Hair/Crazy in Love")
- Going around in circles ("Sit Down, You're Rocking the Boat")
- Butt-slapping ("Push It")
- Jumping up and down ("Jump")
- Cowboy hats and line dancing ("Last Name")
- Mercedes on a chair ("Hate on Me")
- "Single Ladies" dance ("Single Ladies")
- "Say a Little Prayer" Cheerios dance ("Say a Little Prayer")
- Fist pumps and sitting onstage ("It's My Life/Confessions Part II")
- Making halos ("Halo/Walking on Sunshine")
- Faux grinding ("Push It")
- Couples walking together ("Somebody to Love")
- Standing in lines, facing each other ("Keep Holding On")
- Doing the "Thinker" ("Sit Down, You're Rocking the Boat")
- Hairography ("Hair/Crazy in Love")
- Circling each other ("Somebody to Love")
- Tipping Artie's wheelchair ("Proud Mary")
- Slapping their legs ("I Kissed a Girl")

"Don't Rain on My Parade" (Rachel)
Funny Girl (1964)
Nothing is going to stop New Directions now and they are going to do whatever it takes to win: not missing their coach, not their male lead showing up late, not the stolen numbers, not the internal drama that's happening. And what better way to show the haters and disbelievers that they mean business than Rachel's fabulous rendition of Barbra Streisand's signature song. Originally written for the 1964 musical (and 1968 film adaptation) of *Funny Girl*, "Don't Rain on My Parade" is the classiest tell-off of all time.

"You Can't Always Get What You Want" (New Directions)
The Rolling Stones, *Let It Bleed* (1969)
The Rolling Stones taught legions of fans a very important life lesson with their accidental hit inspired by the partying culture of 1960s London. Selected as one of *Rolling Stone*'s 500 Greatest Songs of All Time, "You Can't Always Get What You Want" reminds listeners that sometimes what you want and what you need are two very different things. Take New Directions, for example. They want three perfect musical numbers and a showstopping performance. Mercedes wants a solo. Will wants to be there. Finn wants everything to return to normal. They don't get these things, but they get what they need: a Sectionals win, group camaraderie, confidence, honesty and a couple of important life lessons.

"My Life Would Suck Without You" (New Directions)
Kelly Clarkson, *All I Ever Wanted* (2009)
"My Life Would Suck Without You" was beloved by fans and critics alike. It had the highest chart jump in history (from #97 to #1) and reignited Kelly's fledgling career. New Directions realizes how much Mr. Schue does for them when they were coachless and directionless at Sectionals. This song demonstrates how much New Directions appreciates Will's guidance and support. But the song's message about how love can often be dysfunctional can be applied to nearly everyone: Finn and Quinn, Quinn and Puck, Quinn and the Cheerios, Rachel and Finn, Will and New Directions, Will and Terri, Will and Emma . . . the list goes on.

gleek speak: lisa
(an extra in "sectionals")

Tell us about the experience of being an extra on *Glee*!
The entire experience was such a trip! I arrived with my friend, Cheyanne, at around 7:00 a.m. to be sure we were close to the front of the line. It paid off because we were seated right in the front row balcony, pretty much securing a spot to be on film! The e-mail had instructed us to wear autumn-like clothing because the scene was taking place in Ohio in the fall. Luckily, the theater had A/C; otherwise it would not be pleasant considering it was actually late July in southern California. The e-mail said that they needed us for about three hours. Those three hours actually turned out to be eight! I had no idea setting up different camera angles would take so long. At first they had everyone in the audience do a standing ovation, and they filmed that, doing about four takes. This was after waiting for about two hours just sitting around watching the crew set up. To make the time go by a little faster, all of the cast members and the creators of the show came up to the balcony in groups throughout the day and did a Q & A with us. After waiting around for what seemed like forever, filming finally got underway. "Don't Rain on My Parade" was the first scene with Lea Michele's character coming through the back door of the auditorium. Poor Lea had to do this take about 25 times from all different angles. After this was complete, Cheyanne and I went for some lunch then came back to see a couple of takes of the whole cast performing "You Can't Always Get What You Want." After that it was getting late and we were all tired, so we decided to head home. On our way out the door we received a red *Glee* t-shirt to thank us for our time. It was a great way to end the day!

Give My Regards to Broadway: Inspired by the history of Motown, *Dreamgirls* premiered on Broadway on December 20, 1981. It was an instant hit and won six Tonys. *Dreamgirls* tells the story of a classic Motown girl group, The Dreams, who become musical superstars. Along the way, hearts are broken and friends are betrayed. Effie was not originally a starring role, but after the original Effie, Jennifer Holliday, quit the play twice over creative differences, the second act was rewritten to heavily feature her. Beyoncé, Jennifer Hudson, Eddie Murphy and Jamie Foxx starred in the 2006 film adaptation, which won two Academy Awards, including Best Actress in a Supporting Role for Hudson.

Off-Key:

- With Sectionals only a week away, they don't have their set list finalized?
- The plot of "Wheels" was an entire episode dedicated to raising the funds to acquire a charter bus for Artie. The bus they take to Sectionals is not a charter bus, but a wheelchair accessible bus owned by "Lima Public Schools."
- Emma wonders if the deaf choir is going to sing "Don't Start Believin'."
- There is a bandage on Rachel's right knee as she makes her way to the stage. Once she's onstage, the bandage is gone.
- When Sue and Will confront each other in the hallway, Sue has a bag over her shoulder in some shots, but not every one.
- The timeline for Sectionals doesn't make any sense. The competition starts at 11, New Directions sees two performances and has an hour to prepare, then the judges meet at 12:15. Unless there's some time travel involved here, this is impossible.

Behind the Scenes:

- Quinn is worried that Puck may be carrying the genes for Tay-Sachs, a "Jewish" disease. In real life, Dianna Agron is Jewish and Mark Salling is Christian.

- "Don't Rain on My Parade" was Lea Michele's dream *Glee* song. Her dream came true. When asked what song he would sing, Ryan Murphy also chose "Don't Rain on My Parade." *Funny Girl* was the first movie he ever saw and he loved singing this song as a kid.

Center Stage:

- Puck broke the first two rules of fight club: You do not talk about fight club. *Fight Club* is a 1996 novel by Chuck Palahniuk, which was adapted into a 1999 film starring Edward Norton and Brad Pitt. Norton's unnamed character is fed up with his all-American white-collar life and joins a secret fight club with Tyler Durden as an escape.
- Artie does def poetry jams. Def poetry was popularized by music producer Russell Simmons when he produced an HBO show called *Def Poetry Jam* from 2002 to 2007. Similar to a poetry slam, up-and-coming spoken word artists would perform on the show. A 2002 stage version of the show appeared on Broadway.
- Altamont Speedway Free Festival was a free concert in Northern California in 1969 that The Rolling Stones organized and headlined. Santana, Jefferson Airplane, The Flying Burrito Brothers and Crosby, Stills, Nash & Young were also featured. 300,000 people attended the concert, which is now infamous for its violence. Fighting was rampant and Mick Jagger was even punched in the face. There was one murder, one hit-and-run, one drowning and a rumored four babies born. Concert-goer Meredith Hunter was murdered by a Hells Angel who was later acquitted of the crime after claiming it was self-defense. It's rumored that the Stones hired Hells Angels to be the security for the concert, something the band and their management deny to this day, claiming the Angels were only supposed to watch the stage and the equipment.

Jazz Hands:

- Tay-Sachs is not technically a "Jewish" disease, but it does occur at higher rates in French Canadians, Ashkenazi Jews and Cajuns than in other populations, and results in mental and physical deterioration, and often death by the age of four. The cause is a genetic recessive mutation, which means both parents need to be carriers in order for their child to possess symptoms.
- When Will accuses Sue of leaking the set list, she claims he's making

a libelous statement. In legal terms, a libelous statement is written. A slanderous statement is spoken.

- According to the Jane Addams Academy advisor, Will has a Jheri Curl. A Jheri Curl is a popular African American hairstyle named after Jheri Redding, where the wearer has glossy, loosely curled hair.
- The girls' Sectionals dresses were designed by Aqua, but the costume department added the red sashes to give the look some more spunk.
- When Will and Emma kiss for the first time, the sign behind them declares "NO SEX." What is Ryan Murphy trying to tell us?

How Sue Cs It: "You will be adding revenge to the long list of things you're no good at, right next to being married, running a high school glee club and finding a hairstyle that doesn't make you look like a lesbian."

♪♫♪

1.14 "hell-o"
Original Air Date: April 13, 2010
Written by: Ian Brennan
Directed by: Brad Falchuk

The Music: ★ ★ ★ ♪
The Drama: ★ ★ ★
The Laughs: ★ ★ ★

Rachel: And that, fellow glee clubbers, is how we say hello!

Rachel wants Finn, but Finn wants freedom, until he wants Rachel, but by then, Rachel wants Jesse. Jesse acts like he wants Rachel, but he might want to destroy New Directions even more. And Will? He has no idea what or who he wants.

"Hell-O" is the perfect title for the spring premiere of *Glee*, as the show said hello to fans new and old after a four-month hiatus. The episode's running theme of introductions, reintroductions and reinventions, and the use of the word "hello" (or just the word's powerful first syllable!) is a bit corny, but it creates an opportunity to introduce new characters, new feelings and new drama.

Two new characters say hello this episode: Vocal Adrenaline's star soloist, Jesse St. James, and their driven director, Shelby Corcoran. Jesse seems like the perfect match for Rachel, with his diva-esque tendencies and bad boy vibe (she did hook up with Puck, after all, so clearly Rachel has an attraction to rebels). He may be nothing more than a scheming spy, but his chemistry with Rachel is electric, and after dealing with Finn's commitment phobia, Rachel deserves someone who likes her for her, coordinating cat calendars and all. Rachel may be a lot of crazy things (like a fame-obsessed drama queen), but she's also extremely self-aware. Just as she knows in "Ballad" that Will's maturity could complement her driven personality, she knows that New Directions has a better chance at winning Nationals than she has of finding a high school guy who understands her high-maintenance needs and supports her relentless ambition. Since Vocal Adrenaline's star performer seems to be Rachel with a Y chromosome and even more confidence, it could be the right fit, and a relationship with Jesse may be a risk worth taking.

While sparks fly between Jesse and Rachel, the introduction of Shelby feels somewhat forced. Will hooking up with a strong woman who makes Will's dedication to show choir look minor league is an interesting idea, but despite the connection their lips make in his living room, Shelby doesn't seem to connect with Will as well as Jesse does with Rachel. It feels unrealistic that their brief conversation about their glee clubs would lead to them getting hot and heavy, yet Shelby's actions are still somewhat understandable. Rachel's jump to his-and-her calendars is the innocent equivalent to Shelby's jump to Will's couch. Shelby, like Rachel, recognizes that glee club–loving single dudes are few and far between and seizes every romantic opportunity she gets. It's too soon to tell what Shelby's role will be, but the prospects are intriguing.

Though Rachel and Will both get a taste of Adrenaline this episode, once again Will's character parallels Finn as both men attempt to rediscover themselves. They're pretty screwed up right now, as both are still recovering from their baby drama fallout and big break-ups, and neither guy deals well with change. Time and again, Finn demonstrates how he will do anything to hang on to his popularity and this episode is no exception, with him kicking Rachel to the curb. And Will? Well, he's been with the same woman since he was 15 (!), and then post-break-up he immediately tries to swap Terri's crazy for Emma's. After continually defining themselves by their relationships with others, it's time for our confused leading men to get a reintroduction to themselves.

With all these new changes and new competition, New Directions had

idina menzel as shelby corcoran

Broadway star Idina Menzel was a huge fan of *Glee* when it premiered. She wanted to see if she could score a guest-starring role, so her team sent out feelers to Ryan Murphy. It worked, and Idina was cast as Shelby Corcoran, the demanding Vocal Adrenaline coach. Born on May 30, 1971, in Syosset, New York, to a therapist and a salesman, Idina dreamed of being a performer and attended university at NYU's Tisch School of the Arts (the same university Matthew Morrison would attend a few years later). Shortly after graduation, she scored her first Broadway role, originating the role of Maureen in the Broadway production of *Rent*. This gig would establish Idina as a breakout Broadway performer, and she even earned a Tony nomination for Best Actress for the part. *Rent* did wonders for Idina's personal life too: she met her future husband, co-star Taye Diggs, whom she married in 2003. After leaving *Rent* in 1997, Idina had small roles in off-Broadway plays and recorded her first album before getting her second big role, playing Elphaba in *Wicked* (opposite fellow *Glee* guest star Kristin Chenoweth) in 2003. She's kept busy since leaving *Wicked* in 2007, recording, performing and enjoying family life. She gave birth to her son Walker in 2009.

better buckle up. It won't be long before today's hellos pave the way for a "highway to hell."

High Note: The tension between Rachel and Finn is very well done, especially during New Directions' "Hello Goodbye" performance. Rachel may be dating Jesse, but this relationship is far from over.

Low Note: Overall, the episode is way too rushed and doesn't flesh out many plot points. *Glee* had a lot of ground to cover, so here's hoping they decrease the tempo in coming episodes.

Behind the Music:

"Hello, I Love You" (Finn)
The Doors, *Waiting for the Sun* (1968)
The Doors' #1 hit, inspired by Cream's "Sunshine of Your Love" and a beautiful girl Jim Morrison saw in Venice Beach, is about lust at first sight. Finn is saying hello to both his inner rock star and his romantic desires. Which girl (Rachel, Quinn, Brittany and Santana or perhaps someone new) will he say "hello" to next?

"Gives You Hell" (Rachel)
The All-American Rejects, *When the World Comes Down* (2008)
Rachel sings The All-American Rejects' first big hit, which is about feeling vengeful toward an ex, after Finn breaks up with her. Rachel is frustrated with Finn's tendency to consistently put his social status ahead of his relationship with her, whereas she's always been open about her feelings for him. The All-American Rejects sing about suburban status symbols, like a 9-to-5 job, new cars and picket fences, and status is something Finn often can't look past. For a Lima Loser like Finn, this suburban dream might be as good as it gets.

"Hello" (Rachel and Jesse)
Lionel Richie, *Can't Slow Down* (1983)
Nothing is more romantic than this #1 hit about discovering the love of your life from the ultimate love balladeer, Lionel Richie. With this song, Jesse and Rachel come together both musically and romantically. Considering Jesse and Rachel just met, it's a bold duet for Jesse to select, but he seems like a bold guy. However, Rachel did sing "Endless Love" with her teacher, so she's not exactly the most adept at recognizing the appropriateness of her song choices.

"Hello Again" (Will)
Neil Diamond, *The Jazz Singer* (1980)
Just as Will explains to Emma, Neil Diamond's love song is about discovering romantic feelings for a longtime friend. Emma may have loved Will for years before they got together, but Will only realizes his own feelings after his marriage falls apart and Emma admits her longstanding crush to him. Will's using this song to reintroduce himself to Emma, this time as a romantic prospect — though as Terri reveals, it's not the fresh start it appears to be.

"Highway to Hell" (Vocal Adrenaline)
AC/DC, *Highway to Hell* (1979)
After describing being on tour as being on a "highway to hell," bandmates Bon Scott, Angus Young and Malcolm Young were inspired to turn this experience into a song, one that became one of the most famous rock anthems of all time. Everyone is on the road toward their dream: Vocal Adrenaline is heading for a fourth-straight national championship, Rachel is searching for love and stardom, and both Will and Finn are in the process of finding themselves. But even the journey toward greatness can be long, painful and hellish.

"Hello Goodbye" (New Directions)

The Beatles, *Magical Mystery Tour* (1967)

Paul McCartney once said that this Beatles classic is about how you can't have it all. Once you acquire something you've wanted, you lose something else in the process. Finn wants Rachel and wants to be popular, but believes he can't have both. Rachel wants a relationship and says hello to Jesse, only to discover that she could have Finn if she wants. New Directions may be saying hello to show choir success, but this success means they'll continue to be at the bottom of the social ladder.

Give My Regards to Broadway: Rachel wants to attend a community production of *Phantom* with Finn. *The Phantom of the Opera* is the tale of a disfigured man who lives below the Paris Opera House. A musical genius, he meets, trains and falls in love with Christine, a young girl who works in the chorus. But while the Phantom's love grows, Christine falls in love with someone else, creating a love triangle doomed to a tragic conclusion. Now considered the most popular musical of all time, Andrew Lloyd Webber was inspired to turn the 1910 French novel *Le Fantôme de l'Opéra* by Gaston

jonathan groff as jesse st. james

Lea Michele has finally been reunited with her real-life BFF Jonathan Groff, and it's all thanks to Ryan Murphy. After Lea and Jonathan starred in *Spring Awakening* together on Broadway, Jonathan filmed Ryan Murphy's pilot project *Pretty Handsome*. While the show wasn't picked up, Ryan was impressed with Jonathan and promised him that if *Glee* took off, he'd write a part just for him. Voilà, meet Jesse St. James! The Ronks, Pennsylvania, native was born to Jim and Julie Groff on March 26, 1985. Jonathan's been busy since childhood, having played the role of Rolf in the national tour of *The Sound of Music* and having a recurring role on *One Life to Live* until 2007, when his character was killed off. He and Lea Michele originated the leads of *Spring Awakening*. It was his first big Broadway role, and the part scored Jonathan his first Tony nomination. He's had a handful of small film roles since, but there's definitely more to come from this budding triple threat!

Leroux into a musical after seeing the 1976 musical adaptation by Ken Hill. Webber developed his own adaptation, which opened first in London and made its Broadway debut on January 26, 1988. *Phantom* saw its 9,000th performance take place on Broadway in 2009, making it the longest-running musical of all time.

That's Pretty *Popular*: Adam, a confident, talented, dark and mysterious new senior, admires the Glamazons' talent and beauty and wants to join in "All About Adam." He seems to be a harmless admirer, but in the end his true intentions are revealed: he's out to destroy the Glamazons. As for Jesse's intentions with Rachel? It's too soon to tell, but if he's anything like Adam, Rachel better watch out.

Slushie Facials:
- Rachel, Kurt and Mercedes are slushied in the hallway.
- Sue cuts off a male student's ponytail.

Off-Key:
- Both Emma and Terri refer to the song from *The Jazz Singer* as "Hello." The actual title of the Neil Diamond song is "Hello Again."
- When Quinn and Puck are fighting in the hallway, Quinn's position against the wall changes from frame to frame.

162

- During "Gives You Hell," Brittany and Santana are resting their chins in their hands in one shot, but when it cuts back to them, their hands are in their laps.
- Dakota Stanley, the Vocal Adrenaline choreographer from "Acafellas," doesn't appear and is never mentioned.

Behind the Scenes:

- Despite the fact that Cory Monteith claims he's terrible at basketball, this is the second time he's played a basketball player on television. The first was in *Kyle XY*, when he had a recurring role as high school jock Charlie Tanner in the show's first two seasons.
- Lauren Gottlieb, Jason Glover and Janette Manrara, all former *So You Think You Can Dance* contestants, are Vocal Adrenaline dancers in "Highway to Hell."
- "Dolphins are just gay sharks" is Heather Morris's favorite Brittany-ism.
- Sue was supposed to say the lines "Shut your mouth before I rape it" and "She wears floor-length skirts that make her look like she escaped from a polygamist cult" in this episode, but the producers cut both at the last minute to avoid controversy.

Center Stage:

- Kurt feels like Lady Gaga, a singer who experienced overnight success when she released her 2008 debut album, *The Fame*, which earned six Grammy nominations.
- Ken pulls a "Jessica Simpson," by gaining weight after he and Emma broke up. Between 2007 and 2009, Jessica, an actress, singer and reality television star, had a very public relationship with professional football player Tony Romo. After they broke up in 2009, Jessica revealed a much curvier and heavier new body.
- When Will encourages Finn to find his inner rock star, he offers Mick Jagger and Jim Morrison as two examples. Mick Jagger, the lead singer for The Rolling Stones, has been living the rock star life since the band formed in 1960s. Mick is renowned for dating models, actresses and fashion designers; fathering several children; and headlining music tours around the world. Jim Morrison was the beloved front man for The Doors from 1965 to 1970 and is widely considered one of the most charismatic rock stars of all time. In 1971, Morrison mysteriously died,

supposedly from a brain hemorrhage caused by taking heroin.

- *The Jazz Singer* is a 1980 film starring Neil Diamond, the hugely successful singer-songwriter best known for "Sweet Caroline." Neil plays a young Jewish man who defies his father and follows his dreams of being a pop singer. The film flopped at the box office, but the soundtrack (written and performed by Neil) was a success, selling over five million copies.

- Terri loves to have Jerry Bruckheimer night but left three of the successful film and television producer's action flicks behind when she moved out: *Armageddon, Bad Boys* and *Con Air*. Will Smith and Martin Lawrence star in *Bad Boys*, a 1995 film about two police officers who need to track down $100 million worth of heroin or their police division will be shut down. *Armageddon* is a 1998 film starring Ben Affleck and Bruce Willis as oil drillers recruited to destroy an asteroid heading toward Earth. *Con Air*, headlined by Nicolas Cage and John Cusack, is a 1997 film about a group of prisoners in transport who successfully take over the plane they're traveling in. All three films grossed over $100 million each at the box office.

- One of the McKinley High old maids spends her Friday nights watching *Ghost Whisperer*, the CBS drama that ran from 2005 to 2010 and starred Jennifer Love Hewitt as Melinda Gordon, an antique shop owner who tries to reunite ghosts with their living loved ones so the undead can find eternal peace.

- Rachel is afraid of turning into Barbra Streisand's character in Sydney Pollack's 1973 Oscar-nominated film *The Way We Were*, which also starred Robert Redford. Barbra and Robert played Katie Morosky and Hubbell Gardiner, a couple whose differences drive them apart and who, years later, come to regret their parting of ways but realize they can't relive the past.

Jazz Hands:

- When Rachel, Mercedes and Kurt are walking down the hall in the opening scene, an instrumental version of "Don't Rain on My Parade" is playing, harkening back to Rachel's Sectionals solo, and reinforcing the glee club's belief that, thanks to their win, McKinley's hallways are a walk of fame, not shame.

- Maharishi, which is what Sue called Principal Figgins, is the Hindu term for saint that literally translates to "great seer."

- Take a good look at the relationship calendars Rachel created: she

just like jesse (st.) james

Jesse St. James is the name of Vocal Adrenaline's star, and it's a name he shares with several other notable folks:

1. **Jesse Woodson James:** The original Jesse James was an outlaw and gangster who robbed banks and trains and committed murder in the late 1800s in the American Midwest. He was never captured but was eventually murdered by a fellow outlaw he considered an accomplice, Robert Ford.
2. **Jesse Gregory James:** Another notorious Jesse James is a motorcyle customizer and star of the reality show *Monster Garage*. He's known for his reality television appearances and his womanizing ways. He's been married three times, including to actress Sandra Bullock, a relationship that ended with a very public divorce.
3. **Jessie St. James:** Jessie St. James was one of the porn industry's most famous female stars in the 1970s and 1980s. Her most famous role was in the 1980 film *Insatiable*, one of the best-selling pornographic films of all time.
4. **Brian Gerard James:** A professional wrestler better known by his ring name "The Road Dogg" Jesse James, Brian James was active in the World Wrestling Federation (now World Wrestling Entertainment) from 1994 to 2000, where he was a five-time tag team champion with partner Billy Gunn.
5. **Jessica Rose James:** Jessica, who goes professionally by Jessie James, is an American country/pop singer whose first album, *Jessie James*, debuted on August 11, 2009, on Mercury Records, the same label *Glee* star Matthew Morrison is signed with.

superimposed her and Finn's faces onto the heads of the cats!

- Puck asks Quinn to stop "supersizing," the term McDonald's used until 2009 to upgrade the size of their fries and soft drink for a small cost.
- Hurricane Katrina, the devastating storm that caused the levies of New Orleans to collapse and flood the city in 2005, was the most expensive natural disaster in North American history, as well as one of the deadliest. 700,000 residents whose homes were destroyed were given trailers or supplied hotel rooms to live in by FEMA, the Federal Emergency Management Agency. These trailers were controversial, as they were often not properly equipped or hooked up, and the supply of trailers was limited. Five years later, hundreds of families are still living in trailers and the area that was affected is still being rehabilitated.
- Alexander Graham Bell, the inventor of the telephone, indeed used "Ahoy" (the traditional greeting two ships used when approaching each other) as his usual telephone greeting. It was Thomas Edison, as

Will states, who persuaded the Central District and Printing Telegraph Company to adopt "Hello" as the standard telephone greeting.

- "Pearly white harbor," Will's toothy assault on Emma, references the unexpected Japanese attack on the United States at Pearl Harbor in Hawaii on December 7, 1941, during World War II. Six Japanese aircrafts bombed the naval base, resulting in four battleships sinking and causing nearly 2,500 deaths.

- Sue threatens Santana and Brittany with a Japanese ritual belly slitting, also known as *seppuku* or *hara-kiri*. This suicide method was popular during the Japanese medieval period and was considered an honorable way to end one's life.

- Sue claims she gave a cheerleading seminar to Sarah Palin, the former governor of Alaska and John McCain's 2008 controversial vice-presidential nominee. Largely unqualified and unvetted by the McCain campaign, Palin caused some unease with American voters due to her lack of experience, contradictory statements, conservative viewpoints and difficulty with media interviews.

- When Rachel is searching for a "hello" song in the library, she passes on the sheet music for *The Jazz Singer* soundtrack, which includes "Hello Again," the song that Will and Emma dance to in his apartment.

- Rachel's outfits make her look like an Israeli Pippi Longstocking, an unusually strong redhaired girl known for her stockings and her braided pigtails. Pippi was the star of many popular children's books, a 1949 movie and two television series.

- Rachel compares her and Jesse's romance to that of Romeo and Juliet, a Shakespearean couple whose love was doomed from the start, thanks to their dueling families.

- "Mr. Schue, we have a problem" is a line lifted from the Apollo 13 radio transmission. "Houston, we've had a problem" was often misquoted as "Houston, we have a problem" and is now a catchphrase that gained popularity when the erroneous version was used for the 1995 Ron Howard film *Apollo 13*.

- Kurt calls Rachel "Benedict Arnold," a general in the American Revolutionary War who betrayed the Americans and joined the British army. While still with the American army, he tried to take command of White Point, New York, and hand it over to British control. After that plan failed, he abandoned his double-agent ways and joined the British army.

- Those cute black dresses from "Hello Goodbye" are from Target. The costume department added the white bows for fun.

How Sue Cs It: "I am engorged with venom and triumph."

♪♫♪

1.15 "the power of madonna"
Original Air Date: April 20, 2010
Written by: Ryan Murphy
Directed by: Ryan Murphy

The Music: ★ ★ ★ ★
The Drama: ★ ★ ★
The Laughs: ★ ★ ★ ♪

Emma (to Will): We will change the world one girl at a time. We'll be like a girl-saving team.

Sue and Will both use Madonna to empower their students, while the New Directions guys get a lesson in girl power.

While *Glee* occasionally hits us over the head with their theme of the week, the Madonna spin on the "equality for all" theme made the concept feel shiny and new. The *Glee* ladies tend to get a lot of crap from their male counterparts so it's about time somebody helps them stand up for themselves and demand some respect. And it appears the boys are getting the message that's being blasted through the loudspeaker. Jesse transfers to McKinley and Will files for divorce; both men are working hard to prove that they're worthy of their lady's love. Finn's also fighting the good fight, trying to reconcile his feelings for Rachel and his desire for popularity. Aside from caving to Santana's sexual pressure, Finn shows a lot of maturity in this episode, from telling the guys that they need to make things right with the girls to being the bigger man by welcoming Jesse to New Directions. If Finn wants to win Rachel back, he's on the right track.

While at first this episode appears to be about boldly taking control, it's also about knowing yourself, and the "Like a Virgin" montage brings the intersection of these two themes into sharp focus. It's particularly interesting that Finn decides to get physical while the girls both abstain. Is this an indication that the ladies are more mature, more sensitive and ultimately more concerned with how they see themselves instead of how others see them? Or are their choices a reflection of the stereotypes that the Material Girl herself challenges — that women are only seen as either virgins, like Rachel and Emma, or whores, like Santana? (In Freudian psychoanalysis this tendency is called a Madonna/whore complex, where Madonna refers to the Virgin Mary, not the "Like a Virgin" singer.) But Santana playing the seductress is in control of the situation and her own body. It's a welcome counterpoint to the abstinence of Rachel and Emma, proving it's not about the morality of the choices they make but about being true to themselves in those choices.

Kurt and Mercedes finally get their chance to shine by joining the Cheerios in this episode. They make it pretty clear that they dislike how Mr. Schue continually favors Rachel and Finn for solos, but he's still not getting the message, as he very rarely lets anyone else get a turn in the spotlight. Sure, it is sneaky for Kurt and Mercedes to join the squad behind Will's back, but it's understandable that these two are sick of being second best, especially when they're both such first-rate performers. Sue's acceptance of Mercedes and Kurt harkens back to the role she played as co-director of the glee club in "Throwdown," and this shake-up is another embodiment of Madonna's message of equality and empowerment, as well as Sue's (sometimes hidden) mantra of inclusion and diversity. Sue loves putting Will in his place, and when she can send Will a message while ruining his club (and giving her Cheerios a competitive advantage), she'll jump at the chance to take it. It's a nice play on how Sue aspires to be like Madonna: both are contradictory, ambitious women who go after what they want and try to teach men a lesson or two along the way.

This episode is so jam-packed with musical numbers that there isn't a lot of room left for plot development. As a result, other storylines like Sue's "Vogue" video and makeover felt rushed and under-developed. Nonetheless, Sue's singing debut is well worth waiting 15 episodes for — her re-creation of one of Madonna's most iconic music videos is one for the yearbook.

Despite a few bad notes, the Madonna messages of empowerment and equality seem to get through to everyone. Girls or guys, geeks or Cheerios, New Directions' success comes from respecting each other and working together. When they do, the result is simply "Madge-ical."

High Note: "Like a Prayer" is beautiful and uplifting, the perfect end to a powerful episode.

Low Note: Jesse better not be dating Rachel as part of a Vocal Adrenaline ploy, because trying to woo her into sleeping with him before she's ready takes it way too far.

Behind the Music:

"Express Yourself" (Rachel, Quinn, Mercedes, Tina, Santana and Brittany)
Madonna, *Like a Prayer* (1989)
Expressing yourself through song is nothing new to New Directions, and Madonna's catchy top ten hit about female empowerment sets the tone for the rest of the episode, as New Directions explores Madonna's message of equality of the sexes. The girls pay tribute to Madonna in more ways than one with their rendition of "Express Yourself," as their costumes and choreography are directly lifted from Madonna's dystopian music video, considered one of the greatest videos of all time.

the making of a material girl: the madonna discography

Madonna has recorded and released 11 studio albums, six compilation albums, three soundtrack albums, three live albums and three remix albums throughout her illustrious career. Here we briefly examine the importance of her original studio albums:

1. **_Madonna_ (1983):** Madonna's debut record has sold ten million copies worldwide and established her as an up-and-coming dance artist, while her unique look made her an immediate fashion icon.

2. **_Like a Virgin_ (1984):** Madonna's second album incorporates more rock-infused beats and Motown influences, thanks in part to her increased creative control. _Like a Virgin_ surpassed even the astonishing success of the budding superstar's debut album, and in its lifetime has sold over 21 million copies around the world.

3. **_True Blue_ (1986):** Madonna's third album, largely considered to be her breakthrough record, explores her feminine side, the concept of love and her relationship with then-husband Sean Penn. Despite mixed reviews from critics, Madonna dominated the charts, and has sold over 24 million copies of _True Blue_ worldwide.

4. **_Like a Prayer_ (1989):** Madonna's music took a darker turn with _Like a Prayer_ as she musically explored her divorce from Sean Penn, her childhood and her difficult relationship with her stepmother. Despite being less commercially successful than _True Blue_ (having sold just over seven million copies worldwide), _Like a Prayer_ was adored by critics and is considered one of Madonna's greatest records.

5. **_Erotica_ (1992):** Each song on this concept album explores a different aspect of sexuality, but in this case, sex didn't sell. Despite the infectious hip-hop and jazz-infused dance pop style, it is the Material Girl's least commercially successful record, selling only four million copies around the world since it dropped. Many critics argued that Madonna took the concept of "erotica" too far and that her exploration was too clinical rather than sexual, but the album has come to be revered over time.

6. **_Bedtime Stories_ (1994):** After the critical and commercial backlash to _Erotica_, _Bedtime Stories_ saw Madonna move into more radio-friendly R&B sounds, and, as a result, scored the pop star her first Grammy nomination and double platinum status within a year of its release. It went on to sell over six million copies worldwide. Despite the record's more welcoming vibe, Madonna still tackled controversial subjects with her music, including the public's reaction to _Erotica_.

7. **_Ray of Light_ (1998):** Recorded after the birth of her daughter, _Ray of Light_ marks a shift toward a more mature and adventurous sound, exploring trance and electronica, and covering personal topics like motherhood and fame. This shift resulted in one of

Madonna's biggest successes, with the album going triple platinum in the U.S. within nine months of its release, winning in four of its six Grammy-nominated categories and eventually selling over 20 million copies worldwide.

8. **Music (2000):** *Music* was recorded to bolster the set list and generate interest for her Drowned World Tour. Musically it is an extension of *Ray of Light* and highlights Madonna's transition to Euro dance pop, while maintaining her signature rock vibe. The album was nominated for five Grammys, winning one, and has sold 11 million copies worldwide.

9. **American Life (2003):** This concept album explores materialism, fame, nationalism and the American identity. Despite the push from "Die Another Day," the theme song for the James Bond film of the same name, *American Life* was Madonna's second-lowest-selling album (after *Erotica*), and got a lukewarm critical reception.

10. **Confessions on a Dance Floor (2005):** *Confessions on a Dance Floor* marks Madonna's return to her dance music roots, incorporating '70s and '80s influence with modern and Euro dance music. The return to her dance style was a success: she nabbed the Grammy for Best Dance/Electronic album and has sold eight million copies worldwide since its release.

11. **Hard Candy (2008):** Madonna continues her exploration of modern dance music with *Hard Candy*, but this time she added an urban edge, thanks to collaborations with artists and producers like Justin Timberlake, Timbaland and Pharrell Williams. The album received mixed reviews and sold a respectable four million copies worldwide.

"Borderline/Open Your Heart" (Rachel and Finn)

Madonna, *Madonna* (1983)

Madonna, *True Blue* (1986)

Madonna sings about unfulfilled love and male chauvinism in "Borderline," her first top ten hit. Until Finn is mature enough to accept Rachel for who she is and accept everything that comes with dating her — the good and the bad — Rachel feels he doesn't deserve her. "Open Your Heart," a song about opening yourself up to love, was originally written with a rock and roll bent and Cyndi Lauper in mind. Madonna snagged it instead, rewriting some of the lyrics and changing the beat to make it her fifth #1 hit. When sung by Finn, it emphasizes his desire to prove to Rachel that he's matured, and that he's ready for a relationship with her and all her crazy.

"Vogue" (Sue)
Madonna, *I'm Breathless* (1990)
"Vogue" was inspired by New York's vibrant gay dance scene. It samples several disco hits, including "Love Is the Message" by MFSB, "Ooh, I Love It (Love Break)" by Salsoul Orchestra and Madonna's own "Like a Virgin." The video was inspired by 1930s Hollywood and several of the scenes are recreations of Horst P. Horst's photographs of stars, many of whom are mentioned in the song. In an episode where Kurt and Mercedes reinvent themselves as Cheerios, they are inspired to recreate Sue Sylvester's look. Since Madonna is all about reinvention, what better way to do that than using Madonna's greatest dance hit as the soundtrack for the ultimate makeover?

"Like a Virgin" (Rachel, Jesse, Santana, Finn, Will and Emma)
Madonna, *Like a Virgin* (1984)
"Like a Virgin," one of Madonna's signature hits, was inspired by the songwriters' own romantic experiences. Madonna didn't like the song when she first heard the demo, but it eventually grew on her. Despite the ambiguity of the song's lyrics, *Glee* takes it literally: Rachel, Emma and Finn are all hoping to lose their virginity. Madonna's accompanying music video asserts her sexual strength and independence, which is what the girls do: Santana by unapologetically offering sex to Finn, and Rachel and Emma by realizing they aren't ready.

"4 Minutes" (Mercedes and Kurt)
Madonna featuring Justin Timberlake and Timbaland, *Hard Candy* (2008)
Thanks to "4 Minutes," two social outcasts are suddenly the coolest kids in school. Madonna was inspired to write this song as a reaction to global environmental destruction, social inequality and economic disparity, and to encourage immediate response to these plights. Kurt and Mercedes may not change the world, but they change the social structure at McKinley when they join the Cheerios and receive a standing ovation for their performance.

"What It Feels Like for a Girl" (Finn, Puck, Kurt, Artie, Mike and Matt)
Madonna, *Music* (2000)
"What It Feels Like for a Girl" showcases the struggles girls face every day in contemporary society, the very message Mr. Schue wants to teach the boys. Artie's spoken word introduction is from Ian McEwan's 1978 novel *The Cement Garden*, a modern gothic tale about four orphan siblings left to their own devices.

Actress and singer-songwriter Charlotte Gainsbourg starred in the 1993 film adaptation of *The Cement Garden* and lends her voice to the original recording.

"Like a Prayer" (New Directions)
Madonna, *Like a Prayer* (1989)
"Like a Prayer" explores the intense emotions of a highly charged relationship, and New Directions' rendition compares these feelings with the ones they get when performing. Routine, ritual and channeling a greater power are elements found in religion, relationships and performance, and New Directions' version of "Like a Prayer" showcases all three. Being onstage with each other is like a religious experience and, if they want to maintain this positive feeling and sense of empowerment, the glee clubbers should take a page from a religious book and follow the golden rule: do unto others as you would have them do unto you, a Madonna-approved message.

The Sound of Music: Madonna may currently dominate the world of music, but her origins were humble. Born Madonna Louise Ciccone on August 16, 1958, to a French Canadian mother and Italian American father in Bay City, Michigan, Madonna was the third of six children. After high school, she received a dance scholarship to the University of Michigan but dropped out to pursue a career in dance in New York City. There, she caught the eye of DJ Mark Kamins who introduced her to Sire Records, which signed her and released her debut album in 1983. Madonna went on to garner worldwide success and critical acclaim, and constantly reinvented herself for her audience. She also dabbled in acting, starring in *Desperately Seeking Susan* in 1985 and *A League of Their Own* in 1992. Madonna's personal life has also been a wild ride. After a whirlwind romance, she married Sean Penn in 1986, a relationship that would end in a very public divorce in 1989. In 1996, Madonna had a daughter, Lourdes, with her former personal trainer, Carlos Leon. She married her second husband, Guy Ritchie, in 2000, and that same year they had a son, Rocco. In 2004, Madonna developed an interest in humanitarian issues, partnering with Live Aid. She also adopted a son, David, in 2006 and a daughter, Mercy, in 2009, both from Malawi.

Give My Regards to Broadway: Jesse chooses to meet Rachel at the library near Stephen Sondheim's biography, and Mark Eden Horowitz's *Sondheim on Music* falls on the floor, a collection of interviews with the

express yourself: the madonna references

This very special episode deserves a very special sidebar to celebrate all the Madonna-isms that occurred:

- The episode's title references Madonna's 1998 single "The Power of Good-Bye," which is about how freeing and empowering saying good-bye or ending a relationship can feel.
- The compilation album Sue gives Figgins is 2009's *Celebration*, Madonna's third greatest hits collection.
- Sue is "desperately seeking Susan," referencing the 1985 film of the same name. Madonna starred as Susan, a New Yorker whose life intrigues several people, including suburban housewife Roberta, played by Rosanna Arquette. Hijinks ensue when Roberta decides to find Susan.
- Sue mentions that Madonna owns a British estate. In 2001, Madonna and then-husband Guy Ritchie purchased the 200-year-old Ashcombe House in Wiltshire, U.K., a property that was previously owned by renowned photographer and designer Cecil Beaton. When Madonna and Guy divorced, Guy retained ownership of the property, but she still regularly rents property in the English countryside.
- Sue encourages her Cheerios to date younger men, just like Madonna. Madonna's second husband, Guy Ritchie, was ten years younger than her. After they divorced in 2008, Madonna became involved with Jesus Luz, a male model 28 years her junior.
- Eight Madonna look-a-likes from her music videos ("Like a Virgin," "Material Girl," "Holiday (Live)," "Human Nature," "Nothing Really Matters," "Don't Tell Me," "Open Your Heart" and "Lucky Star") make appearances during Finn and Rachel's duet.
- Just like Madonna, Kurt is "going to Kabbalah." Kabbalah is a set of teachings based on Jewish mysticism and focusing on the universe in nature. Madonna took up the practice in 1996 and is a devout follower.
- Kurt says his video is going to be "Madge-ical," referencing Madge, the nickname the British tabloids gave Madonna.
- "Burning Up," "Frozen" and "Justify My Love" were all heard over McKinley's loudspeakers.

composer examining his work and creative process. Stephen Sondheim is an award-winning Broadway composer whose body of work includes the iconic shows *A Funny Thing Happened on the Way to the Forum*, *Sweeney Todd* and *West Side Story*. He celebrated his 80th birthday in 2010 and has received several lifetime achievement awards. His work is so influential that a Broadway show highlighting his music, *Sondheim on Sondheim*, was developed in 2010. Madonna even recorded a Sondheim song, "Sooner or Later (I Always Get

My Man)," for the 1990 film *Dick Tracy*, which won Sondheim an Academy Award for Best Original Song.

That's Pretty *Popular*: While the Sue Sylvester re-creation of Madonna's "Vogue" is truly epic, it isn't the first time a Ryan Murphy character channels the Material Girl. Cheerleader Nicole Julian does her own re-enactment of "Vogue" in the second season episode "Coup," and Nicole and Mary Cherry partially remake Madonna's "Music" video in "Ur-Ine Trouble." Like Emma and Rachel, Brooke certainly feels like a virgin in the pilot episode after she realizes sexy lingerie doesn't mean you're ready for sex. And in "Caged!" we learn that bad girl Nicole pulled a Santana when she seduced golden boy Josh into doing the deed after he and Brooke broke up, an effort designed to boost both their popularity points.

Slushie Facials:
* Quinn draws a not-so-flattering picture of Rachel while the girls are hanging out in the choir room.
* Sue pushes three kids in the hallway after Will insults her hair.

Off-Key:
* During the Cheerios' "Ray of Light" performance, some of the signs on the gym walls are backwards. The film was most likely flipped in post-production.
* Quinn's baby bump looks significantly smaller in her "Express Yourself" costume than it does in her regular clothes. That's a mighty tight corset she's got on!
* Madonna isn't blasting through the loudspeakers when Kurt and Mercedes approach Sue about doing "Vogue."
* There are no male Cheerios participating in the "4 Minutes" performance or Sue's "What Would Madonna Do?" chat, even though they are around for the "Ray of Light" performance.
* Sue claims she was six years old when *True Blue* came out in 1986, which would make her seven years old when she spoke at Palladium.

Behind the Scenes:
* Madonna originally wasn't keen on the idea of licensing her music to *Glee*. To get her to agree to offer her entire catalogue, Ryan Murphy

wrote her a personal letter, explaining why he was longtime fan and why her message of equality was important for fans of the show. It didn't hurt that Madonna's publicist, Liz Rosenberg, pushed for the episode, in part thanks to her *Glee*-obsessed stepdaughter. "I begged Madonna to allow them to use her music because my stepdaughter would never forgive me if I didn't get Madonna to OK the usage of the songs," Liz explained.

- The "Vogue" re-creation (which took three months to put together) was shot with the actual Madonna video being played in front of the cast so that they could emulate the original exactly.
- The hands above Jane Lynch's face during the "Vogue" video are the hands of Heather Morris and Naya Rivera. Heather also stars in the video as the dancer wearing the cone bra.
- Nathan Trasoras from the sixth season of *So You Think You Can Dance* makes an appearance in the "Vogue" video and in the "Ray of Light" Cheerios performance.
- The marching band that plays at the Cheerios' "4 Minutes" performance is the University of Southern California's marching band, the Trojans.
- "Mr. Schue, is he your son?" is a line improvised by Heather Morris during rehearsals. Ryan Murphy thought it was hilarious and added it to the script for Brittany.
- The woman Mercedes is dancing with in the choir for "Like a Prayer" is Amber Riley's mom! When Ryan Murphy mentioned he needed people for the choir, Amber suggested her mother, and Ryan made sure she was front and center so she could sing with her daughter.
- New Directions wore their "Like a Prayer" outfits for their White House Easter Egg Roll and *Oprah* performances in April 2010 and during the 2010 *Glee* Live Tour.
- Several costumes were custom-made for this Madonna-specific episode, including the "Express Yourself" looks, the Cheerios' stilt legwarmers and Santana, Rachel and Emma's nightdresses (which are all the same shade of lavender).

Center Stage:

- Sue believes Madonna is more powerful than Angelina Jolie and Catherine the Great. Angelina is an Academy Award–winning actress who is just as famous for her personal life as her acting career. She and longtime partner Brad Pitt are renowned for their humanitarian work and many children. Catherine the Great was the Empress of Russia from 1762 until her death in 1796. Under Catherine's rule, Russia emerged as one of Europe's economic, political and cultural leaders.

- Sue claims she said, "I'm tough. I'm ambitious. And I know exactly what I want. If that makes me a bitch, OK," at Palladium in 1987. Madonna said this in 1992 to *People* magazine. Palladium was a popular new wave night club in New York that showcased artists like Frank Zappa, Blue Öyster Cult, Iggy Pop, Kiss, Iron Maiden and Def Leppard before shutting down in 1998.

- Rachel and Jesse went to see the Wiggles, an Australian musical group who is very popular among the toddler set. They've sold over 17 million DVDs and 4 million CDs worldwide.

- Emma thinks girls are troubled because their role models include Britney Spears and her shaved head, Lindsay Lohan and her *Lord of the Rings* look and Ann Coulter. Singer Britney Spears had a public breakdown in 2007 that saw her shave her head and enter a treatment facility. Lindsay Lohan is a young actress better known as an adult for her hard partying ways and high-profile relationships. J.R.R. Tolkien's *Lord of the Rings* is a fantasy trilogy adapted by Peter Jackson into a successful movie franchise, and the Lohan reference likely points to the sickly, emaciated Gollum. Ann Coulter is a political commentator, author and activist well known for her right-wing opinions and controversial actions.

- Sue smells the cookies of the elves in Will's hair. Keebler elves are the mascot for Keebler, the second largest baked goods company in the United States. Many of their television commercials feature elves baking Keebler products in their treetop bakery.

- Finn would rather pay homage to Pantera than Madonna. Pantera was a popular 1990s heavy metal band. Formed in 1981 and disbanded in 2003, Pantera pioneered "groove metal" and is widely regarded as one of the best heavy metal bands of all time.

- Sue "allows" Will to have his Barbras, Chers and Christinas, referring to recording artists Barbra Streisand, Cher and Christina Aguilera.

- Will comments on Sue's "Florence Henderson look." Florence played Carol Brady on *The Brady Bunch* and was known for her short shag hairstyle. Coincidentally, Jane Lynch played Carol Brady for the live comedy show *The Real Live Brady Bunch* in Chicago in the early 1990s.

- Sue calls Mercedes "Whoopi" and Kurt "Don Knotts." Whoopi Goldberg, an actress who starred in films *Sister Act* and *Ghost* and is a current co-host of the talk show *The View*, is one of an elite group of performers who have won the four major entertainment awards: Emmy, Grammy, Oscar and Tony (occasionally referred to as the elusive EGOT). Don Knotts is an American actor best known for his Emmy-winning role as Barney Fife in the popular 1960s television show *The Andy Griffith Show* and for his role as Ralph Furley, the landlord on the 1980s show *Three's Company*.

• Sue calls Kurt a "future center square," referring to the 1966–2004 game show *Hollywood Squares*, where celebrities sat in a tic-tac-toe board and helped contestants answer trivia. The center square on the board was usually a quirky, flamboyant celebrity.

Jazz Hands:

• Rachel won Jesse a Care Bear, a stuffed animal based on the American Greetings characters. A cartoon based on the characters ran from 1985 to 1988. Since then, they've appeared in films, in computer games and as toys.

• Emma's new brochures include "Loose," "Toxic Shock," "Congratulations, You're Pregnant!," "Do I Have Asperger's?," "YUK! My Privates," "Proper Wiping: Easy as 1-2-3," "Why Is There Blood?," "Autism: the . . . ," "I Still Breastfeed . . . But How Old Is Too Old?" and "Help! I'm In Love With My Stepdad!"

• Rachel says "Noted" to Finn, just like Shelby said "Noted" to Will in "Hell-O."

• Finn is as sexy as a Cabbage Patch Kid, a line of cute dolls with plastic heads and soft bodies that looked like babies. The dolls were very popular in the 1980s.

• Sue calls the glee club "Up with People rejects." Up with People is an international organization founded in 1965 that creates musical groups with students from diverse backgrounds and sends them around the world to perform. However, New Directions couldn't be Up with People rejects because you must be at least 18 years old to audition.

• Will falsely claims that Madonna's catalog is in the public domain. In order for an artist's work to be in the public domain in the United States, the artist must have passed away over 70 years ago.

• Will suggests that Sue should fix her hairstyle with a Flowbee, a hair-cutting vacuum attachment that was popular — and the butt of many jokes — in the 1980s.

- Sue tried to bleach her hair with napalm and ammonia. Napalm is a flammable liquid used by militaries to cause fire, make flamethrowers and firebombs and burn enemies.

How Sue Cs It: "Oh hey, William. I thought I smelled cookies wafting from the ovens of the little elves who live in your hair."

♪♫♪

1.16 "home"
Original Air Date: April 27, 2010
Written by: Brad Falchuk
Directed by: Paris Barclay

The Music: ★ ★ ♪
The Drama: ★ ★ ★
The Laughs: ★ ★ ♪

Will: You'll always be empty inside until you find a home.

Kurt, Finn, Mercedes, Will and April Rhodes (yup, she's back!) all get a lesson on what home means to them and the importance of finding a place that feels like, well, home.

With "Home," *Glee* does its best to remind everyone that there's no place like home. It's an interesting concept for an episode, as many members of the glee club come from non-traditional homes — Kurt, Finn and Puck all have single-parent families, Rachel has two gay dads and Quinn is bouncing between houses but no longer has a home.

This idea of "home" and its importance in one's life manifested itself in different ways for different characters. Finn, for example, is clinging to the idea of a home that doesn't actually exist, thinking that home should be an unchanging physical place and not an adaptable emotional space. Considering how we've continually seen that Finn struggles with change, his vision isn't surprising. He's caught up in the physicality of a home (for example, his obsessive devotion to his dad's chair) and he doesn't realize that

q&a: michael benjamin washington as tracy pendergrass

Born and raised in Dallas, Texas, Michael Benjamin Washington has been working professionally since he was 11 years old. After graduating from high school, he enrolled at the Tisch School at New York University. From there, Michael scored parts on Broadway, including a role in the original production of *Mamma Mia!* Recently, Michael has been focusing on his film and television career. We contacted Michael about what it was like to have a role on the hottest new show, and he happily answered our questions:

Have you always wanted to be an actor? How did you get into acting?

I was a Presidential Scholar in the Arts my senior year of high school and performed excerpts from *Othello* and *The Colored Museum* for [the] president and Mrs. Clinton at the Kennedy Center! I trained in theater at New York University with a little-known actor named Matthew Morrison, who has remained one of my best friends in the world. It was a thrill to get the offer to play Tracy Pendergrass, although Ryan Murphy had no idea Matt and I were buddies!

How did you prepare to play Tracy?

I have a minor in journalism from NYU and have NEVER done anything with it until this part! Thanks, *Glee*. My parents appreciate it.

What song would Tracy sing?

I've had visions of Tracy discovering Artie on a cafeteria loading dock, and they launch into "Sittin' on the Dock of the Bay." Kevin and I are from the same hometown, Plano, Texas, so, I think our ears like the same tones/tunes. He's fantastic! And a very nice, stylish, down-to-earth, WALKING dude!

What was it like on the *Glee* set, specifically working with Jane Lynch?

Jane Lynch is not only a brilliant comedienne, she is a FANTASTIC actress. The long days/nights that are required to be in the *Glee* ensemble would suck if there wasn't 100% commitment to craft, energy and attitude. Ms. Lynch is a consummate professional and never missed a laugh. She's always present and, despite her iconic status as THE most formidable villain on television, I've never worked with someone more generous and open. My goal was to help the audience see another side of Sue, and, I think, they did.

his home has evolved to something of greater value (his mother's happiness and the support she gives him). For Kurt, home is about acceptance — his dad is his fiercest advocate, and his home is a refuge for him, a place where he can escape the torment he suffers from at school. For Quinn, home is about support — something she needs desperately from her family but now seeks from her friends. For Will, home is memories of his glory days and of happier times. Terri's absence reinforces his sense of homelessness now that he's unsure of who he is. A house is a physical place meant to shelter us from the storm, and for all of these characters, a home is an emotional shelter.

The most interesting use of the "home" theme is the one that's most abstract: Mercedes' quest to feel at home in her Cheerios uniform. Mercedes has always been comfortable in her body, but joining the Cheerios reminded her that skinny girls still rule the school. Now that she's popular, there's a different set of rules for her to follow, but conforming isn't something our sassy confident diva is at home with. Thanks to Quinn's kind guidance, Mercedes figures out how to balance where she's from with where she's going, and the result is one of most touching musical moments this season.

April is back on the scene, acting as a catalyst for Will's home-related discoveries. Although she helps Will come to terms with his need for a sense of place, her reintroduction is a stretch, and her storyline is veil thin. "The Rhodes Not Taken" already focused on April's journey back home (for April, home is where the spotlight is). For *Glee* to revisit this plot line again is frustrating, but it made sense for someone who falls off the wagon as often as April does. Sometimes people need a little more help finding their way home.

New Directions gets a new home in the April Rhodes Civic Pavilion, but for the club's members, things are a little more complicated. Here's hoping they can simplify things in the future by remembering that home is where the heart is.

High Note: Finn opening his home to Burt is a big moment. He's learning to put the needs of others ahead of his own, and wanting his mom to be happy is a good place to start.

Low Note: Kurt standing outside the Hudson window is just plain creepy. The poignancy of a Finn/Burt truce and Kurt's resulting heartbreak is evident without making him look like a stalker.

Behind the Music:

"Fire" (Will and April)
Bruce Springsteen, *Live/1975–85* (1987)
Originally intended for Elvis Presley (and famously covered by the Pointer Sisters), "Fire" sets up the dynamic between April and Will for the rest of

the episode. The song is about a man who pursues a woman who claims she doesn't want him. April has a crush on Will and the two clearly have chemistry. Will, however, is confused by his recent divorce and multiple romantic exploits and is reluctant to pursue anything with anyone, let alone the alcoholic April.

"A House Is Not a Home" (Kurt with Finn)
Dionne Warwick, *Make Way for Dionne Warwick* (1964)
Kurt uses this Burt Bacharach and Hal David–penned song to demonstrate to Finn that Finn's mom is right — a house is not a home, living together does not make you family and a chair can't be a stand-in for a father. Kurt's rendition of this song is beautiful, although it's also a tad creepy and self-serving: if Finn accepts his mother's romantic life, he has no choice but to hang out with Kurt more often.

"One Less Bell to Answer/A House Is Not a Home" (Will and April)
Barbra Streisand, *Barbra Joan Streisand* (1971)
Barbra Streisand was the first artist to record this mash-up of two Burt Bacharach songs, both of which explore loneliness. "One Less Bell to Answer" examines living alone after a break-up, something Will is experiencing for the first time and something April is perpetually terrified of. Will can pretend moving will give him a fresh start and April can pretend that her relationship with Buddy is the real thing, but both are avoiding their solitude.

"Beautiful" (Mercedes)
Christina Aguilera, *Stripped* (2002)
Christina's Grammy-winning ballad about not letting the criticism of others get you down reminds Mercedes about the importance of both being true to yourself and loving yourself. These messages are important ones for *Glee*, as many of the characters regularly question who they are, try to change or hide their true selves and feel left out, cast out or judged.

"Home" (April with New Directions)
The Wiz (1975)
What better way to sum up an episode about the importance of finding one's sense of place than a touching rendition of "Home," a song that asserts there's no place like it? New Directions is singing this song in their new home. April,

gleek speak: clare hitchens
(*glee* fan and disability advocate)

As a mother of a son with Down syndrome, how did you and your family feel about the character Becky Jackson?
We were thrilled! Kids with Down syndrome are increasingly included in regular education classes, community sports and clubs, church groups and workplaces. But you'd never know it if you watch TV — there's very little representation. It's important for people with disabilities to see themselves represented in media, in popular culture, etc. If I recall correctly, she goes to high school but is in a special education class. Although many kids are included in regular classes, this is still rare in high school and special ed is still the norm. But good schools will get the kids with disabilities involved in extra-curricular activities and will make allowances if their audition or tryout is not up to the mark. It's about community, or it should be.

I also want to counter the opinion out there that this side of Sue is unrealistic. I know some real jerks that have a soft side when it comes to kids with disabilities. Let's face it, families of people with disabilities are not a homogenous group. But there's something about these kids that brings out the good in people. It totally made sense to me that Sue would be like that with her sister and that she would carry that into her experience with Becky. To me it didn't cheapen her character, it enriched it. I thought Jean [Robin Trocki] was wonderful, by the way. I'm not sure why she's always in bed, though. I'd like to see her up and about more rather than perpetuating the idea that disability = illness. But don't get me started on institutions. It may be where many older people with Down syndrome are, but that is changing as well. Then again, maybe Sue only visits at bedtime. I'd like that explored a little, because it bugs me. On the whole, though, I'm happy to see Down syndrome portrayed positively in both characters.

in turn, is searching for a place she can call home, and Will wants to recreate the feelings of home he had when his marriage was happy and stable.

Give My Regards to Broadway: Premiering on Broadway on January 5, 1975, *The Wiz*, a remake of the classic tale *The Wizard of Oz*, reinterprets the adventures of Dorothy in Oz from an African American perspective and changes the location from Kansas and Oz to Harlem and a fantastical New York City. The musical was a success, winning seven Tony awards, including Best Musical, and ran for 1,672 performances. In 1978, a film adaptation starring Michael Jackson and Diana Ross was released, but it was a critical and commercial bomb.

That's Pretty *Popular*: Enemies Brooke and Sam see their parents get together early on in the show, and much of the first season is about the girls' attempts to break them up. Like Finn, Brooke eventually comes around and supports her dad and the union, but Sam goes to great lengths to ruin the marriage because she's terrified of the bond Brooke and her mom are developing.

Off-Key:

- Will renting a roller rink seems like a stretch. There are plenty of options at McKinley, including the choir room and the gymnasium. And if the Cheerios need the auditorium all week, why are Kurt, Mercedes, Brittany and Santana always with the glee club?
- In "Hell-O," Brittany and Santana inhale their Breadsticks meal (and con the waitress into giving them seconds), but here they tell Mercedes they only consume Sue's cleanser.

Behind the Scenes:

- The roller rink band is Mulatto, a six-member group that blends rock, hip hop, jazz, funk and soul. The band formed in 2005 in Long Beach, California, and has been touring with Nas since 2008.
- Kurt's many tears are real! While television and movie sets have drops to create the illusion of crying, Chris Colfer refuses to use them.
- "A House Is Not a Home" was added to Kristin Chenoweth's 2010 Broadway show, Burt Bacharach's *Promises, Promises*, because it wonderfully showcases her voice.

Center Stage:

- Mercedes and Kurt should have a show on Bravo, an American cable network known for its ground-breaking reality television shows including *Project Runway*, *Queer Eye for the Straight Guy* and the *Real Housewives* franchise.
- Journalist Tracy Pendergrass may be named after 1970s R&B singer-songwriter Teddy Pendergrass, whose biggest hit was "If You Don't Know Me By Now."
- Finn's mom got *Pretty Woman*–ed up, referencing the 1990 movie that made Julia Roberts a huge star. In the film, Julia plays a prostitute hired by a wealthy man (Richard Gere) to be his escort for the week. In order to take her from trashy to classy, she undergoes a very famous wardrobe

makeover on Rodeo Drive.

- Rachel and Jesse would love nothing more than to be Beyoncé and Jay-Z, music's power couple who were married in April 2008. Jay-Z is an immensely successful producer and recording artist, and Beyoncé is one of the most success female recording artists of all time.
- In the cafeteria, Rachel praises Fanny Brice, a singer, actress and comedienne who was the inspiration for the 1964 Broadway musical and 1968 film *Funny Girl*.
- Kurt made his dad sit through *Riverdance*, an Irish stepdancing show that became very popular in the late 1990s and was even on Broadway in 2000.
- Sometimes April just needs a little Burt Bacharach, a pianist, composer and music producer known for his romantic ballads and Broadway-ready show tunes.
- Kurt feels like the "guy who set up Liza and David Gest." Liza Minnelli is an actress and singer who married concert promoter David Gest in 2002. The couple divorced only 18 months later, and he sued her for $10 million, citing physical and emotional abuse. The claim was dismissed in 2006.
- Sue called Tracy Pendergrass "Rerun." Freddy "Rerun" Stubbs, known for his red beret, shoddy grades and talented dancing, is a character on the 1970s sitcom *What's Happening!!* The show, about three black teens growing up in L.A., lasted for three seasons from 1976 to 1979 and was a modest hit.

Jazz Hands:

- If you look closely at the New Directions crew in the roller rink, you'll see that Artie is wearing roller skates!
- The Hudsons and Hummels are merging just like the Bouviers, a wealthy and prestigious family, and the Kennedys, an emerging political dynasty, did when Jacqueline Bouvier and John F. Kennedy married in 1953. John was elected the president of the United States in 1960, a position he held until he was assassinated on November 22, 1963.
- The Pulitzer Prize, for which Tracy Pendergrass was previously shortlisted, is an annual award given to the best journalism, literature and music produced in the United States. *Newsweek*, with a circulation of nearly two million copies, is the second largest weekly news magazine in the U.S..
- The first Gulf War, which took place from August 1990 to February

1991, is often called Operation Desert Storm. The Americans became involved after Iraq invaded Kuwait and the United Nations initiated military response. The Iraqi invasion quickly ended, but approximately 3,500 civilians and 150 coalition soldiers (including Finn's dad) lost their lives along the way.

- Duke University in Durham, North Carolina, has one of the best college basketball programs in the United States. They won the 2010 NCAA championship. Despite their success, Burt hates them as much as he hates the Nazis, the German political party that is responsible for World War II and the Holocaust, murdering nearly six million Jews.

The Buckeye State: Kurt's dad offers Finn tickets to see the Cleveland Browns, Ohio's only professional football team, and one of four NFL teams that have never played in a Super Bowl game. Tracy Pendergrass wrote an article about high school athletes immediately going pro. One of the most successful athletes to make this move is Ohio's own LeBron James, who grew up in Akron, 137 miles northeast of Lima. LeBron was drafted by the NBA's Cleveland Cavaliers in 2003 and is now one of the league's best players.

How Sue Cs It: "Now, if you'll excuse me, I have to put in a call to the Ohio Secretary of State, notifying them I will no longer be carrying photo ID. You know why? People should know who I am."

♪♫♪

1.17 "bad reputation"
Original Air Date: May 4, 2010
Written by: Ian Brennan
Directed by: Elodie Keene

The Music: ★ ★ ★
The Drama: ★ ★ ★
The Laughs: ★ ★ ★

Rachel: In this age of celebrity sex tapes, a good reputation does no good at all.

While the New Directions kids attempt to sully their reps in hope of improving their social status, Will and Sue both flail under the weight of a bad image.

In the age of celebrity sex and drug scandals and Perez Hilton, it's no wonder that the members of New Directions often struggle with being slushie-stained nobodies. Thanks to the Quinn-penned Glist, the glee clubbers decide it's time to step it up a notch and move from being "asses to badasses," as Jesse put it.

Quinn spent years cultivating a good girl image (she was president of the celibacy club, after all), but, as she points out near the end of the episode, a bad reputation is better than no reputation at all. As long as she's pregnant, Quinn knows that she'll never get back in the good social graces at McKinley, so she thinks that destroying the few threads of supposed decency she has left will at least get her noticed again. Her plan parallels one of the main issues in "The Power of Madonna," as it reminds us that, largely, girls can either be good (virgins) or bad (whores) in order to have value. Now that her baby bump proves she's lost her v-card, Quinn feels she needs to slide all the way down to the bottom of the naughty list and reinvent her reputation in order to regain a place in the spotlight.

The problem with bad reputations, as Quinn learns, is that unless you have a PR army readily at your disposal, they're impossibly hard to control. Rachel's been doing her best to establish a rep since birth, and her desire to control her own image has never been more evident than with her "Run Joey Run" video. This project is a Rachel Berry dream, as it allows her to play leading lady, writer and director, exercising complete creative control over her own story. But the determined diva quickly discovers that she can't exert that same control in real life, and that her careless actions make her less of a "bad girl" and more of a bad person. Everyone already knows Rachel's unwilling to compromise her chance at superstardom, but the video debacle really showcases how willing she is to compromise her relationships with others, even the most promising romance she's had yet. But what is curious about Rachel's creation is that she only shows the video to the 12 people involved in glee club, and they won't be the ones who will make or break her reputation. Is this a sign that the project is less about building a reputation than revising her own self-image?

While the New Directions crew tries to bring down their reps in the hopes of raising their social status, Will and Sue learn that a bad rep doesn't provide the same social currency in the adult world. Men are often lauded

olivia newton-john

Olivia Newton-John was one of the biggest music artists of the 1980s. Born in Cambridge, England, on September 26, 1948, Olivia moved to Australia when she was six years old. There, she honed her musical talent, winning a contest on the television show *Sing, Sing, Sing*. The prize was a trip to England, and, after a brief stint in the Monkees-style band Toomorrow, she eventually pursued a solo musical career. She released her first solo album, *If Not For You*, in 1971, and after modest musical success in England, she headed for America and eventual superstardom. After meeting *Grease* producer Alan Carr at a dinner party, she was offered the part of Sandy, a role that would spur a successful music career.

for being players, so Will's newfound pariah status caused by his promiscuous ways is an interesting switch, reminding viewers (and the glee club) that developing bad reputations outside of high school and Hollywood isn't usually the best way to get ahead. While Will means well (his treatment of Quinn in this episode proves his passion for these kids), the occasional reminder that he's a role model might put him in his place, as neither his womanizing ways nor his dishonesty with Emma are examples the glee clubbers should be following.

Speaking of Will's women, the recurring theme of Emma's inability to assert herself pops up again, but this time Miss Prim and Proper isn't afraid to call it like she sees it. Although this showdown is spurred on by a meddling Sue Sylvester, it's a worthwhile device because Sue's motivations are revealing: sure, she wants to see Will get humiliated, but malicious intent aside, there is actually some logic (and perhaps some empathy) underneath Sue's rough exterior. It's a move that gives the track-suited tyrant a bit more depth but is completely in character, since after "The Power of Madonna," there's no doubt that Coach Sylvester is a fierce advocate for good old-fashioned girl power.

Both Will and Sue react to their humiliation in similar ways. Will, embarrassed by his public shaming by Emma, takes out his frustration with a move that seems straight out of the Sue Sylvester playbook — grilling the glee clubbers to solve the mystery of the Glist. Sue, mortified by Brenda Castle and the rest of the McKinley staff mocking her, handles her rage by hurling back insults at her attackers. While the two teachers initially use anger to cope with their disgraceful situations, both of them later reveal their softer sides (Will reaches out to Quinn and apologizes to Emma, and Sue opens up to her sister) in order to come to peace with their pain. Through this parallel treatment, *Glee* helps to blur the lines between the show's hero and villain, again proving the idea that being good or bad is only based on one's perception.

"Bad Reputation" starts with an assignment to rehabilitate the bad rep of a song, but by the episode's end, many of the glee club members have to put their own reps through rehab. Public opinion is a flaky, often illogical beast, and hopefully these kids (and kids at heart) can live the lyrics of Joan Jett's song and learn to love themselves a little more and care about what others think a little less.

High Note: Rachel's re-creation of "Run Joey Run" deserves to go into the music video hall of fame.

Low Note: Will may be a good guy deep down, but he needs to do more than simply give Emma flowers as an apology for his manwhoring ways.

Behind the Music:
"Ice Ice Baby" (Will with New Directions)
Vanilla Ice, *To the Extreme* (1990)
As the first hip-hop single to ever top the Billboard Hot 100, it's surprising how far and fast "Ice Ice Baby," which samples Queen and David Bowie's "Under Pressure," has fallen. Vanilla Ice (real name: Robert Van Winkle) wrote the song at 16 years old, inspired by his experiences growing up in Florida. As a former hit that is now only appreciated ironically, it's a great example for Mr. Schue (who teaches New Directions the dances moves from the original video!) to use for his "musical rehabilitation" project.

"U Can't Touch This" (Artie, Kurt, Tina, Mercedes and Brittany)
MC Hammer, *Please Hammer, Don't Hurt 'Em* (1990)
Artie, Tina, Mercedes, Kurt and Brittany use MC Hammer's signature song (again with dance moves replicated from the original music video) to develop a bad reputation. If Hammer's loud music, loud clothing and loud dance moves can't rock a library, nothing can. Our determined glee clubbers try to prove to everyone, including the creator of the Glist, that no one can touch them. They're "badasses" and they'll dance wherever, whenever.

molly shannon as brenda castle

If anyone can go toe-to-toe with Jane Lynch, it would be fearless performer Molly Shannon, born on September 16, 1964, to an Irish Catholic family in Shaker Heights, Ohio, a small town only 140 miles from Lima. When Molly was four years old, she was involved in a car accident that took the lives of her mother and younger sister. She threw herself into performing at a young age, entering the film industry immediately after high school, and scored a handful of small film roles. Her big break came when she was cast on *Saturday Night Live* in 1995. While on the live comedy show, she developed groundbreaking characters like Mary Katherine Gallagher. In 2001, she left the show to focus on her film and television projects. Her personal life also blossomed: she married Fritz Chestnut in 2004, and the couple has two children.

"Physical" (Sue and Olivia Newton-John)
Olivia Newton-John, *Physical* (1981)
As Olivia herself pointed out, "Physical," a romp about wanting to get it on (a declaration that can sometimes result in a bad reputation), was the biggest hit of the 1980s. Sue and Olivia try to give this song's video a revamp, as the original video, despite winning the 1983 Grammy for Best Music Video, was scorned by the public. This re-creation, which replaces chubby men with hot boy toys, is a slight improvement.

"Run Joey Run" (Rachel with Finn, Puck and Jesse)
David Geddes, *Run Joey Run* (1975)
Rachel's "musically promiscuous" video, a re-creation of David Geddes' all-but-forgotten story song about a doomed relationship, encapsulates the many themes of the episode: trying to develop a bad reputation (as she thinks making this video will do), rehabilitating bad music and the complexity of romantic relationships. Rachel may think this video presents her as a desirable and promiscuous budding star, but in reality it shows that she's a confused and insecure girl who is intrigued by (and attracted to) three very different boys.

"Total Eclipse of the Heart" (Rachel and Jesse with Finn and Puck)
Bonnie Tyler, *Faster Than the Speed of Night* (1983)
Bonnie Tyler's oft-parodied #1 hit about losing a lover is the perfect song to showcase Rachel's devastation and confusion about wrecking not one but

the glist

Everyone's bad reputation was inspired by their Glist ranking. Here's how they all stacked up:
1.) Quinn +45
2.) Santana +43
3.) Puck +38
4.) Brittany +33
5.) Jesse +29
6.) Finn +19
7.) Mike +11
8.) Matt +5
9.) Rachel -5

three relationships with her "Run Joey Run" video. The song also includes lyrics about going insane, which is what happens to Rachel when she decides the "Run Joey Run" video would be a good idea, and about falling apart, which is what she's doing now that it appears she's lost Puck, Finn and, most notably, Jesse, forever.

Give My Regards to Broadway: *Grease*, the story of 1950s high schoolers, originated as a play in a Chicago trolley barn. It eventually made its way to Broadway, premiering on February 14, 1972, and running for a then-record 3,388 performances. The critically acclaimed 1978 film adaptation cast the unknown Olivia Newton-John alongside the budding superstar John Travolta, and the two introduced star-crossed lovers good girl Sandy and bad boy Danny to a whole new audience via the big screen, in the most commercially successful movie musical of all time.

That's Pretty *Popular*: Creating and maintaining reputations is a recurring theme on *Popular*, but it's most evident when Sam tries to show off her own bad reputation in "Mo' Menace, Mo' Problems" by getting a nose ring.

Slushie Facials:
- The glee club posts Sue's "Physical" video on YouTube.
- Figgins says that Sue made a list of McKinley's ugliest red-haired students.
- Students at West Dayton High posted a video of their superintendent riding a pony while wearing women's lingerie.
- Quinn posts a list that ranks members of the glee club according to their

promiscuity and sexual deeds.

- Puck mentions how he likes to set stuff on fire and beat up people he doesn't know.
- Artie reveals that someone likes to flush his glasses down the toilet.
- Puck tells Rachel that he sprays people with fire extinguishers, despite every intention not to.

Off-Key:
- Is making noise in the library the worst thing they can come up with? Really? These kids need to watch more *Gossip Girl*.
- Mercedes and Kurt aren't in their Cheerios' uniforms when Mr. Schuester interrogates them.

Behind the Scenes:
- The producers were surprised by the positive response to the Puck and Rachel relationship in "Mash-Up," a pairing nicknamed "Puckleberry" by fans. As a result, the producers decided to revisit the Puck/Rachel romance.
- Olivia Newton-John was always embarrassed by the "Physical" video, even though it won the 1983 Grammy Award for Video of the Year. When Ryan Murphy approached her about recreating it for *Glee*, she jumped at the chance to make fun of herself.
- Doing "Physical" was a dream come true for Jane Lynch, as it gave her an opportunity to work with Olivia, someone she's admired since high school. Jane's dog is even named after the *Grease* star!
- Three *So You Think You Can Dance* alumni are in this episode. Brandon Bryant shows up in both the "Physical" video and Rachel and Jesse's ballet class. Melissa Sandvig plays a fellow ballet student. Ben Susak, who made his first *Glee* appearance in "Acafellas," is also in the "Physical" video.

Center Stage:
- The episode's title is inspired by Joan Jett and the Blackhearts' song "Bad Reputation," which was the theme song of another high school-centric show, NBC's *Freaks and Geeks*. The song is about doing what you want and not caring about what others think of you.
- Sue does the Cabbage Patch Dance in her jazzercise video, which became popular thanks to Dr. Dre and DJ Yella's 1987 song "The Cabbage Patch."

gleek speak: darryl pring
(co-founder of *Gleeks: An Improvised Musical!*)

Tell us about your Toronto-based show, *Gleeks: An Improvised Musical!* Amanda Barker [a comedian and writer] approached me about doing a spoof of *Glee*. I had already been successful with other parody shows like *Don't You Forget About John Hughes* and *Dr. Whom*. I was a fan of *Glee* and didn't hesitate to say yes. The key to satire or parody is to love what you are satirizing, so that it translates to the audience. Our biggest obstacle with this show was (and continues to be) cast size. We had 11 improvisers in this show, plus a pianist and I was pulling lights [editing scenes]. Sometimes, when you have too many cooks in the kitchen, the kitchen gets really messy. Usually an improv show would not dare have more than six performers, maybe seven. The problem is, with a show like *Glee*, there are SO MANY compelling characters. In hindsight (or for the next show) we may have a smaller cast. But overall, the show went very well. As with any improv show, some scenes didn't drive the narrative so they fell a little flat, and I felt we didn't quite grasp the show's id [creative energy], but the duet toward the end between Mr. Shooter and the guidance counselor was just magic. Those kinds of moments I cherish, because they can't be duplicated.

The dance consists of making fists and moving them in circles.

- West Dayton High School, where scandalous photos of superintendants make the rounds, is not a real school. However, West Dayton High is the name of the high school White House press secretary C.J. Cregg attended on NBC's *The West Wing*. She goes to her West Dayton High School 20th reunion in "The Long Goodbye."

- In her "Run Joey Run" video, Rachel plays the tragic heroine who dies at the end like Nicole Kidman in *Moulin Rouge!* This 2001 movie musical tells the tragic love story of a poet, Christian (Ewan McGregor), who falls in love with doomed cabaret star Satine (Nicole Kidman). The film was nominated for eight Academy Awards and was the first musical to be nominated for Best Picture in 22 years.

- Olivia discovers Sue's "Physical" video because of her daughter, Chloe. Chloe Lattanzi, a singer and actress, is Olivia's only child, born on January 17, 1986, to Olivia and her first husband, Matt Lattanzi.

- Just like on *Glee*, Olivia is a busy activist, raising awareness for environmental issues, animal rights and breast cancer.

- *Law & Order* is a popular television franchise that dramatizes aspects of the justice system. The franchise began in 1990 and has since expanded to include several different spin-offs.
- Kurt, Tina, Artie, Mercedes and Brittany are as menacing as Muppet Babies, infant versions of Kermit, Miss Piggy and other Muppets, who appeared in the 1984–1990 cartoon series *Jim Henson's Muppet Babies*.

Jazz Hands:

- Terri Schuester has gone AWOL, marking the first time a regular cast member didn't appear in three episodes in a row.
- Sue needs to figure out the difference between slander and libel, two concepts she also mixes up in "Sectionals."
- Jesse's black T-shirt says "*UTGÅNG*," which means "exit" in Swedish.
- Perez Hilton is a popular celebrity gossip blogger, known for his snarky attitude, "outing" celebrities and discovering new music.
- Foot binding, which began around the tenth century, was practiced on young girls and women in China (not Imperial Japan, as Sue claims) as a way to ensure their feet remained small and dainty. It resulted in lifelong deformed feet and chronic pain.
- Jazzercise, the combination of jazz dance and aerobics, was developed in 1969 and quickly became a workout phenomenon.
- Sandy Ryerson makes a brief reappearance playing Rachel's dad in her "Run Joey Run" video.
- The picture book Sue reads to Jean is *I'll Always Love You* by Paeony Lewis and Penny Ives, about the strong bond between a mother bear and her baby.

The Buckeye State: Olivia Newton-John is chairing a benefit on Kings Island, a theme park in Mason, Ohio. It is the sister theme park to the previously mentioned Cedar Point. It's one of the most popular theme parks in North America, with over three million people visiting every year.

How Sue Cs It: "I might buy a small diaper for your chin, because it looks like a baby's ass."

♪♫♪

1.18 "laryngitis"

Original Air Date: May 11, 2010
Written by: Ryan Murphy
Directed by: Alfonso Gomez-Rejon

The Music: ★ ★ ★
The Drama: ★ ★ ★
The Laughs: ★ ★ ✦

Will: The glee club has lost its voice. It's time for us to get it back.

Feelings of loss and longing abound as Rachel loses her voice and fears she'll never sing again, Puck loses his Mohawk and fears he'll never be cool again and Kurt tries to lose his lady fabulous image out of fear of losing his dad.

The title of this episode may refer to losing one's voice, but in "Laryngitis" we see three main characters lose a key part of themselves and struggle to deal with the implications of that loss.

When Rachel is felled by losing her voice, she explains the symbolism behind this loss very clearly: Who is Rachel Berry without her voice? Just as a chair is not a chair in "Home," here a voice is not just a voice; it's a commonly used metaphor for identity. For Rachel, being a singer is her purpose in life, her true reason for being. Sure, it seems somewhat over the top for her to feel at *such* loose ends over what's bound to be just a brief illness, but then again, most of what Rachel does is over the top. As with her "Run Joey Run" video, Rachel will do whatever it takes to achieve success, even alienate herself from the people she loves, so losing her ability to sing would be understandably terrifying for her. Furthermore, Rachel uses her talent and her quest for celebrity status to hide her fears, and if she loses her voice she also loses the mask she hides behind. By meeting Finn's paralyzed friend, Sean, Rachel learns to understand that there are people worse off than her and that losing her voice isn't a death sentence. As Rachel is starting to realize, no one should be solely defined by one thing, because you're ultimately limiting yourself if you do. High school politics are all about slotting people into convenient categories (jock, geek, bully, stud), and sometimes living with a label is easier than learning about yourself.

While Rachel and Puck learn similar lessons about labels this week, they come to very different conclusions. Puck no longer needs his Mohawk to keep his mojo, but he doesn't get the message that he can be more than just a bully, choosing instead to continue living within his already crafted stereotype. When Mercedes talks to him about the importance of being true to who he is, there is a glimmer of understanding in Puck's eye, but it seems like that's all we ever get from him: fleeting moments of nice guy potential that are quickly squashed by badass behavior. Puck follows the exact same pattern in "Mash-Up" when he briefly dates Rachel (even serenading his love interest once again). Yet both times he ends up reverting to his badass ways. Will we ever get to see Puck truly explore his nice side or is he too afraid of losing the security his bully persona gives him?

The most interesting use of the loss motif is Kurt's attempt to lose his "capital G gay" image motivated by his fear of losing his dad. Out of the three characters dealing with loss this episode, Kurt is the only one who actually chooses to lose an essential part of his identity. Facials and show tunes are out, flannel and Mellencamp melodies are in, all just so he can establish a greater bond with his father. But Kurt limiting himself by trying to become a stereotype is something Burt has never expected of his son. Though Kurt is remarkably cool in the face of bullies and prejudice at school, this wholesale transformation really highlights his well-masked insecurities. Seeing Kurt go to such great lengths for his father's love is touching, but by the end of the episode the storyline feels a bit too familiar. We've already seen Kurt and Burt talk about their unbreakable bond and love for each other multiple times. In fact, it's pretty much the only thing Burt does on the show. These two are a great portrayal of a complicated father-son relationship, but it's time for them to explore some new storylines.

Will's also fighting with loss; that is, the collective loss of his students' drive and focus. If New Directions can't shake off their laziness and disinterest, they may face their biggest loss yet: the Regionals title.

High Note: Nothing can top the riveting emotion of a heartbroken Kurt singing "Rose's Turn" and his touching reconciliation with his father afterward.

Low Note: "One" might be the worst group performance since "Hair/Crazy in Love," but at least that performance was supposed to be awful. "One" is the lowest musical note of *Glee* thus far.

Behind the Music:

"The Climb" (Rachel)

Miley Cyrus, *Hannah Montana: The Movie* (Original Motion Picture Soundtrack) (2009)

Several artists rejected this pop country ballad about how life can be a difficult journey before it found its way to the teen pop princess. Rachel, upset that not everyone is pulling their weight in glee club, selects this song to reinforce that she's the hardest working person in New Directions. The song was the most popular audition choice for the 2009 season of *American Idol*, and Rachel's off-key version appears to be a playful poke at *Glee*'s sister show.

"Jessie's Girl" (Finn)

Rick Springfield, *Working Class Dog* (1981)

Rick Springfield wrote his breakout hit about unrequited love after he developed a crush on his friend Gary's girlfriend. After spotting a jersey with "Jessie" on it, Rick changed the name in his song to Jessie, and *Glee* fans will forever thank him for that. "Jessie's Girl" might be the most literal song *Glee*'s ever done, but it's a perfect choice for Finn, the lovesick classic rock fan.

"The Lady Is a Tramp" (Puck and Mercedes)

Babes in Arms (1937)

Several artists have covered this musical spoof on high society from the musical *Babes in Arms*, including Frank Sinatra and Ella Fitzgerald, The Supremes and Sammy Davis Jr. "The Lady Is a Tramp" is about a woman who doesn't follow New York's high society social conventions, but it also applies to Mercedes at modern day McKinley High. She doesn't look, sound or act like a regular Cheerio, but thanks to her cheeky attitude and vocal talent, she's at the top of the social heap. Puck chooses this song to woo Mercedes because he wants to show her that he, too, defies the rigid social structure of high school, though by the end of the episode we can see that Puck will do anything to cling to his place at the top.

"Pink Houses" (Kurt)

John Cougar Mellencamp, *Uh-Huh* (1983)

John Cougar Mellencamp's anthem is not about "bold interior design," as Kurt originally thinks, but instead it's about the struggles of those who live in

zack weinstein as sean fretthold

Zack Weinstein is as inspirational as the character he plays. Growing up in Saratoga Springs, New York, he dreamed of being an actor, and after he graduated from high school, he majored in theater at Skidmore College in his hometown. In the summer after his freshman year of college, Zack was in a canoeing accident and broke his neck, which paralyzed him from his upper chest down. He took a year off from school to recover and rehabilitate, but did not give up on his dream of being an actor. He returned to school, graduated in May 2009, married his college sweetheart and moved to Los Angeles to pursue his dream. *Glee* is his first professional role, and here's hoping there's many more to come!

blue-collar Middle America. Kurt tries to connect with his father by not only giving himself a butch makeunder, but also by covering Burt's favorite artist. "Pink Houses" is also about masking a reality, as the pink paint hides the poverty and desperation living within, just like Kurt's flannel and trucker's cap hide his show tune–loving flamboyant self.

"The Boy Is Mine" (Mercedes and Santana)
Brandy and Monica, *Never Say Never* (1998) and *The Boy Is Mine* (1998)
Brandy and Monica's tale of loving the same man was the first #1 hit for both singers. It garnered the two artists a Grammy Award for Best R&B Performance by a Duo or Group with Vocal. While the original song played up the rumored rivalry between Brandy and Monica, *Glee*'s version highlights the rivalry that ignites between Mercedes and Santana after Mercedes starts dating Puck.

"Rose's Turn" (Kurt)
Gypsy (1959)
In the musical-turned-film *Gypsy*, overbearing stage mother Rose Lee sings "Rose's Turn," a song about regret and missed opportunities, after she realizes she's pushed her daughters away from her and she's lost her chance to find her own success and happiness. Kurt's afraid that he's pushed away his father by being himself and introducing Finn into his father's life. Several of the lyrics were changed to reflect Kurt's personal situation.

"One" (New Directions)

U2, *Achtung Baby* (1991)

U2's "One" came about when it looked like the band might break up for good. Instead, they came together to write this number about the difficulties of maintaining relationships, which rings true for New Directions. The glee clubbers realize they need to put the group ahead of their personal problems and that they need to work hard to maintain important relationships.

That's Pretty *Popular*: Brooke gets petty and tries to win Josh back after she dumps him and he starts dating the unpopular Carmen in "Lord of the Flies." Nicole, Mary Cherry and Poppy Fresh all battle for a hot new guy's affections in "Hope in a Jar," having a weight loss showdown (instead of a singing showdown) to determine who most deserves his adoration. Kurt and Burt's father/son drama mirrors Sam's relationship with her mother. Sam becomes upset and jealous when her mom starts planning her wedding with Brooke, an activity that's up Brooke's alley but of no interest to Sam.

Slushie Facials:

- Puck gets thrown in the Dumpster by a group of nerds led by Jacob Ben Israel.

- Puck forces Jacob to give up his lunch money and buy Mercedes an iced coffee.
- When Puck gets his mojo back, he gets his revenge by overseeing the tossing of all of the nerds into the Dumpster, one at a time.

Off-Key:
- Why is Finn allowed in the doctor's office with Rachel? They're not related or married or having a baby together.
- Not only is Jesse going on Spring Break with his Vocal Adrenaline pals a lame excuse for his absence, but it seems hard to believe that any parents, even ones in Bali, would allow their son to miss a week's worth of school. Also, why doesn't his continuing friendship with his former teammates raise any concerns within New Directions?
- Mr. Schue hypocritically gives Rachel a hard time for working out her relationship issues in song in glee club when she performs "Gives You Hell" in "Hell-O," but applauds Finn for doing the same thing here with "Jessie's Girl."
- Puck claims the video game *Super Mario Bros. 3* has star worlds, but only *Super Mario World* has star worlds.
- When did Mercedes and Santana decide to get together to practice and produce a song that showcases their fight over Puck?
- While realizing that she's more than just her voice is an important lesson for Rachel to learn, there are several *Glee* regulars Rachel could've learned a similar lesson from instead of Sean, like the disabled, talented and underused Artie.

Behind the Scenes:
- This episode has Jane Lynch's favorite Sue line in it: "So you like show tunes. It doesn't mean you're gay, it just means you're awful."
- When filming the Kurt and Brittany make-out scene, the producers kept asking Chris Colfer to be a worse kisser, as he looked too experienced for Kurt's first-ever liplock.
- Kurt's rendition of "Rose's Turn" was Chris's idea. After visiting New York City and seeing *Gypsy* on Broadway, he was blown away by the song and asked Ryan Murphy if he could sing it in a future episode.
- Chris loved seeing Kurt's name in lights so much that, for a while, he made a snapshot of the stage his iPhone's background photo.

Center Stage:

- Kurt claims he has the same vocal range as Orlando de Lassus, a 16th century Belgian musician who composed over 2,000 songs and had the ability to sing in any genre, as well as in four languages. Kurt plans to use this vocal range to sing a Whitney Houston number. Whitney is a singer and actress known for her power ballads, including her mega-hit rendition of "I Will Always Love You."

- Puck downloads every single one of Sammy Davis Jr.'s songs. Sammy was an entertainer best known for being the only African American in Frank Sinatra's "Rat Pack." Sammy, who converted to Judaism in 1954, became famous for his performances on Broadway and in Las Vegas. He joined the Rat Pack in 1950. He continued to perform until shortly before his death from throat cancer in 1990.

- Rachel is like Tinker Bell, Peter Pan's fairy sidekick. Tinker Bell loves attention and becomes jealous of Peter's friendship with Wendy in J.M. Barrie's classic play, *Peter Pan*. The play, which debuted in 1904, became iconic after Disney turned it into an animated film in 1953.

- Santana calls Mercedes "Weezie," the nickname of Louise Jefferson, George Jefferson's wife on the 1975–1985 CBS sitcom *The Jeffersons.*

- Mercedes was supposed to sing a Mariah Carey song at cheerleading nationals. Five-time Grammy winner Mariah Carey is the first artist to ever have their first five singles top the Billboard Hot 100 chart. Mariah currently sits at #2 on the list of artists with the most #1 singles, behind The Beatles.

Jazz Hands:

- When Puck compares himself to the guy who lost all his hair, then all his strength, he's referring to the professional tennis player Andre Agassi. Widely considered one of the greatest tennis players of all time, Andre is the only male player to have won the Career Golden Slam — winning Wimbledon, the U.S. Open, the Australian Open, the French Open and Olympic gold. In 1995, in an attempt to revamp his image, Andre shaved his head completely bald. While 1995 was the most successful year of his career, he also began using drugs, and in 1997, he suffered from an injury that nearly ended his career.

- Although Puck's alluding to Andre, Santana thinks he's referencing the biblical tale of Samson and Delilah. According to the story, Samson was one of the strongest men in the world, who derived his strength from his long locks. His enemies hire Delilah to take away his strength and she has a servant shave Samson's head while he's sleeping. He loses his strength and is captured and blinded by his enemies.

- Somebody should report this typo to the city of Lima: The sign on the Dumpster Puck is thrown in reads "Waste Managment."

- Puck tells Rachel that Wikipedia states Martin Luther King, Jr. loved the Jews. Martin Luther King Jr. was an influential civil rights activist and Nobel Prize winner. Originally a Baptist preacher, King started organizing protests, and in 1963, led the March on Washington, when nearly 300,000 marched for civil rights. By the time he was assassinated in 1968, he was considered one of the most influential civil rights activists in the world. In 1965, the American Jewish Committee honored King with the American Liberties Medallion for his efforts.

- Rachel "narcs" on the glee club when she points out who isn't pulling their own weight. A narc, short for narcotics officer, is an undercover police officer, often investigating crimes involving drugs.

- Puck tries to win Mercedes over by telling her she has more curves than a Nissan ad. Nissan is a Japanese car company and their commercials often feature cars driving on long, winding roads.

- Burt thought Kurt's note was the first clue in one of his murder mystery dinners. Murder mystery dinners are a popular form of entertainment, where a host of a dinner party sets up a mystery for his guests. Each guest plays a different suspect in the crime, and through a series of clues, the murderer is revealed.

- Puck's mom won't let Quinn eat bacon. Kosher Jews aren't allowed to eat bacon, but this is a weird restriction since the family regularly indulges in sweet and sour pork, as shown in "Mash-Up."

- Puck believes *Super Mario Bros.* changed civilization when it launched in 1985. The iconic video game developed by Nintendo features two plumber brothers, Mario and Luigi, as they try to save the princess of Mushroom Kingdom. It was the best-selling video game of all-time for 20 years and spawned several sequels.

The Buckeye State: Burt takes Finn to see the Cincinnati Reds, a Major League Baseball team. The National League team has won five World Series championships, the most recent in 1990. Cincinnati is 116 miles from Lima, meaning Burt and Finn enjoyed quite a bit of quality time together.

How Sue Cs It: "So you like show tunes. It doesn't mean you're gay, it just means you're awful."

♪♫♪

1.19 "dream on"
Original Air Date: May 18, 2010
Written by: Brad Falchuk
Directed by: Joss Whedon

The Music: ★ ★ ★
The Drama: ★ ★ ★
The Laughs: ★ ★ ✦

Jesse: A dream is something that fills up the emptiness inside. The one thing that you know if it came true all of the hurt would go away.

Bitter at never attaining his show biz dreams, Will's high school rival Bryan Ryan is back at McKinley High and making trouble for Will and New Directions. Meanwhile, Rachel dreams of finding her birth mother, and Artie struggles with his seemingly impossible dream of being a dancer.

While this episode continues *Glee*'s trend of heavy-handed themes, it works better than hairography, hello or home, because at its core, *Glee* is a show about dreams. From dreams of being a Broadway star to dreams of having a slushie facial–free day, every character struggles with balancing their aspirations with their reality. And with no need to stretch the dream theme to fit the characters, it's one of the most realistic topics the show has ever tackled.

If New Directions and Mr. Schuester have taught the glee clubbers anything, it's to believe in themselves and in their dreams, no matter how ambitious. But it's not all sunshine and roses — the higher you let your hopes soar, the greater the potential fall if things don't work out. There's a delicate balance between goals (achievable feats that can be accomplished with some hard work, such as Will's desire to star in a community play), dreams (long-term goals that may be realized with perseverance, such as Rachel's quest to star on Broadway) and fantasies (long-shot dreams that are incredibly unlikely, such as Artie's longing to walk again). Dreams bridge goals and fantasies and can morph into one or the other, depending on circumstance, hard work (or lack of it) or a little luck.

The tension between these various levels of dreaming is achieved beautifully with Artie's storyline, where he literally rises and falls along with his dreams of being a dancer. While Artie's desire to dance is more of a fantasy at first, his growing commitment to making this desire a reality turns it into more

205

of a dream, albeit one that's very far off in the future. Artie moves from hopeful to upset to realistic throughout the course of the episode, realizing in the end that dreams aren't like wishes granted from a fairy godmother. They take time and work, and the long road is a lot easier to navigate when you have support. Artie takes a big step in sharing his dream with Tina and finally opening up to her, unlike in "Wheels" when he pushes her away. Here's hoping these two can continue to strengthen their bond — Artie helped Tina overcome her stutter, and maybe Tina can help Artie one day achieve his dream too.

While Rachel and Shelby's connected dream of reuniting with each other is more achievable than Artie's, it's just as complicated. Not only is there legal tape and dealing with her dads' feelings, there's also the possibility of Rachel's own disappointment if her real mother doesn't live up to the dream mom she's built up in her mind. By burying her dream deep inside, Rachel can continue to delude herself about why her mother was willing to give her up. Once again, we see Rachel trying to protect herself with a fiction of her own creation — it's easier for the wannabe star to create an elaborate back story that validates her Broadway dreams than to integrate reality into her already vulnerable self-image.

With the appearance of Will's high school rival Bryan Ryan, this episode also revisits one of Will's own dreams, his desire to be a star. Will faces these lingering aspirations in "Acafellas," and with Bryan on the scene, Will's leading man fantasies bubble back to the surface. But while Bryan is back on his spotlight-chasing track by the end of the episode, once again, Will decides to enable the dreams of New Directions rather than follow his own, an act we've seen Will do time and time again. Considering this pattern, we can't help but wonder if Will is really looking out for what's best for his students, or if he, like Rachel, is too afraid of his dreams not going according to his plan. But given cautionary tales like Bryan Ryan and April Rhodes, is Will taking an equally great risk by abandoning his dreams altogether? On the other hand, it's a sign of maturity to be able to distinguish between dreams and fantasies, and Will does this, realizing that while his return to showbiz is a fantasy, helping New Directions win Regionals is a dream that he can help become a reality.

Artie, Rachel and Will all have big dreams, but it's recognizing the potentially terrifying reality of their desires that brings them down to earth: Artie may not walk again, Rachel's mother may be an untalented "teen trollop" and Will may never shine on stage again. Whether you take a chance on your dream, or keep it tucked between the covers, there's always a risk of losing it. Sometimes you have to take a leap of faith and bring your dream out into the daylight, because it takes more than wishing upon a star to make a dream come true.

High Note: Just when "I Dreamed a Dream" was getting overexposed thanks to Susan Boyle's star turn on *Britain's Got Talent*, Rachel and Shelby's version makes it a sob-inducing showstopper once again.

Low Note: It's frustrating how *Glee* repeatedly revisits the same storylines, such as someone attempting to destroy New Directions and Will putting himself on the line to stop it. *Glee* needs to get past finding new threats to New Directions and focus on developing other plot points.

Behind the Music:

"Daydream Believer" (Bryan)
The Monkees, *The Birds, The Bees & The Monkees* (1968)
The irony of The Monkees' bittersweet ode to dreams of happier times and places is probably lost on teenage Bryan Ryan and Will Schuester. Back in high school, when Bryan wooed the girls with The Monkees' last #1 hit, both Bryan and Will had big Broadway dreams. While neither man's life turned out how they expected, Will is content with helping his students achieve their dreams and reflecting on his glory days, whereas Bryan is resentful that he never had a chance to shine.

"Piano Man" (Will and Bryan)
Billy Joel, *Piano Man* (1973)
Billy Joel's first major hit recalls his time as a lounge singer and piano player in Los Angeles. This song is about recalling lost dreams, just as Will and Bryan are doing with their drunken duet. Their rendition of "Piano Man" is a more solemn finish to the message that "Daydream Believer" was setting up. With "Daydream Believer," both men were young and full of hope, with "Piano Man," they're older, tired and filled with yearning for the better days, when they were glee studs with big dreams.

"Dream On" (Will and Bryan)
Aerosmith, *Aerosmith* (1973)
Aerosmith's debut single about making your dreams come true captures what

neil patrick harris as bryan ryan

Older fans of *Glee* will remember Neil Patrick Harris as the bright-eyed preteen prodigy Doogie Howser. The former child star was born on June 15, 1973, in Ruidoso, New Mexico, to restaurateurs. After being discovered at drama camp, Neil began to work regularly in television and film before being cast as the career-defining Doogie on *Doogie Howser, M.D.* at the tender age of 16. When the show ended in 1993, Neil returned to guest work in film and television and worked occasionally on Broadway until 2005, when he scored a regular role on the current CBS sitcom *How I Met Your Mother* as the womanizing, suit-loving Barney. Most recently, Neil also starred in Joss Whedon's musical web series, *Dr. Horrible's Sing-Along Blog*. The openly gay actor has been in a relationship with actor-turned-chef David Burtka since 2007.

Will and Bryan are trying to do by auditioning for *Les Misérables*, as both are turning to community theater as a way to recapture the joy that glee club brought them in high school. Their singing showdown reinforces the dueling nature of auditioning for this role, as only one man will be successful, and the performers both think their rival should "dream on."

"Safety Dance" (Artie)
Men Without Hats, *Rhythm of Youth* (1982)
Canadian band Men Without Hats scored their biggest hit with "Safety Dance," a silly homage to the joy and power of dance. With the new wave movement, innovative styles of dance were introduced, including pogoing, when dancers simply jumped up and down. This type of dance brought no joy to club owners and was often banned, as it was considered dangerous. Men Without Hats wrote this song to protest the banning. As silly as the song may be, this celebration of movement is the perfect soundtrack for Artie's greatest, if elusive, dream.

"I Dreamed a Dream" (Rachel and Shelby)
Les Misérables (1980)
One of the signature songs from *Les Misérables*, "I Dreamed a Dream" is sung by Fantine, who dreams of being reconnected with her long-lost daughter, just as Shelby dreams of a reunion with Rachel. Being reunited with her mother is a dream Rachel has harbored for most of her life, but she has kept it so buried

that she's not ready to face the possibility of it coming true, or at least the possibility of it not turning out as she imagined. When Shelby's dream of being a star didn't come true, she turned to a dream of reuniting with her family and building the life she gave up in her quest to become a star.

"Dream a Little Dream of Me" (New Directions)
Ozzie Nelson (1931)
Several artists, including Louis Armstrong and Ella Fitzgerald, Barbara Carroll, the Nat King Cole trio, Bing Crosby and Dean Martin, recorded this sweet tune about encouraging a loved one to dream of them. Artie has big dreams of being a dancer, but he's also worried that his disability may keep him and Tina apart. If they can't even dance together for glee club, a place where big dreams are encouraged, how can Artie achieve his dreams of being a star and of being with Tina?

Give My Regards to Broadway: Brenda Castle auditioned for the role of Miss Adelaide in *Guys & Dolls*, a musical about petty criminals in 1940s New York. The show, based on Damon Runyan's short stories "The Idyll of Miss Sarah Brown" and "Blood Pressure," premiered on Broadway on November 24, 1950, running for a successful 1,200 performances and snagging a Tony for Best Musical. Miss Adelaide is a nightclub singer eager to marry her fiancé of 14 years, gambler Nathan Detroit. The musical follows Nathan's misadventures as he concocts his most elaborate gamble to date: he bets another big-shot gambler that he can't lure a good girl to Havana. What starts as a mission of corruption quickly turns to an infectious romance that will have both couples in its hold by the show's conclusion. The musical was made into a 1955 film starring Marlon Brando, Frank Sinatra, Jean Simmons and Vivian Blaine, and was the most commercially successful film of the year.

That's Pretty *Popular*: When everyone is asked to write down their biggest secrets for a school assignment in "Caged!," Nicole swipes them and forces the girls to reveal whose secret is whose. As for mother/daughter bonding, in the season one finale Brooke reconnects with her mother, who abandoned her when she was eight years old, and in "It's Greek to Me," Nicole, who was adopted, bonds with her birth mother.

Off-Key:

- Will doesn't get to do anything for himself? What is "Acafellas" about then?
- During Artie's dream sequence, you can see the fast food chain Jollibee in the background. Jollibee currently has franchises in three states (New York, Nevada and California) but not in Ohio!
- Kurt would never jump at the chance to own a bedazzled jean jacket, even if it was free.

Behind the Scenes:

- John Michael Higgins plays Russell, a fellow recovering show tune addict. John worked with choreographer Zach Woodlee and Heather Morris on 2009's *Fired Up!* and played Molly Shannon's love interest Phil on the American version of the sitcom *Kath & Kim*, whose single season aired on NBC from 2008 to 2009.
- Artie's flash mob dream sequence was filmed at Eagle Rock Plaza in Los Angeles, which was open to the public that day. In order to make the flash mob feel authentic, real patrons stumbled upon the filming and several of them appear in the episode!
- Heavy Impact's Isaac Tualaulelei, from the fifth season of *America's Best Dance Crew*, was one of the principal dancers in the flash mob scene. He made his first *Glee* appearance in "Preggers" as a "Single Ladies"–dancing football player. This time, Isaac's entire dance crew gets to join him. Watch for his fellow members in the flash mob.
- Sue references the recent phenomenon of administrations protecting glee clubs and other arts programs. This movement is in large part thanks to *Glee* itself, whose success has spurred renewed interest in arts and music programs around the world.
- Neil Patrick Harris was the person who suggested that Bryan and Sue get it on. He felt that Bryan and Sue were such intense people that the scene could be taken up a notch, and that "anger sex" would fit for both characters.
- Before she got her big break on Broadway, Idina Menzel was a wedding singer, and "I Dreamed a Dream" was on her regular set list.

Center Stage:

- Artie pulls the book *Godard on Godard: Critical Writings by Jean-Luc*

Godard. Jean-Luc Godard was a film critic and filmmaker, and this 1986 book is a collection of Godard's essays and interviews about other filmmakers' work and his own ideas about film. French New Wave was the name given to several French filmmakers in the 1950s and 1960s who experimented with filmmaking techniques and often used film to comment on social and political issues.

- Christopher Reeve was an American actor, screenwriter and filmmaker best known for portraying Clark Kent in the four original Superman films. A 1995 horseback riding accident left him paralyzed, but he continued his career in the film industry, making his directorial debut with the 1997 HBO film *In the Gloaming*, which starred several Hollywood notables and received five Emmy nominations.

- Rachel wants to star in three Broadway shows: *Evita*, *Funny Girl* and *Oklahoma!*. *Evita* is about Argentina's first lady Eva Perón, *Funny Girl* is about American singer and actress Fanny Brice and *Oklahoma!* is about the romance of farm girl Laurey and cowboy Curly McLain. All three musicals feature strong female characters with numerous solos, which makes them roles that are right up Rachel's alley.

- Patti LuPone and Bernadette Peters, Rachel's potential mothers, are both big Broadway stars. Born on April 21, 1949, in Long Island, New York, Patti is best known for her Tony-winning turns in the 1979 musical *Evita*, in which she played the title character. Bernadette Peters is a seven-time Tony-nominated singer and actress. The Queens, New York, native has 32 films to her credit and several Broadway shows, most

joss whedon (special guest director)

Love *Buffy the Vampire Slayer*, *Angel*, *Dollhouse* or *Firefly*? You have Joss Whedon to thank for that. The American screenwriter, director and producer created all of these shows as well as the online sensation *Dr. Horrible's Sing-Along Blog*. The third-generation television writer was born on June 23, 1964, in New York City and attended Wesleyan University before heading to Hollywood to find TV writing work. After a stint on the sitcom *Roseanne*, Joss tried his hand at film for a few years (including writing the original *Buffy the Vampire Slayer* movie and co-writing *Toy Story*) before developing his own television shows. A lifelong lover of comics, he wrote a 24-issue arc of *X-Men* for Marvel and will direct a film adaption of *The Avengers* in 2011. Joss and his wife, Kai, live with their two children in Los Angeles.

notably *Annie Get Your Gun* and *Sunday in the Park with George*. She's also an accomplished television star, winning Emmys for her guest stints on *The Muppet Show* in 1977 and *Ally McBeal* in 2001. Both actresses have played Rose in *Gypsy*, a pushy stage mother who drives her daughters to stardom, an effort Rachel surely would appreciate.

- Patti often toured with Mandy Patinkin, an American singer and actor known for his work on Broadway in *Evita*, *Sunday in the Park with George* and *The Secret Garden*. He's also had a successful film career, starring in *The Princess Bride*, *Yentl* and *Dick Tracy*.

- The song playing in the bar before Will turns on "Piano Man" is Gary Wright's 1976 hit "Dream Weaver" (which was rerecorded and released for the 1992 film *Wayne's World*), about how dreams are possible, thanks to makers of dreams, or "dream weavers."

- Bryan locks away his *Playbills*, the monthly magazine that is distributed for particular shows on Broadway to accompany the performance.

- Will and Bryan are competing for the role of Jean Valjean in *Les Misérables* (see page 60).

- Will's original audition song was going to be "The Impossible Dream," the signature song from the 1965 Tony-winning musical *Man of La Mancha* — a fictionalization of the life of *Don Quixote* author Miguel de Cervantes. The musical tells the story of what would eventually become one of the most influential works of fiction ever written. "The Impossible Dream" is about following your destiny, which is what Will and Bryan are trying to do by auditioning for the musical.

- On Rachel's bedroom wall, there is a poster for the musical *Annie*, the 1977 Tony-winning Broadway show about an orphan named Annie who is eventually adopted by a wealthy and loving businessman, Oliver "Daddy" Warbucks.

- Jesse wants to do a CSI investigation, naming the popular CBS Las Vegas–based forensics investigation show that has spawned spin-offs based in Miami and New York.

Jazz Hands:

- Bryan sells Hummers, a GM off-road vehicle known for its immense size, gigantic tires and ability to drive through difficult terrain. They became very popular in the 1990s, but were discontinued in April 2010.

- Global warming, the concept that the Earth's median temperature is

gleek speak: adam wright
(television blogger at tvdonewright.com)

As someone who uses a wheelchair, how did you react to Artie and his two major story arcs, in "Wheels" and "Dream On"?
When I first saw Artie's character, I said "FINALLY!" It was so refreshing to see a fellow physically disabled person prominently featured in a hit show, which is a rarity in television today. But I was also curious to see HOW they were going to portray him. Were they going to reinforce the typical stereotypes of what people have of disabled people, or were they going to do this right? "Wheels" was an episode where Artie was viewed as strong and confident. Now with "Dream On," it's like they completely dismissed "Wheels." Artie's dream is to be a dancer, a dream that's pretty much unattainable. That part was okay. But they made him look so weak, from the part where he fell helplessly and stayed down, to the part where he watched on as Tina danced with another boy. I feel like "Dream On" was cheaply written to get an emotional response from the audience. They made the minority, Artie in this case, the pitiful victim. Why didn't they add a wheelchair dance sequence in "Dream On" anyway? The [flash mob] scene itself was beautifully shot, and I gave full credit to Kevin McHale. My main issue is the audience's response to this. I've read responses like "Awww, I wish they would show Artie dance more often" or "That was so cool, I want more!!!!" Well guess what, folks . . . real disabled people don't have that on and off trigger. I've never had a problem with having a non-disabled actor play a disabled character until they showed THAT scene. I want to see, in the future, more of what we saw in "Wheels." But I also want to see Artie featured with other problems that have nothing to do with his disability.

increasing because of human activity, is just a theory, according to Bryan. Bryan is not the only opponent to global warming, as many members of the political right wing and religious groups also dispute this phenomenon.

- Rachel's dream was "HUGE STAR," Quinn's was "no stretch marks," Puck's was "3 some" and Artie's was "dancer."
- Artie might finally be front and center, but star status doesn't come with a new wardrobe — that perfectly starched collared shirt is the only one he ever wears!
- Did you notice Artie's fellow glee clubbers in "Safety Dance"? In order of appearance, Mike, Matt, Brittany, Tina, Mercedes and Kurt show up to take part in the flash mob.
- According to the American Cancer Society, Sue's statistics on high school activity and obesity are correct.

- Sue may have a secret sex room, but it's unclear whether David Letterman actually had one for his own secret sex. In October 2009, the popular late night host revealed he had multiple affairs with junior female staff members throughout the course of his career at CBS.

The Buckeye State: Patti LuPone performed at E.J. Thomas Hall in Akron, Ohio. This performance venue is part of the University of Akron, seats 3,000 people and showcases Broadway performers, ballets, musicals and more every year. Since her appearance there in 1994, Patti has returned to perform at the venue several times, including in February 2010 alongside Mandy Patinkin. Akron is approximately 150 miles east of Lima.

How Sue Cs It: "Is it a tad over-the-top to bill the district for skydiving lessons to have the Cheerios parachuted onto the football field? Perhaps. But what I do here makes a difference."

♪♫♪

1.20 "theatricality"
Original Air Date: May 25, 2010
Written by: Ryan Murphy
Directed by: Ryan Murphy

The Music: ★★★
The Drama: ★★★
The Laughs: ★★

Shelby: You just have to radiate emotion, express what's deep inside you. That's what theatricality is truly about.

Mr. Schue encourages the glee clubbers to let their freak flags fly, but Finn's still too scared to completely express himself. Parent-child drama abounds when Burt defends Kurt, Shelby reunites with Rachel and Puck serenades his unborn baby girl.

No matter which way you slice it, the members of New Directions are a theatrical bunch, and in this episode they learn to get their freak on and

glee gets gaga-fied

The New Directions girls, plus Kurt, Finn and the members of Vocal Adrenaline wear costumes inspired by different Lady Gaga looks. Here's what you need to know about each outfit and how it suits the character that sports it:

Vocal Adrenaline: Vocal Adrenaline's full body Chantilly lace looks are inspired by the 1998 Alexander McQueen dress Lady Gaga wore to accept the award for Best New Artist at the 2009 MTV Video Music Awards. The costumes conceal Vocal Adrenaline's faces, reinforcing the idea that they are not individuals. New Directions, on the other hand, are allowed to choose looks that showcase their unique personalities and they're all about self-expression.

Kurt: Kurt's look was inspired by Lady Gaga's "Bad Romance" music video, where she wore a crystal mini-dress and 12-inch heels from Alexander McQueen's final collection in Spring 2010. Gaga and the designer collaborated to create this futuristic alien look. Kurt gives the look a presidential twist with a George Washington–inspired wig, highlighting that he won't lie about who he is, even if that means being overly theatrical.

Tina: Lady Gaga's champagne bubble costume made its appearance during her 2009 American *Fame Ball* tour. Hussein Chalayan, who created the original bubble dress for his 2007 collection, inspired Gaga's costume designer. Tina picks this look to show off her "bubblier" side.

Quinn: Quinn models her look after Lady Gaga's custom Giorgio Armani Privé gown worn to the 2010 Grammy Awards. The space-age look symbolizes the alienation Quinn feels now that she's pregnant and not a Cheerio.

Mercedes: Mercedes showcases her diva side and love for loud color by knocking off Lady Gaga's purple bow wig from the August 2009 cover of *Billboard*. While Gaga paired the wig with a black suit, Mercedes' dress was inspired by the Armani Privé bodysuit Gaga wore to perform at the 2010 Grammys, but Mercedes opts for sleek silver instead of Gaga's glittery green.

embrace what makes them different. Being yourself is a dangerous prospect in high school, and Kurt, Tina and Finn learn that the hard way in this episode. Even though both Kurt and Tina are repeatedly told to change who they are and to try harder to blend in with the crowd, *Glee* makes it clear that muting your true personality and style isn't the right decision, and it's better

Rachel #1: Rachel's first attempt at a Lady Gaga look was modeled after Gaga's custom creation made entirely out of Kermit the Frog puppets. Gaga donned this look for a 2009 interview on German television and claimed it was a statement on the use of fur and other animal products in fashion. Rachel has a different rationale: this look represents the simple childhood she now longs for.

Brittany: Lady Gaga first donned the lobster headpiece, which was designed by Irish hat designer Philip Treacy, when she went out to dinner in England during her 2010 *Monster Ball* tour. Gaga paired her headpiece with a see-through plastic dress, while Brittany opted for a more modest (and more functional) structured jacket and leggings. It makes sense that Brittany would combine her interest in everything aquatic with her desire to dance like a demon for her Gaga look.

Santana: Santana's lacy look was inspired by the Jeffrey Bryant bodysuit and Charlie Le Mindu headpiece Lady Gaga wore to the March 2010 MAC Viva Glam Launch in London. Santana makes the look her own by swapping the oversized floral headpiece for an oversized bow, showing the world that she's God's gift to McKinley High.

Rachel #2: Rachel finally shines like the star she is with her second look, inspired by Gaga's black cocktail dress and mirrored triangle embellishment (complete with sunglasses). Lady Gaga wore this look to her April 2009 concert at the Ritz Byor in Tampa, Florida. She donned a similar all-silver look later that year, but Rachel and Shelby prove they are serious artists with a flair for the dramatic by opting for the stunning original.

Finn: Finn turns a shower curtain into a knock-off of the Atsuko Kudo red PVC dress Gaga donned when she met Queen Elizabeth and performed at the Royal Variety Show in December 2009. While Finn goes out on a limb to dress like Gaga for Kurt, he chooses her most conservative look to date, which makes sense for the boy who wasn't going to be caught dead doing Gaga in the first place.

to shout it out loud than to tone it down.

Theatricality isn't just about big songs and bigger headpieces. In a broader sense, it's also a safe space for the New Directions crew to express themselves as they slip out of their designated high school roles and into new ones. It can be used to amplify feelings or to find a mask to hide behind, all under the protection of dramatic devices, as the glee clubbers sort out who they are and who they want to be.

This makes theatricality a perfect backdrop for Kurt's story, since theatrics like costume and song allow him to experiment with who he is. Nevertheless, he faces resistance to his experimentation everywhere, first from jock bullies Karofsky and Azimio, and then from Finn. And while Finn's in the wrong by telling Kurt that he should try harder to fit in, our confused leading man has admittedly been thrown into a tough situation. Finn has repeatedly shown that he struggles with change, and when he's bombarded with dramatic set changes like a new home and plot twists like a surprise party, the jock who likes to keep it simple probably can't help but feel like he's been mistakenly cast in someone else's drama.

Of course the most threatening of those dramas seems to be Kurt's overly optimistic attempts at upgrading their budding bromance to budding romance. Finn may need to be more flexible about the roles he'll play, but Kurt also needs to stop drawing others into his dramatic plots. The tension between Kurt and Finn yields even more drama when Burt steps in to play the hero. Burt's fierce love and loyalty for his family has never seemed stronger, and having him reveal his regrets about the past is a wonderful touch. But is Burt yelling at his own high school self as much as he's yelling at Finn? His hard-fought acceptance of Kurt's sexuality has been a difficult journey for him. He may be a supportive parent, but he's still dealing with the long-ingrained prejudices he mentions to Finn. In any case, Burt's consistently unconditional love for Kurt is one of the highlights of this show.

The Hummel-Hudsons aren't the only family unit getting theatrical, as this episode also explores the relationships between Rachel and Shelby and between Puck and his unborn child. Rachel and Shelby's foray into being mother and daughter doesn't go as either of them plan, but their portrayal of the situation feels much more realistic than a happy, problem-free reunion. Shelby may coach teenagers all day at work, but when she comes face-to-face with her teenage daughter she balks at the commitment and responsibility. Both Rachel and Shelby have built up this reconnection in their minds, but the reality of motherhood to Rachel is too much for Shelby and she believes it's better to rip Rachel's bandage off hard and quick, in true mom fashion, before Shelby has time to create a bigger wound by hurting Rachel further down the line. She may think this is what's best for Rachel, but she's really looking out for herself, which is what many driven talents do, her daughter included. Rachel has repeatedly put her own needs ahead of New Directions, so Shelby's self-centered attitude comes as no surprise. Like mother, like daughter.

While Shelby shows a lot of immaturity, Puck shows a great deal of maturity. For the first time, Puck uses a song for something other than seduction when he serenades his unborn child and baby momma as a showcase of his love and support. In a move that subtly elevates the bad boy to leading man status, Puck's plot line mirrors Finn's in the first half of the season, right down to the bad baby-naming. Finn getting past his own baby-daddy drama by singing "Beth" alongside Puck and owning up to his family-fueled frustrations are two big steps forward for him. He may not know it yet, but he's emerging as the leader he so desperately wanted to be in "Mattress." It looks like it took dressing up as someone else to show Finn and the rest of New Directions that the most radical, most dramatic role you can play in high school is yourself.

High Note: Gaga = greatness. From the costumes to the dance moves, the girls' (and Kurt's!) homage to Lady Gaga is over-the-top theatrical fun.

Low Note: Although Tina's storyline kicks off the glee clubbers' missions to express themselves, it quickly melts into the background in favor of others' personal trials. It's refreshing to see Tina in a non-Artie plotline, but it's a shame that her individuality quest isn't developed beyond her faux vampire heritage.

looking as loud as kiss

The boys of New Directions opt for another show-stopping act by performing in complete Kiss gear. Let's look at who chooses what and why:

Finn: Finn, ever the leader of New Directions, takes on the costume of Kiss's leader, Gene Simmons. Gene was known as "the Demon" because of his dark side and love of comics. Finn has a dark side too, which comes out whenever someone questions his popularity or sexuality, and he has an ugly moment later in this same episode.

Puck: Puck adapts Paul Stanley's "Starchild" persona as his own. Puck is the romantic ladies' man of McKinley High, having dated nearly every girl in New Directions. He makes the costume more personal by replacing Paul's traditional five-pointed star with the Jewish symbol of the six-pointed Star of David.

Artie: Artie takes on Ace Frehley's "Spaceman" persona, which was inspired by Ace's love of space and out-there personality. Claiming Artie is from outer space is a bit of a stretch, but he's certainly the biggest fish out of water here as the only original glee club member to join the Kiss side.

Mike: Peter Criss's "Catman" persona was inspired by Peter's difficult childhood. He had been through so much before he joined the band that he believed he had nine lives. Mike, on the other hand, seems to be an easy-going football player whose smooth dance moves and quick reflexes are quite catlike.

Matt: Matt gets his first-ever line to explain he's the band's fifth wheel. He gracefully took on the role of Tommy Thayer, the replacement Spaceman. Ace Frehley quit the band in 2002 and Tommy was asked to take on the Spaceman persona to encourage continuity. Poor Matt always gets the shaft when it comes to costumes, lines and backstory!

Behind the Music:

"Funny Girl" (Shelby)

Funny Girl (1968)

Fanny Brice, the protagonist in *Funny Girl* (see "Give My Regards" below), is an outsider. She's the girl who makes people laugh, not the girl people fall for, and she sings about this in "Funny Girl." Both Shelby and Rachel feel the same way. They are talented performers who can command an audience, but they feel like something is missing in their lives. Shelby wants to correct the mistakes of her past and start a family, and Rachel wants to find her mom and be treated with the respect a budding star deserves. Like Fanny, they are theatrical performers who are drawn to drama, both on stage and in life, and it makes sense that a song by one of Rachel's idols would be the piece of music that brings them together.

"Bad Romance" (Rachel, Quinn, Mercedes, Tina, Santana, Brittany and Kurt)
Lady Gaga, *The Fame Monster* (2009)
Inspired by the techno music Lady Gaga heard while touring eastern Europe, "Bad Romance" expresses what it's like to be in love with your best friend and relates how love has its ups and downs. The members of New Directions love performing, but sometimes this love can come with painful consequences, whether it's harassment from the football team or having a showdown with Vocal Adrenaline. Romantically, everyone in New Directions has faced a "bad romance," with Kurt's unrequited crush, Puck and his multiple romantic exploits, Quinn dealing with the consequences of a bad romantic choice, Rachel's back and forth with Jesse and Finn and Will still trying to figure out who he is and who he wants.

"Shout It Out Loud" (Finn, Puck, Artie, Mike and Matt)
Kiss, *Destroyer* (1976)
"Shout It Out Loud" was a modest hit, but became a concert staple for the theatrical Kiss. The song is about getting out and having some fun, not sulking about things you can't change and about partying hard even if you're broken-hearted. Finn did all of this when he took control of the Gaga situation. The boys may not have wanted to do Lady Gaga, but they certainly made the right choice, choosing a song that's about having fun on your own terms and being larger than life, with a rock and roll twist. All of the boys have situations they can't change, including Finn and Kurt's new home life, and Puck's impending fatherhood, but despite these heavy issues, the boys are still going to have some fun.

"Beth" (Puck and Finn with Artie, Mike and Matt)
Kiss, *Destroyer* (1976)
Puck may want to name his baby girl "Beth," but Kiss's song also expresses the way he feels about his soon-to-be-born daughter. Drummer Peter Criss

221

penned Kiss's first million-selling single with his original band, Chelsea, after his wife told him about how she missed him when he was on the road. Fellow band mate Mike Brand's wife, Becky ("Beck," which was later changed to "Beth" for the song), often made similar comments and would call the band regularly when they were practicing and on tour. Puck hasn't always been there for Quinn, but he sings this song to prove to her that even if they aren't together (physically or emotionally), he still supports her.

"Poker Face" (Rachel and Shelby)
Lady Gaga, *The Fame* (2008)

Lady Gaga's Grammy-winning song (Best Electronic/Dance Recording) may be about boyfriends and comparing those relationships to gambling, but when *Glee* does it, it becomes a sweet mother/daughter duet about how all relationships can be a gamble. Shelby takes a gamble when she sends Jesse to McKinley High to help her reunite with Rachel. She thinks meeting Rachel will give her what she wants, but later realizes that inviting herself into Rachel's life at this time would just make the teen girl more confused. Rachel takes a gamble herself by accepting Shelby and trying to make her part of her life. Some gambles, like this one, don't pay off, but neither Shelby nor Rachel regrets the meeting, reinforcing that life without risk isn't a life worth living.

The Sound of Music: Lady Gaga and Kiss come from different eras, but they're cut from the same cloth: both are over-the-top artists who know how to put on a show. From costumes to song choices to dance moves, these are the artists you want to see in concert because you never know what to expect. Born Stefani Joanne Angelina Germanotta on March 28, 1986, in New York City, Lady Gaga began performing in New York in the early 2000s, when she was attending New York University's Tisch School of the Arts. Interscope Records signed the budding superstar, and in 2008 she released her debut album, *The Fame*. From there, her own fame grew as she released several hit singles, all original dance floor–ready beats, and the album was nominated for six Grammys. Lady Gaga's elaborate costumes (which she likens to performance art) have become increasingly high concept and difficult to wear. While Gaga has named Madonna, David Bowie and Michael Jackson among her influences, Kiss can't be that far down the list. Formed in New York City in 1973, their elaborate costumes and stage performances (which included fireworks, blood and smoking guitars) quickly garnered them attention. Like

222

gleek speak: danielle bruno
(fashion blogger at What Would Emma Pillsbury Wear? wwepw.blogspot.com)

If you could pick any designer to make costumes for New Directions, who would it be? Why?
Chris March, of course! Who else but the *Project Runway* alum could create perfect stage looks for New Directions? In "Acafellas," Rachel says, "We're going to win because we're different." Throw aside the traditional show choir costumes, where the guys' ties match the girls' dresses. BORING. Chris March would take New Directions to a whole new level, and I, for one, would like to see Kurt in at least one headdress.

Gaga, members took on alternate egos on stage (see "Looking as Loud as Kiss"). The band saw huge success throughout the 1970s and anchored an extremely successful reunion tour in the 1990s. They've sold over 100 million albums worldwide but, despite their iconic look and commercial success, have yet to be inducted into the Rock and Roll Hall of Fame.

Give My Regards to Broadway: Fanny Brice, a singer, comedienne and actress, was the inspiration for the 1964 Broadway musical (and 1968 film) *Funny Girl*, both starring Barbra Streisand. Ray Stark, Fanny's son-in-law, commissioned a biography about Fanny. When the manuscript didn't pan out, he was encouraged to turn the story into a musical. *Funny Girl* focuses on Fanny's rise to fame and her tumultuous relationship with her husband, Nick Arnstein, who was an entrepreneur and gambler. The show opened on Broadway on March 26, 1964, ran for 1,348 performances and was nominated for eight Tony Awards. In 1968, Barbra reprised her role as Fanny for the film adaptation, winning the Academy Award for Best Actress, an honor she shared with Katharine Hepburn.

Slushie Facials
- Jocks Karofsky and Azimio push Kurt and Tina into the lockers.
- Karofsky and Azimio threaten Finn in the bathroom.
- The two jocks taunt Kurt and Tina, ruining Kurt's bedazzled heels.
- Tina threatens Principal Figgins with a midnight visit from her father, "the King of the Vampires."

- Karofsky and Azimio nearly beat Kurt up for the third time, but thankfully Finn and the rest of New Directions stop them.

Off-Key:
- Jesse doesn't make an appearance and isn't even mentioned, even though he's back from spring break and he and Rachel reconcile in "Dream On."
- The Hummels' house is twice as big as the Hudsons', yet Kurt and Finn have to share a room.

Behind the Scenes:
- "Theatricality" was originally supposed to follow "Funk" as the 21st episode of the first season. It's rumored (but has never been confirmed) that the swap was done to coincide with the *American Idol* finale and May sweeps, as family drama and a Gaga-fied *Glee* would attract more attention from casual television viewers and the media.
- Lea Michele may be a pro on stage, but she's no match for Lady Gaga. The "Bad Romance" number gave Lea a serious lump on her knee to remember the experience by!
- While New Directions' costumes aren't exact replicas of Lady Gaga's looks they come pretty close, thanks to Lady Gaga's own costumer, who was on hand to make the looks authentic. The costume department deliberately went for a home-sewn Gaga look because they wanted to reinforce the notion that the kids made the costumes themselves. (See "*Glee* Gets Gaga-fied" above.)
- Chris Colfer kept the handmade ten-inch heels as a memento because walking in them was one of the hardest things he's ever had to do.
- Chris may have had a hard time with the heels, but he wasn't the only actor to struggle with his or her costume: Jenna Ushkowitz's bubble dress would clink so much that she had to hold her breath during other people's dialogue; Heather Morris's lobster headpiece took 45 minutes to put on and take off, as it had several mechanisms attached so that it wouldn't fall when she danced; and the Kiss paint took forever to remove.
- Artie may rock the guitar on several performances for New Directions, including the boys' Kiss performance, but in real life, Kevin McHale can't strum a tune! Instead, the show brought in instructors to teach Kevin how to fake it.

Center Stage:

- The girls at McKinley High are Twihards, the name for fans obsessed with Stephenie Meyer's *Twilight* series of books and their film adaptations. In the film version, Kristen Stewart plays Bella Swan, a human who falls in love with a vampire, Edward Cullen (Robert Pattinson). Throughout the series, Bella is torn between Edward and her werewolf best friend, Jacob Black (Taylor Lautner), prompting fans to choose "Team Edward" or "Team Jacob" and openly support this cause by donning T-shirts, like the McKinley High students.

- Kristen Stewart is known for her awkward public appearances and frank personal interviews. She's very uncomfortable with the constant Twilight spotlight on her and, as a result, some people have questioned her appreciation for the series and its fans. Tina's mom thinks that this makes her a bitch.

- In high school, Will used to dress up like Kurt Cobain, the lead singer of the grunge band Nirvana. Kurt was known for his flannel shirts, long hair and generally unkempt appearance. After forming Nirvana in high school, Kurt and his bandmates made it big in 1991 with the release of their second album, *Nevermind*. The band is credited with launching the grunge movement and has since sold over 50 million albums worldwide. They broke up in 1994 after Kurt committed suicide.

- Principal Figgins used to dress up like Elvis Presley, "the King of Rock and Roll" and the best-selling solo artist of all time. Elvis helped popularize rockabilly in the 1950s and eventually became a superstar and music icon, recording in several different genres including gospel, blues, country and pop. He was known for his gyrating hips, greased hair and jumpsuits, and he developed a huge teen girl following. After making 33 films and releasing over 102 songs, he mysteriously died in 1977.

- As Puck mentioned, David Bowie "dresses weird." David Bowie is a British musician and actor who broke through in 1969 with his first single, "Space Oddity." Over the next few years, he would perfect "glam rock," a genre of music where performers were known for their over-the-top costumes, elaborate hairstyles, makeup and glitter galore. David continued to transform his look and music throughout the decades and today is considered one of the most critically acclaimed and influential artists of the past 30 years.

- Will mentions Lady Gaga's Haus of Gaga, a collective of artists and designers who help Lady Gaga put together her costumes, hairstyles, makeup and props. Gaga was inspired to start the collective, which is modeled after Andy Warhol's Factory, when she started to make money as a songwriter and wanted to channel these funds into something creative that would help further her work as an artist.

- Will calls the Gaga-fied glee club "little monsters," the term Lady Gaga uses for her fans.
- Although they're not singing along yet, Vocal Adrenaline is prepping for a performance of Lady Gaga's "Bad Romance" when they're in the red Chantilly lace outfits.
- Lady Gaga's "Speechless" is playing in the background when Kurt is fixing his Gaga heels and Finn is removing his Kiss makeup. The song, aptly about appreciating and respecting your family, is on Gaga's 2009 album *The Fame Monster*.
- Marlene Dietrich and Gary Cooper in *Morocco* inspired Kurt's new bedroom décor. *Morocco* is a 1930 film about a man (Gary Cooper) who works for the French Legion and falls in love with a seductress (Marlene Dietrich). The film, made infamous for its on-screen girl-on-girl kiss, was nominated for four Academy Awards and is considered to be one of the most culturally significant films ever made.
- Rachel was named after Rachel Green, the spoiled fashion-loving roommate on the NBC sitcom *Friends*. The show premiered in September 1994 and ran for ten years as one of NBC's Thursday night staples. Rachel Berry was born in December 1994, meaning *Friends* was on the air for only three months when she was named. Her dads must have been really big fans!

Jazz Hands:

- Three major players were missing from this episode: Jane Lynch, Jayma Mays and Jessalyn Gilsig.
- Tina's goth style is a look that originated in the U.K. in the 1980s, when bands like The Sisters of Mercy and The Mission gained popularity. Goth is associated with horror films, the Victorian era, dark clothing and heavy makeup.
- Prior to the redecoration, Kurt's room is painted Dior Gray, a shade of paint made by Benjamin Moore and inspired by the color of French designer Christian Dior's dressing rooms.

- The Hudsons and Hummels are playing *Sorry!*, a game that was patented and produced by the Parker Brothers in 1934. Players race around the board to get all their pieces "home" first and can bump others back to the start. It's an apt game to ask Finn to play, considering he was just bumped from his home and no one really feels all that bad about it.

- Tina feels like an "Asian Branch Davidian" when she isn't allowed to wear her preferred clothes to school. Branch Davidians are a Protestant sect who are collectively preparing for the second coming of Jesus Christ, but the group is most commonly associated with the Waco, Texas, cult governed by David Koresh according to his own loose interpretation of Branch principles. In 1993, suspicions arose that illegal activity was taking place on the Waco commune. After an unsuccessful search warrant, the FBI began a 50-day siege that ended in a deadly fire, killing 76 people, including David Koresh. Branch Davidians are still active today, but have far fewer followers.

- Shelby's lack of stardom feels like the Fisher King's wound. According to legend, the Fisher King is one of the keepers of the Holy Grail, but his perpetual wounds prevent him from being able to move. Whenever he is injured, the soil becomes infertile, leaving the land barren and his people unable to grow food. Like the Fisher King's land, Shelby feels a constant loss and her own field, her uterus, is barren.

- Puck wants to name their daughter Jack (or Jackie) Daniels, after one of the best-selling whiskeys in the world. Founded in 1866, by the original Jack Daniel (legend states he started the company at the tender age of 16), Jack Daniel's is currently produced in Lynchburg, Tennessee, and is known for its iconic black-and-white label.

- Karofsky and Azimio encourage Kurt to go from Gap to Banana Republic. Both chains are owned and operated by Gap Inc., along with the clothing chains Old Navy, Piperlime and Athleta. While Gap is known for its generic casual wear, Banana Republic is a mainstream luxury retailer.

- Supercuts, a budget hair salon chain in the United States, has over 2,000 North American locations, servicing hundreds of walk-ins every day.

♪♫♪

1.21 "funk"
Original Air Date: June 1, 2010
Written by: Ian Brennan
Directed by: Elodie Keene

The Music: ★ ★ ♪
The Drama: ★ ★ ♪
The Laughs: ★ ★

Artie: They call it a funkification, meaning they show us what they've got and we spiral into a deep cloud of funk.

Jesse's back with Vocal Adrenaline and New Directions has fallen into a pre-Regionals funk. Meanwhile, Will seeks naughty revenge on Sue.

"Funk" is another theme-of-the-week episode and this one feels pretty funky, as it fails to really build up excitement for the finale. Larger character arcs, important to the second half of the season, are rushed through, while side plots that start and finish within this episode are given priority treatment.

One key example is Jesse's speedy return to Vocal Adrenaline. Although he's been crucial to Rachel's character development since his first appearance in "Hell-O," Jesse is quickly cast aside in this episode. His explanation of why he rejoined his former glee club barely grazes the surface of the truth, as he doesn't even acknowledge his part in Shelby's reunion plan. It doesn't help matters that his and Rachel's break-up (which, knowing Rachel, was probably quite dramatic) happens offscreen. It seems unfair to the importance of Jesse and Rachel's storyline, considering how strongly this relationship affected New Directions' leading lady.

Similarly, the budding friendship between Quinn and Mercedes that's been dropped in sporadically throughout the last few episodes came to a sudden and rather unexpected high point. Comparing the different prejudices both Quinn and Mercedes suffer from was a tricky choice. Being unpopular and ridiculed, whether it's for being a pregnant celibacy club prez or for being a curvy black girl, is the worst shame to deal with as a high schooler. For Quinn to equate her struggles with Mercedes' feels believable for a privileged, sheltered girl. Getting pregnant, after all, is the worst thing that's ever happened to Quinn. Mercedes' acceptance of this comparison, on the other hand, feels off for a girl who is proud of her heritage, proud of her body and proud of her "chocolate thunder." You'd think she'd take a teeny bit more offense to the comparison of a stupid decision to years of systemic oppression. That said, she's also a lonely, sometimes insecure gal, and Quinn and Mercedes have had a few solid bonding moments and appear to understand each other. They're both women after all, and Quinn's performance isn't just about how hard it is to be pregnant. It's also about the consequences and difficulties of living in a man's world, something they both deal with every day. The new BFFs moving in together feels like a leap, but this is *Glee*, and *Glee* only knows how to drive in the fast lane.

With the Jesse and Rachel and Quinn and Mercedes developments brushed past quickly, one of the main focuses becomes the funky twist Will and Sue's relationship takes this episode. Hilarious scenes aside, Sue's new-found lust for Will feels as believable as her follicle jealousy back in "The Power of Madonna." While it is hard to watch Will be so purposefully malicious, his cruel scheme further exposes the insecurities beneath Sue's rough exterior, as well as her hidden compassion for her Cheerios, and it was one of the more believable revelations of Sue's kinder side. Despite her Hall of Fame hallways, the Cheerios are all Sue has, and it's always refreshing to see genuine vulnerability from *Glee*'s resident villain. But Will's Casanova charade also reveals a bit of his own vulnerability. Bouncing from Terri to Emma to Shelby to April proves that Will thrives on female attention, and after the finalization of his divorce, his Sue seduction is probably as much about picking his ego back up as bringing Sue down.

Perhaps the title of this episode comes across a bit *too* strongly — "Funk"s depressing theme puts us in a funk. By the end New Directions may have shifted from being in a funk to getting funky, but can these self-admitted "losers" really pull off a win at Regionals?

High Note: It doesn't matter that "Good Vibrations" isn't a funk tune. Pucky Puck and Finny D are the musical highlight of the episode.

Low Note: This episode was originally intended to air before "Theatricality" and the swap in order shows. From no mention of Shelby being Rachel's mom to Quinn moving in with Mercedes after Puck's touching plea last episode, several plotlines take too many steps back.

q&a: kent avenido as howard bamboo

Kent Avenido and his Sheets 'N Things counterpart Howard Bamboo are both hilarious, but at least with Kent you're laughing with him rather than at him! Born and raised in Kentucky, Kent studied acting at Yale University's School of Drama in New Haven, Connecticut, and has snagged roles in feature films such as *50 First Dates* and *Get Smart*. In addition to numerous theater credits, Kent has also been featured in over a dozen national commercials for companies such as Starbucks, Wendy's, Heineken, Toys "R" Us and Toyota. Kent currently lives in Los Angeles, where he has spent roughly the past 15 years living his dream of being a performer. We contacted the comedic actor, and he graciously took the time to give us further insight into the mind of Howard Bamboo.

We haven't really gotten to see any of Howard's personal life. How do you imagine the rest of his life?

Howard seems to be a simple guy just trying to make it in life and survive each day working at Sheets 'N Things with Terri. I imagine the time from the moment he clocks out at night to the moment he clocks back in the next morning to consist of a comedy of errors. (Possible spinoff or webisodes, Fox?!) Judging by his work with the Acafellas, I think he secretly would love to be a performer, but he would never have the courage and confidence to actively pursue it.

Did you have a musical background before getting your role on *Glee*? Did you know right away that your character would be singing?

Like many actors, I started out in the theater, which definitely included musicals here and there. On the day I filmed the pilot episode back in October 2008, Ryan Murphy asked me if I could sing and dance, both of which I confirmed. He then mentioned that if Fox picked up the show, there was a storyline in the third episode for which Howard would be perfect. Fortunately, Fox did pick up the show and that storyline would later become the Acafellas.

What was your favorite song to perform and why?

The night I shot the Acafellas performing "Poison" with Matthew Morrison, Patrick Gallagher and John Lloyd Young was quite possibly my most favorite single day as an actor thus far in my career. Earlier in the week, we had been in dance rehearsals, and I had had my first *Glee* recording studio session, so the night that we filmed the number in a bar in Van Nuys was the payoff of a lot of hard work. It was also the night I first met Jane Lynch, Jayma Mays, Iqbal Theba, Victor Garber and Debra Monk. I didn't want the night to end, and in the following days back on the *Glee* set at Paramount Studios, I joked with everyone that I was going through a bit of "Poison" withdrawal.

Is there a character in particular you'd most like to see your character interact with? Or, alternatively, a cast member you'd like to work more with?
If Will and Emma don't end up working out, I could see Howard possibly finding a love interest in Emma. I think Howard has a lot of love to give and would be kind, loyal, patient and nurturing to her. Plus, they could both find some common ground sharing war stories about Terri. Or how about a complete fantasy scene with Howard, Finn and Brittany facing off in a game of *Jeopardy!*? It would end up being like one of those *Saturday Night Live* skits with Alex Trebek and Sean Connery!

The cast member with whom I would like to work more would be Jane Lynch. In the "Vitamin D" episode, I filmed a scene with her, and she is one of the nicest and most talented people. Unfortunately, that scene did not survive the cutting room floor, but I was truly honored just to be breathing the same air as she.

What's it like working with Ryan Murphy?
It's an absolute privilege and pleasure working with Ryan. I have been witness to his genius from very early on, as he was present at all of my callbacks and directed me in the pilot episode. He has played such a pivotal role in all of the show's success, and I've been so fortunate to benefit greatly as an actor from his creativity and sheer brilliance. Plus, he's so in tune to what's funny, which has been extremely helpful in developing a character like Howard Bamboo.

If you had to narrow it down to just one thing, what's the best part about working on *Glee*?
It's incredibly difficult to narrow it down to just one thing, but I would have to say the people. By that, I include all of our wonderful fans as well as everyone from the cast and the crew. Gleeks are the most amazing and devoted fans from literally all across the world. In particular, Howard Bamboo has developed a bit of a cult following and a legion of his own fans, whom I have affectionately named "Hobos." Shout-out to the Hobos!

Behind the Music:

"Another One Bites the Dust" (Vocal Adrenaline)
Queen, *The Game* (1980)
"Another One Bites the Dust," Queen's best-selling single and only Grammy-nominated song, tells the story of a man down on his luck reverting to a life of crime and murder as payback. Vocal Adrenaline doesn't go as far as to murder their competition, but they're certainly doing everything they can to make sure New Directions dies a show choir death.

"Tell Me Something Good" (Will)
Rufus and Chaka Khan, *Rags to Rufus* (1974)
Stevie Wonder penned Rufus and Chaka Khan's first hit about encouraging a love interest to acknowledge their romantic feelings. The song's lyrics, about a person who puts pride before all else, describe Sue to a tee. Will may be singing this song to get back at Sue, but the message is bang-on: despite a house full of hardware, Sue's life is empty without love, and happiness would come easier if she put her ego aside and opened herself up to another person, rather than replacing companionship with competition.

"Loser" (Finn and Puck with Sandy, Howard and Terri)
Beck, *Mellow Gold* (1994)
The surprise hit that launched Beck's career, "Loser," with its surreal and sometimes nonsensical lyrics, is often considered the song that sums up the Generation X slacker culture of the 1990s. Puck and Finn are Lima Losers, dismayed that they work at Sheets 'N Things with Howard have to serve Sandy and have to answer to Terri. If these sad-sack adults are any indication of what their lives might be like after high school, Puck and Finn are not looking forward to it.

"It's a Man's Man's Man's World" (Quinn)
James Brown, *It's a Man's Man's Man's World* (1966)
James Brown's exploration of how, despite all the great things men have done for civilization, men would be nothing without their women, takes on a more poignant meaning when sung by Quinn, the most conservative girl in glee club. No longer a Cheerio, she is now stared at, made fun of and homeless, not to mention dealing with pregnancy hormones and a changing body every day. Her baby daddy, Puck, on the other hand, gets by relatively unscathed, with an undamaged reputation and girlfriends galore.

"Good Vibrations" (Finn, Puck and Mercedes)
Marky Mark and the Funky Bunch, *Music for the People* (1991)
Marky Mark's first #1 hit may not be funk, but it shares funk's desire to feel the music and provide an authentic expression of the artist by sharing "good vibrations" with fans. Puck and Finn may have chosen this song because of its appearance on "the iTunes" search, but it encapsulates the message Will is trying to teach his students: music can free you from a funk, allow you to focus on other things and help you feel good about yourself.

"Give Up the Funk (Tear the Roof off the Sucker)" (New Directions)
Parliament, *Mothership Connection* (1975)
Originally released as "Tear the Roof off the Sucker (Give Up the Funk)," iconic funk band Parliament's biggest mainstream hit explores how funk is an authentic expression of emotion. Since Vocal Adrenaline's members are self-declared "soulless automatons," New Directions uses this song to show them how authentic and soulful they are in comparison. They may not have fancy dance moves and complicated vocal arrangements like Vocal Adrenaline, but they do have more passion, heart and soul, and they can find the fun in funky.

The Sound of Music: Will argues that funk is "soul meets anger." Funk emerged in the 1960s, when African American artists experimented with combining soul, jazz and R&B into a more danceable type of music by bringing electric bass, guitar and drums to the forefront of the song. James Brown is credited with developing funk music in the 1960s when he scored with hits like "Cold Sweat" and "Get Up (I Feel Like Being A) Sex Machine." In the 1970s, George Clinton (with his two bands Parliament and Funkadelic), along with artists like Chaka Khan and Sly & the Family Stone, helped bring the genre into the mainstream. Funk largely influenced disco and go-go music, and faded out of the mainstream when these two genres became popular.

That's Pretty *Popular*: "Funk" tries to touch on oppression and racism with the Quinn/Mercedes plotline, but Ryan Murphy hit viewers with a quadruple whammy of discrimination with *Popular*'s second season episode "Fag." Sam and George face discrimination for their interracial relationship, Sugar Daddy deals with size-ism when he's rejected for a job because he's fat, Lily tries to stand up for a fellow student being subjected to homophobia and Brooke's date is subjected to religious discrimination.

Slushie Facials:
*   Vocal Adrenaline covers New Directions' choir room in toilet paper.
*   Will breaks Sue's trophy.
*   Puck gave his first-ever wedgie at four years old.
*   Puck and Finn slash the tires of Vocal Adrenaline's Range Rovers.
*   Jesse and Vocal Adrenaline egg Rachel.

Off-Key:

- Twice in this episode Kurt is in regular clothes and when he should be in his Cheerio uniform.
- What happened to the job Finn got in "Wheels"? Did he quit after he discovered he wasn't the father of Quinn's baby?
- Rachel claims to be a vegan, but it's odd that a vegan would make someone venison (as Rachel serves Will in "Ballad") and eat pepperoni pizza (as Rachel does with Finn during "The Rhodes Not Taken").
- With Regionals next week, it's surprising that no set list has been picked yet — or even mentioned, for that matter.

Behind the Scenes:

- Courtney Galiano from season 4 of *So You Think You Can Dance* was one of Quinn's pregnant back-up dancers, and she also joined Vocal Adrenaline for "Another One Bites the Dust."
- While Rachel claims to be a vegan, Lea Michele actually is one.
- When filming "Hell-O," Brad Falchuk asked Heather Morris and Naya Rivera to link pinkies when approaching Finn about their date, but the two actors decided to incorporate it into future interactions between their characters. You'll notice it in this episode when the twosome leaves the choir room after being given their funk assignment and when they enter Will's apartment with Sue.
- It may be hard to believe, but the deep voice that opens "Give Up the Funk" is really Chris Colfer's!

Center Stage:

- Sue wants her trophy annex to look like Elvis Presley's Gold Record Room. Graceland, Elvis' home, is open for tours for his fans and each room has a distinctive theme, such as the Jungle Room and the Trophy Room. His Gold Record Room displays the 110 albums the King had go gold and platinum during the course of his career.
- Rachel's heart is crushed like the floor in *Stomp*, the show by the U.K. dance troupe of the same name that generates beats using everyday objects and is known for its high-energy, physical style of dance.
- Will's "Funkytown" riff is from funk band Lipps Inc.'s 1980 single "Funkytown," a song about a place with limitless soul and energy.
- KC and the Sunshine Band was an American 1970s funk and disco

group known for their dance-ready hits like "That's the Way (I Like It)" and "(Shake, Shake, Shake) Shake Your Booty."

- Artie loves KC and the Sunshine Band's "Boogie Shoes," a disco song that became a hit when it appeared on the soundtrack for the 1977 John Travolta film *Saturday Night Fever*.
- Quinn names her band "The Unwed Mothership Connection," inspired by the title of funk master George Clinton's fourth album with his band Parliament, *Mothership Connection* (1975), widely considered to be the greatest funk album of all time.
- Jayne Mansfield, a 1950s blonde bombshell, might appreciate Sandy's tribute bathroom, as the actress and *Playboy* playmate decorated her entire Beverly Hills home in pink and dubbed it the Pink Palace.
- Sandy says he needs his Kenny G, referring to the most successful instrumental artist of all time, who has sold over 75 million albums worldwide. The Grammy-winning artist broke through in the late 1980s and is known for his smooth jazz saxophone. He's an excellent example of muzak, the instrumentals often heard in department stores and elevators.
- The New Directions boys want to go all *Braveheart* on Vocal Adrenaline, referencing Mel Gibson's 1995 movie about warriors seeking Scottish independence in the early 1300s. The film was nominated for ten Academy Awards, winning five, including Best Picture.
- Kurt performed a 14-and-a-half minute Céline Dion medley, entirely in French. Céline Dion is a French Canadian singer best known for her "titanic" 1999 hit "My Heart Will Go On."

Jazz Hands:
- Again, no Jayma Mays! At least Jane Lynch and Jessalyn Gilsig are back, with Jessalyn making her first appearance since "Hell-O."
- Artie is wearing a surgical mask and Brittany is trying to put the toilet paper back on the roll when New Directions is cleaning up their TPed choir room.
- Sue tells the glee clubbers "whose hearing has not been damaged by massive doses of Accutane" to pay attention to her. Accutane, a medication used to treat severe acne, has been marketed and sold as Roaccutane.
- If Shelby had finished her math, she'd know that Puck and Finn owe her $20,800.
- The Great Chicago Fire was supposedly started when a cow knocked over

a lantern in Patrick and Catherine O'Leary's barn. However this claim has since been proven false. The fire lasted for two days, destroying hundreds of acres of land and killing hundreds of people. Abraham Lincoln, the 16th president of the United States, is credited for seeing the country through the 1861–1865 civil war and is considered one of the greatest presidents the country ever had. However, since he was assassinated in 1865, and the Chicago fire was started in 1871, Sue might need a history lesson or two.

- Puck claims he has fromunda cheese on his fingers, which isn't a real cheese, but a stinky cheese-like substance that sometimes grows on male genitalia.

- In 2006, NPR reported that the Frito-Lay product Hot Cheetos had addictive properties, causing students to act jittery and wired and experience withdrawal symptoms when they didn't get their chip fix. Several schools banned the cheesy snack, but kids traded them from their backpacks and lockers. Eating the chips causes the body to release endorphins, which is why Sue supports the snack.

- Will attempts to seduce Sue with his own version of the bend and snap, a move popularized by the 2001 film *Legally Blonde*. Doing the bend and snap involves purposely dropping something to show off your butt, then picking it up quickly and smiling to show off your chest.

- Howard says that Sandy Ryerson gave him Bell's palsy, a condition that causes sufferers to lose control of one side of their face. The condition isn't contagious, however, and can only be contracted through paralysis-causing illnesses like tumors, strokes and Lyme disease.

- When the cheerleaders are all distraught, Brittany's uniform is on backwards.

- Sue isn't just a cheerleading champion; she's also a bowling and tennis champion (if she actually won all those trophies in her house).

- Sue is the Michael Jordan of cheerleading, referring to the time he won six NBA championships with the Chicago Bulls. Unlike Sue, Michael's six championships were not consecutive. His first string of consecutive championships came in 1991, 1992 and 1993 and the second string in 1996, 1997 and 1998.

- When Kurt spoke French to the reporter, he said, "Vive la différence!," which translates to "Long live the difference!" and is usually used as a call to celebrate diversity.

The Buckeye State: Will had to drive all the way to Dayton to get Sue's protein shake. Dayton, the fourth largest city in Ohio, is known for its tech industry and is 75 miles south of Lima.

How Sue Cs It: "You know, for me trophies are like herpes. You can try to get rid of them but they just keep coming. Sue Sylvester has hourly flare-ups of burning, itchy, highly contagious talent."

♪♫♪

1.22 "journey"
Original Air Date: June 8, 2010
Written by: Brad Falchuk
Directed by: Brad Falchuk

The Music: ★ ★ ★ ★
The Drama: ★ ★ ★ ★
The Laughs: ★ ★ ★

Will: Now, I was going to quit once, but you guys brought me back with "Don't Stop Believin'." It was a nine, but we are going to make it a ten.

It's all been leading up to this. New Directions has finally made it to Regionals, but can they beat out Vocal Adrenaline?

If you've been watching *Glee* all season, you've probably felt like you've been on quite the journey. The show's had its ups and its downs, has made you laugh and cry (sometimes at the same time) and has offered up its share of amazing songs and, well, awful songs. But through it all we've stayed the course, and here we are, at the finale. Calling this episode "Journey" fits perfectly, not only because of the Journey medley of songs that New Directions performs at Regionals, but also because it feels like we are watching the end of a journey. Win or lose, New Directions has come insanely far since we saw them at the beginning of the year (as Will points out, there were five of them . . . and they really sucked), and the "full circle" nature of this episode worked extremely well.

Bookending the season with "Don't Stop Believin'" is obviously an iconic choice, but it is also wonderfully symbolic of New Directions' growth. While originally the song was mainly a Rachel-Finn duet with background choral work from the rest of the glee club, this time everyone gets a turn in the spotlight, reinforcing that the glee club belongs to all of its members, and they all belong to the glee club. The "journey" statements before their "To Sir, with Love" performance contain all of *Glee*'s reoccurring themes — acceptance, tolerance, self-confidence and self-discovery — perfectly summing up how glee club has affected these kids, and how they've grown from being caricatures into characters. Even the very act of making these public declarations shows how the members of New Directions have grown, since one of Mr. Schue's key ideas is that glee club is about expressing yourself.

In fact, all three leading men can't stop expressing themselves this episode, with Finn, Puck and Will all making declarations of love. These men have struggled with romance this season, and they each finally get up the courage to confess their true feelings. On the other hand, all of their declarations come during dramatic moments: Finn says "I love you" right before going on stage at Regionals, Puck tells Quinn how he feels while still basking in the glow of their new baby girl and Will admits his love for Emma during a heated discussion about the future of glee club. Are these confessions made only in the heat of the moment, or will these guys "hold on to that feelin'" through 'til next year?

bill a. jones as rod remington

Bill Jones has spent most of his career behind the camera, working as a radio host, voicing characters and doing commercial work. He started out as a radio host and performing in local theater before moving to Los Angeles to give acting a full-time try-out in 1987. There, he balanced his blossoming voice career with prominent radio gigs. The Nashville, Tennessee, native has had his fair share of on-screen success as well, appearing in television shows like *7th Heaven*, *Just Shoot Me!* and *Las Vegas*. When he's not doing guest stints on television shows, his voice work keeps him busy, with clients like Fox, Disney, McDonald's and American Airlines. Rod Remington may not belt out a tune on *Glee*, but Bill enjoys a successful side career as a lounge singer, performing the great American standards at clubs and on cruise ships.

While romances may come and go, at least glee club is here to stay, thanks to the heroic actions of McKinley's favorite villain, who realizes she actually has a lot in common with glee club's determined underdogs. Though some of *Glee*'s biggest laughs come from exploiting pervasive high school stereotypes, the show's courageous decision to turn New Directions' greatest villain into their savior prevents viewers from slotting anyone into convenient categories.

Through all of this, *Glee* keeps the focus on the most important parts of the episode: the Regionals competition and Quinn being in labor. The parallel between the two events works well, for after inauspicious beginnings and nine months of slow growth, both New Directions and Quinn can finally present the fruits of their labors. Watching our heroes lose is heartbreaking, but fitting. Vocal Adrenaline is simply the better team. New Directions may have more heart, but their rivals are stronger singers and dancers. And it's a fitting conclusion for the group that started as losers to finish as losers, but with one notable difference — being losers doesn't really matter anymore. They've found their passion, their confidence and more support than they could have imagined. Though they may still be losers, it's clear that thanks to glee, they won't stop believin'.

High Note: Just when an eight-minute Journey medley astounds viewers, *Glee* goes and blows minds with an epic mash-up of Vocal Adrenaline's "Bohemian Rhapsody" and the birth of Quinn's baby, then makes us bawl with "To Sir, with Love" and "Over the Rainbow." The music in this episode is *Glee* at its best.

Low Note: While Shelby adopting Quinn's baby brought those two storylines to a nice close, people just can't go into a hospital and pick out a baby to adopt — it takes years of payment and paperwork. The plot decision is also troubling as it suggests that Rachel is less desirable as a "used" child whereas Beth is brand new.

Behind the Music:

"Faithfully" (Rachel and Finn)
Journey, *Frontiers* (1983)
Journey's power ballad (and their second top 20 hit) about strangers falling in love again and the difficulties of maintaining a relationship on tour is

the perfect theme song for our on-again off-again glee lovebirds, Finn and Rachel. Thanks to the chaos New Directions brings into their lives, they haven't been able to find a groove that works for them as a couple. Now, with Jesse back in Vocal Adrenaline, Rachel needs to fall in love with Finn all over again. In the song, the man insists he'll always love and be faithful to his girlfriend, something Finn insinuates with his simple declaration before the song begins.

"Any Way You Want It/Lovin' Touchin' Squeezin'" (New Directions)
Journey, *Departure* (1980)
Journey, *Evolution* (1979)
Irish rock band Thin Lizzy inspired "Any Way You Want It," a song about the dizzying elation you feel in a happy relationship. Finn and Rachel are on the mend and New Directions is rediscovering their passion for the stage, which they lost when they began focusing solely on winning. "Lovin' Touchin' Squeezin'" comes full circle since its original appearance in the pilot. There are no major break-ups in this episode, but New Directions is about to feel the heartbreak, as the trophy they've yearned for all season finds its way into the hands of Vocal Adrenaline. It also cleverly foreshadows the twist Will and Emma experience later in the episode.

"Don't Stop Believin'" (New Directions)
Journey, *Evolution* (1979)
Ah, *Glee*'s unofficial theme song makes a triumphant return. New Directions learns, once again, to don't stop believin', because as long as you believe, great things can happen. Winning isn't everything and passion for what you do makes you a winner no matter what the nameplate on the trophy says. Will and his team are ready to give up, believing they can't win Regionals with Sue as a judge. Yet, when they refocus on what's most important — how much they love performing and how they've grown as a team — winning becomes secondary. They rediscover their belief in themselves and even win over their perennial nemesis, Sue. Unlike in the original version of this song in the pilot, everyone gets a chance to shine vocally, demonstrating how far the group has come literally (everyone is a much better singer and performer) and metaphorically (New Directions is now truly a team, working together, supporting each other and looking out for one another).

"Bohemian Rhapsody" (Vocal Adrenaline)
Queen, *A Night at the Opera* (1975)
Queen's masterpiece is a crazy and complex journey through different musical genres and heavy emotions, which is what *Glee* is week in and week out. Freddie Mercury revealed that the song was about a man who killed someone and sold his soul to the devil, an apt comparison for Vocal Adrenaline, who would do whatever it takes for another national title. Queen's two-time #1 hit (in the U.K.; it only reached #4 in the U.S.) does not have a traditional structure; instead it features six distinct parts with abrupt changes in tempo, style and lyrics. New Directions is a complicated mesh of people and musical styles, and their "rag-tag" style could be considered bohemian compared to the polished and professional Vocal Adrenaline. By intersecting this song with Quinn's labor, they showcased how birth is a rhapsody with extreme emotions and severe pain, but this song highlights more than that. It represents New Directions' struggle throughout the season: they've faced near demise from several people wanting to shut the club down, survived Jesse's arrival and departure and dealt with the romantic ups and downs of everyone within the group. Yes, Vocal Adrenaline comes out on top by flawlessly executing one of the most difficult songs ever written, but as everyone points

241

glee by the numbers

Different names Sue calls Emma: 8
Names Sue uses twice: 1
Sue uses Emma's real name: 1
Sue insults Will's hair: 11
Kurt references designers: 3
Track suits Sue owns: 35
Rachel wears knee socks: 43
Physical ailments Sue has: 5
People (including Will) quit New Directions: 13
New Directions wears Converse: 9
How Sue Cs It segments: 5
Rachel storms out: 4
Sue's show choir rulebook appearances: 3
Sue's journal appearances: 4
Quinn cries: 8
Kurt cries: 10
Justin Timberlake references: 4
Barbra Streisand references: 7
SYTYCD alum appearances: 12
Rachel and Finn do their signature dance move of spinning around each other: 4
Others do Rachel's and Finn's signature dance move: 2
Slushie facials: 26

out in this episode, New Directions is the team with soul and passion, and this is what will carry them through.

"To Sir, with Love" (New Directions)
Lulu, *To Sir, with Love* (1967)
The 1967 British film *To Sir, with Love*, tells the tale of teacher Mark Thackeray (played by Sidney Poitier), who inspires a group of students at a high school in a tough neighborhood. Mark takes the teaching job to bide his time while waiting for an engineering job to come his way, and along the way, changes students' lives. "To Sir, with Love," the film's theme song and #1 hit, expresses just how much Mr. Thackeray meant to his students and how much he did for them. New Directions uses this song to say the same thing to Mr. Schuester, and this literal song choice perfectly conveys their message of gratitude.

"Over the Rainbow" (Will accompanied by Puck on guitar)
Israel Kamakawiwo'ole', *Facing Future* (1993)
The Wizard of Oz made "Over the Rainbow" famous, but Will is actually singing the lesser-known ukulele version by Israel Kamakawiwo'ole', which he released as a mash-up with "What a Wonderful World" in 1993. Judy Garland's signature song is about the promise of tomorrow, of a place and time where things will be happier. Judy, as Dorothy, sings this song as she yearns for a better, more cheerful place. Now that New Directions has been offered another year at McKinley, they can look "over the rainbow" to next year, when they have another chance to continue to do what they love, and maybe, just maybe, can give Vocal Adrenaline a run for their money.

The Sound of Music: New Directions pays homage to American rock band Journey with their Regionals set list. Journey, known for their power ballads, gained prominence in the late 1970s and early 1980s and is now considered one of America's most beloved bands. Worldwide, they've sold over 75 million albums, but have yet to be inducted into the Rock and Roll Hall of Fame. Santana alums Neal Schon and Gregg Rolie formed Journey in San Francisco in 1973. After a few name changes, line-up changes and mediocre releases, they hired their most famous lead singer to date, Steve Perry, in 1977. He updated the band's sound, positioning them to finally break into the mainstream market, which they did in 1979 with the release of *Evolution*. Today, the band continues to tour internationally, and "Don't Stop Believin'" is the most popular iTunes download of all time.

That's Pretty *Popular*: Quinn's mom takes a lesson from Josh's mom, who leaves her controlling and abusive husband and supports her son's choice to be a singing football star in "Booty Camp." This isn't Ryan Murphy's first big musical season finale, either. The first season finale of *Popular*, "Two Weddings and a Funeral," has an epic original musical number with all the main cast members singing — a first for the show.

Off-Key:
- Puck's make-out scene Mohawk is absurdly fake looking.
- The Regionals announcer says Sue just won her fifth consecutive national cheerleading championship, but according to previous episodes, it was her sixth consecutive championship.

- The timing for Regionals is tight. The team waits for Quinn in the hospital while she gives birth, then makes it back in time for the judges' announcement. Either Vocal Adrenaline performs the longest version of "Bohemian Rhapsody" ever or Quinn has the shortest labor in recorded history. But the scene is so well done, that we'll let this slide!
- Josh Groban and Olivia Newton-John rip into Sue for being an Ohio wannabe, but leave local news anchor Rod Remington alone. He's trying at least as hard as Sue to claim "celebrity" status.
- How can Sue cry if she got her tear ducts removed?

Behind the Scenes:

- Quinn has a lamb on her pillow in the flashback. Dianna Agron's nickname is "Little Lamb."
- Filming for Regionals took place at Saban Theatre in Beverly Hills. Several contest winners and extras were invited to fill the auditorium, but the show filmed several different endings to make sure the audience had no idea who won.
- Look closely at the back of the audience in the auditorium's main section during Regionals: those aren't extras, they're mannequins!
- *So You Think You Can Dance* alums Lauren Gottlieb and Jesús Solorio appear in the season finale along with Shelby Rabara, Harry Shum Jr.'s girlfriend, as Vocal Adrenaline dancers.
- The "Bohemian Rhapsody" finale was so difficult that four dancers were injured during rehearsals and Jonathan Groff received a five-inch cut on his arm from his partner's stiletto.
- Jonathan Groff had no idea how to play the piano before performing "Bohemian Rhapsody." He set up piano lessons with Brad Ellis (the show's on- and offscreen piano man), who was supposed to teach him how to fake it. Jonathan picked it up so quickly that he actually could play the song.
- Quinn's transformation from bitchy cheerleader to Mercedes' understanding confidante isn't just due to her unexpected pregnancy. Dianna had a big influence on why the character changed direction. She was so vulnerable and sweet that Ryan Murphy felt he needed to include those characteristics in Quinn.
- The Will/Emma kiss wasn't scripted! Brad Falchuk told Matthew Morrison to do it just before they shot the scene so that Jayma Mays'

stage names

Oh, high school, a time when many a nickname is born, most of which aren't very nice. Here's a list of the names being shouted down the halls of McKinley High:

Will: Schue (Figgins); William, Schuester, Buddy, Manwhore, Slut, Pal (Sue); Hot Stuff (April)

Emma: Eleanor, Edie, Irma, Ellen, Alma, Ellen, Arlene, Ella (Sue); M&M, Emster, Sweetie (Ken)

Rachel: Hot Mama, Miss Bossy Pants, Eva Perón, Babe (Mercedes); RuPaul, Man Hands, Treasure Trail, Stubbles, That Thing, Sweetie (Quinn); Yentl (Dakota Stanley); Swimfan, A-Rach (Finn); Boy Hips (Lauren Zizes); Benedict Arnold (Kurt)

Finn: Frankenteen (Dakota Stanley); F-Wrong (Rachel); White Boy, Justin Timberlake (Mercedes); Finnessa (Puck); Finnster (Sean); Mr. Ikea Catalogue (Kurt); Glee Boy (Azimio); Finny D (Finn); Finnocence (Santana)

Quinn: Q (Sue); Quinnie (Quinn's parents); Pretty Blonde with the White Girl Ass (Mercedes)

Puck: Puckerman (Ken, Rachel); Noah (Rachel); Nathan (yearbook); Puckzilla, Puckasaurus, Puckster, Puckerone, Pucky Puck (Puck); Baby (Mercedes)

Mercedes: Effie (Dakota Stanley); Aretha, Whoopi, Brassy Hag (Sue); Sugar (Puck); Weezy (Santana)

Kurt: Lance Bass (Puck); Mayor of Gay Town (Mercedes); Gay Kid, Ladyface, Kiddo, Don Knotts, Future Center Square (Sue); Homo (Azimio); Fancy (Karofsky)

Artie: Wheels (Sue)

Tina: Asian (Sue)

Mike: Other Asian (Sue, Tina)

Matt: Shaft (Sue)

Santana: Stick Figure (Mercedes)

Brad: Tinkles, Knuckles (April)

Ken: Tanaka-San (Sue)

Figgins: Maharishi, Figgy (Sue)

Josh Groban: Horsey (Sue)

reaction would be real.

- The other real reaction in this episode? All those tears. Despite the many tear-inducing moments for the glee club, not a single actor used teardrops.

- Matthew sang "Over the Rainbow" (complete with ukulele!) as one of his audition pieces for *Glee*.

Center Stage:

- When Sue is talking about "racist Disney characters" living "on the bayou," she was most likely referring to Disney's 1946 film *Song of the South*, based on Joel Chandler Harris' folk tales about Uncle Remus, an African American, and some trickster animals. The stories were inspired by Harris' collection of folk stories from the southern United States. *Song of the South* scored an Academy Award for Best Original Song with "Zip-a-Dee-Doo-Dah." The movie is considered to be racially insensitive by many and it's rumored that this insensitivity is the reason the film has never been released on VHS or DVD, although this has never been confirmed. Sue may have also been referencing a more recent Disney movie, 2009's *The Princess and the Frog*, which is based on *The Frog Princess*, E.D. Baker's novel about a young woman who mistakenly turns into a frog after kissing a frog prince. In the film's early development, it was met with protests claiming that many of the characters perpetuated negative stereotypes, but changes were later made to appease the critics.

- Aural Intensity's mash-up is of Josh Groban's "You Raise Me Up," a 2003 single that topped the Billboard adult contemporary chart, and Olivia Newton-John's "Magic," a 1980 single that was Olivia's biggest adult contemporary hit, topping both the adult contemporary and pop charts. While both of these songs are about love, they can easily be reinterpreted to be about the special effect celebrities have on other's lives (a message that Olivia and Josh clearly believe in).

- Rod Remington partied with Queen's flamboyant lead vocalist Freddie Mercury. Freddie, widely considered one of the greatest frontmen of all time, was a wild personality onstage but was a rather introverted man. During Queen's heyday, he partied hard and slept with many men and women, resulting in a rock star reputation. Freddie passed away from HIV-related complications in 1991.

- Will apparently tears up more than Michael Landon on *Little House on the Prairie*. Michael Landon was an actor, writer and producer who portrayed father Charles Ingalls in the *Little House on the Prairie* television series, which ran from 1974 to 1982 on NBC. The show, based on Laura Ingalls Wilder's book series of the same name, explores the adventures of a family living on a farm in late 19th century Minnesota.

- The whole episode, from Puck admitting he wouldn't acknowledge

Mercedes after glee club to everyone sharing what they used to be before they joined the club, seems to be inspired by *The Breakfast Club*, the iconic 1985 John Hughes movie about five very different high schoolers (the athlete, the princess, the brain, the criminal and the basket case) coming together and learning about the people behind the stereotype during Saturday detention.

- Quinn's dad was having an affair with a tattooed freak, which is similar to A-list star Sandra Bullock's 2010 marital scandal. The *Speed* and *Miss Congeniality* star's husband, Jesse James, supposedly had an affair with Michelle "Bombshell" McGee, a heavily tattooed woman. The scandal broke shortly after Sandra won her Best Actress Oscar for *The Blind Side*.

- Olivia Newton-John indeed had a band at 14, the all-girl Sol Four, which performed at local Australian coffee shops until Olivia worked her way up to being a local radio and television regular.

- Josh Groban was never in the Mickey Mouse Club, a Disney variety show that aired in the 1950s and was revived in the 1990s, launching the careers of several singers and actors including Justin Timberlake, *Felicity* star Keri Russell, Britney Spears, Christina Aguilera and *The Notebook* actor Ryan Gosling.

Jazz Hands:

- It looks like the New Directions gang is on Facebook, the third social networking site to be mentioned on *Glee*, after MySpace and Twitter.

- The girls don Betsey Johnson's gold strapless evening dress for Regionals. The costume department added the straps. Olivia may think the dresses look cheap, but they retail for nearly $450!

- The Mock UN, which temporarily took over the choir room, is a McKinley club inspired by the Model UN. The Model UN is a school organization that simulates the activities of the real United Nations, in an effort to teach students about international diplomacy and intergovernmental relations. The Model UN has been around in some form in American high schools since the 1920s.

- "Beast with two backs" is slang for sex and dates back to Shakespeare's *Othello*.

The Buckeye State: Emma drinks from a mug courtesy of the *Lima News*, which is a real daily newspaper with a circulation of 87,500. It serves Lima and the surrounding communities in Allen County.

How Sue Cs It: "Your hair looks like a briar patch. I keep expecting racist, animated Disney characters to pop up and start singing about living on the bayou."

questions for season two

1. With Shelby gone and Jesse graduating, will Vocal Adrenaline continue to be a show choir powerhouse?
2. How serious are Emma and her dentist boyfriend? Does Will still have a chance?
3. How long will Rachel and Finn last this time?
4. Will Brittany, Mike and Matt ever get a solo?
5. Will we meet Rachel's dads?
6. What will happen between Quinn and Puck now that baby Beth has been adopted?
7. Will Quinn forgive her mom and move back in with her?
8. Will we ever get to learn more about the home lives of other glee clubbers, such as Tina, Artie or Mercedes?
9. What about Terri? Now that she and Will are divorced, will we ever see her again?
10. And finally, will Brittany's last name ever get mentioned?

sources

can't fight this feeling: the origins of glee

Amorgan. "Amorgan Interviews Ryan Murphy," TelevisionWithoutPity.com. December 3, 1999.

Arado, Matt. "Mount Prospect native helped create new Fox show 'Glee'," *Daily Herald*. Online. May 19, 2009.

Bialas, Michael. "Ryan Murphy Makes His Lighthearted Plea With Glee," Blogcritics. org. May 18, 2009.

Bianculli, David. "The Musical Magic Of 'Glee'," NPR.org. September 11, 2009.

Callaghan, Dylan. "Writing in the Key of Glee," *Writers Guild of America West*. Online. Accessed March 1, 2010.

Gross, Terri. "From 'Nip/Tuck' To High School 'Glee'," NPR.org. May 18, 2009.

Hendrickson, Paula. "Casting the Keys to Glee," Emmys.com. November 1, 2009.

Hernandez, Greg. "My chat with 'Glee' creator Ryan Murphy," GreginHollywood. com. December 17, 2009.

Martin, Denise. "'Glee' team rewrites the school musical," *Los Angeles Times*. Online. April 26, 2009.

Mastony, Colleen. "'Glee Club' TV series creator uses Mt. Prospect high school for inspiration," *Chicago Tribune*. Online. September 8, 2009.

O'Connor, Mickey. "Ryan Murphy on Glee: People Don't Just Break Out Into Song; 'There Are Rules'," *TV Guide*. Online. May 19, 2009.

Roberts, Sheila. "Ryan Murphy, Director of Running with Scissors Interview," MoviesOnline.ca. Accessed March 10, 2010.

Schneider, Michael. "'Glee' co-creator gets big Fox deal," *Variety*. Online. December 1, 2009.

Shapiro, Gregg. "Interview with Ryan Murphy and Joseph Cross of Running With

Scissors," AfterElton.com. October 26, 2006.

Sloane, Judy. "Glee — On set with creator/producer Ryan Murphy who tells about the extraordinary success," FilmReviewOnline.com. February 10, 2010.

Stelter, Brian. "A Long Wait Stirs Enthusiasm for Fox Show 'Glee'," *New York Times.* Online. September 1, 2009.

Tallerico, Brian. "Interview: Ryan Murphy Dances His Way to 'Glee' on FOX," HollywoodChicago.com. May 12, 2009.

Udovitch, Mim. "The Cutting Edge of Television: A Bloody Scalpel," *New York Times.* Online. August 3, 2003.

Weiss, Joanna. "Welcome to the club," *Boston Globe.* Online. August 30, 2009.

Wyatt, Edward. "From 'Cabaret' to Kanye, Songs of 'Glee' Are a Hit," *New York Times.* Online. October 11, 2009.

—. "Not That High School Musical," *New York Times.* Online. May 15, 2009.

this Is how we do it: the making of *glee*

Adalian, Josef. "'Glee' Pilot Doubles as Marketing Trial," TVWeek.com. Accessed June 20, 2010.

AndersMusic.com

Belcher, Walt. "Former Tampa man makes music on 'Glee'," *Tampa Tribune.* Online. April 7, 2010.

Bemn-Yehuda, Ayala. "Q&A: 'Glee' Music Producer Adam Anders," Billboard.biz. October 30, 2009.

Bernstein, Abbie. "Exclusive Interview: The 'Glee' Producers Put on a Show for FOX's New Dramedy," *IF Magazine.* Online. September 9, 2009.

"Brad Falchuk," *Life After Film School.* Hulu.com. 2006.

Erhmann, Brett. "2002 Television Pilots (Incomplete at Best)," DangerousUniverse. com. February 11, 2002.

Falchuk, Evan. "Second Opinion Can Save Lives, Cut Costs," *Benefits & Compensation Digest.* October 2009.

Fernandez, Maria. "What 'Glee.' Show Choir Kids Rule," *Los Angeles Times.* Online. April 26, 2009.

Galas, Marjorie. "'Glee': Fancy Footwork Tells The Story," *New York 411.* Online. Accessed March 9, 2009.

Gianelli, Brian. "Ryan Murphy Talks 'Glee' — The Hottest New Show Of The Season," Fancast.com. May 7, 2009.

Glee — Season 1, Volume 1: Road to Sectionals. DVD. Twentieth Century Fox Home Entertainment, 2009.

Herrera, Monica. "'Glee' Rewrites The Script On TV Music," Billboard.com. October 23, 2009.

Jones, Sarah. "Music: The Joy of 'Glee'," MixOnline.com. January 1, 2010.

Kawashima, Dale. "Writer/Producer Adam Anders Tells How He Co-Wrote The Hit 'More Than That' For The Backstreet Boys," SongwriterUniverse.com. Accessed June 20, 2010.

Kinon, Christina. "'Glee' puts edgy spin on Top 40 tunes," *New York Daily News.* Online. May 16, 2009.

McNamara, Mary. "'Glee' on Fox," *Los Angeles Times.* Online. May 19, 2009.

Shales, Tom. "Sharply, Fox Provides A Reason For 'Glee'," *Washington Post.* Online. May 19, 2009.

Sorrells, Melissa Sue. "Glee! Brad Falchuk '93," *Pulteney Street Survey.* Winter 2010.

Trust, Gary. "Best of 2009: By the Numbers," Billboard.com. December 29, 2009.

"TV's Most Talked About Show: The Cast of Glee," *The Oprah Winfrey Show.* Original Air Date: April 7, 2010.

Willman, Chris. "Journey's 'Don't Stop Believing' as pop-cultural touchstone," Pop & Hiss: The LA Times Music Blog. *Los Angeles Times.* Online. June 29, 2009.

Yamamoto, Jane. "Meet Glee's Music Man — Adam Anders," MyFoxLA.com. October 15, 2009.

you're the one that i want: principal players
matthew morrison

Albiniak, Paige. "Music Man." *New York Post.* Online. September 6, 2009.

Buckley, Michael. "Stage to Screens: 'Glee' on TV: Michele & Morrison," Playbill. com. September 8, 2009.

Carter, Kelley L. "Broadway star Morrison gets all keyed up for 'Glee'," *USA Today.* Online. May 18, 2009.

Cohen, Corine. "Interview with Matthew Morrison (now in The Light in the Piazza)," NYCTourist.com. Accessed March 1, 2010.

Dirmann, Tina. "Matthew Morrison Revealed," *Orange Coast.* Online. December 2009.

Goldman, Andrew. "Matthew Morrison," *Elle.* Online. December 18, 2009.

Gostin, Nicki. "'Glee' Star Matthew Morrison Recalls 'Worst Year' Ever," PopEater. com. January 15, 2010.

Jensen, Michael. "A chat with actor Matthew Morrison of 'Glee'," AfterElton.com. September 9, 2009.

Kroll, Dan J. "Adam Returning Home After 4 Year Absence," SoapCentral.com. October 1, 2006.

Masello, Robert. "'I Want To Do It All,'" *Parade.* Online. November 29, 2009.

Williams, Allison. "I, New York," *Time Out New York.* Online. May 14–20, 2009.

lea michele

Ayers, Michael D. "Interview: Glee Star Lea Michele On Central Park, Comedy, and a Sweaty Co-Star," *Village Voice.* Online. September 9, 2009.

Buckley, Michael. "Stage to Screens: 'Glee' on TV: Michele & Morrison," Playbill. com. September 8, 2009.

Farley, Christopher John. "'Glee' Star Lea Michele on the Golden Globes, the Great White Way, and Twitter," Speakeasy. *The Wall Street Journal.* Online. December

18, 2009.

Godwin, Jennifer. "Glee Boss on Showmance: 'We Have Some Plans to Give the People What They Want,'" EOnline.com. December 18, 2009.

Hedegaard, Erik. "'Glee' Gone Wild," *Rolling Stone*. April 15, 2010

"Lea Michele: Dancing with herself," MSN Entertainment. Online. Februay 2, 2010.

Kinon, Cristina. "Hot New Yorker: Lea Michele's success has Bronx feeling 'Glee'," *New York Daily News*. Online. December 26, 2009.

Kuhn, Sarah. "Life Stages," Backstage.com. September 3, 2009.

Martin, Denise. "Lea Michele's 'Glee'-ful awakening," *Los Angeles Times*. Online. December 2, 2009.

Miller, Gerri. "Glee Club Glory," *JVibe*. Online. August 2009.

"OK! Exclusive: Lea Michele Shares Her Best Diet Secret," *OK!* Online. February 8, 2010.

Riley, Jenelle. "Prime Time," Backstage.com. November 18, 2009.

"Sing it with 'Glee'," Skiddle.com. January 29, 2010.

cory monteith

"Glee on Q TV," Qtv's YouTube Channel. www.youtube.com/Qtv.

Hedegaard, Erik. "'Glee' Gone Wild," *Rolling Stone*. April 15, 2010.

Malan, Daniel. "Candid Cory Monteith," TheTVAddict.com. November 18, 2009.

Malkin, Marc. "Glee's Cory Monteith: High School Dropout to Hollywood Star," EOnline.com. September 9, 2009.

Simpson, Melody. "Meet Cory Monteith & Naya Rivera of Glee." Hollywood the Write Way. Online. March 17, 2009.

dianna agron

felldowntherabbithole.tumblr.com

Hedegaard, Erik. "'Glee' Gone Wild," *Rolling Stone*. April 15, 2010.

Miller, Gerri. "Glee Club Glory," *JVibe*. Online. August 2009.

Waterman, Lauren. "Dianna Agron," *Interview*. Online. Accessed February 26, 2010.

Zuckerman, Suzanne. "Dreaming Big: Dianna Agron of Glee," *Women's Health*. Online. January 28, 2010.

jane lynch

Berrin, Danielle. "Jane Lynch: 'I'm just a goof,'" *Guardian*. Online. January 9, 2010.

Bialas, Michael. "Ryan Murphy Makes His Lighthearted Plea With Glee," Blogcritics. org. May 18, 2009.

Cutler, Jacqueline. "'Glee' hitting all the right notes," *Buffalo News*. Online. September 6, 2009.

Duran, Rick. "Role Models — Jane Lynch Interview," The-Frat-Pack.com. Accessed March 11, 2010.

Forsee, Kari. "The Genius of Jane Lynch," Oprah.com. December 21, 2009.

"Glee's Jane Lynch on Love, Loss, and What I Wore and Her Final Episode of Party Down," *New York Magazine*. Online. October 27, 2009.

Hartinger, Bret. "Interview: Glee's Jane Lynch Got Picked First in High School P.E. (But She's Still No Sue Sylvester!)," AfterElton.com. September 30, 2009.

Holmes, Linda. "Jane Lynch Answers Our Five Unlikely Questions On Fights, Clones & More," NPR.org. October 7, 2009.

Malen, Daniel. "Exclusive Interview: Jane Lynch Talks Glee and Party Down," TheTVAddict.com. April 24, 2009.

"Meet 'Glee' Star Jane Lynch, TV's New Queen Of Mean," NPR.org. October 7, 2009.

Perkins, Tracey. "Jane Lynch: 'I didn't want to be gay — I wanted an easy life,'" Mirror.co.uk. January 31, 2010.

Spitznagel, Eric. "Q&A: Jane Lynch Might Just Slip You a Mickey," *Vanity Fair*. Online. September 4, 2009.

Warn, Sarah. "Interview with Jane Lynch," AfterEllen.com. November 15, 2004.

jayma mays

Friedman, Amy. "From Grundy to 'Glee'," *Roanoke Times*. Online. April 7, 2010.

Sternberg, Alix. "Exclusive Interview: Jayma Mays (Emma) from Glee," TheTVChick.com. December 2, 2009.

Tennis, Joe. "Living A Hollywood Dream," *A! Magazine*. Online. March 2010.

Wampler, Angela. "Believe! Q&A with Jayma Mays," *A! Magazine*. Online. September 28, 2009.

amber riley

"Amber Riley," WendyWilliamsShow's YouTube Channel. www.youtube.com/WendyWilliamsShow.

French, Dan. "Q&A: Glee's Amber Riley," DigitalSpy.com. January 5, 2010.

"GleeFan Exclusive: Amber Riley Q&A," GleeFan.com. August 16, 2009.

Gregg, Gabi. "Amber Riley," YoungFatandFabulous.com. August 10, 2009.

chris colfer

Fernandez, Maria Elena. "Chris Colfer's journey from small town to 'Glee'," *Los Angeles Times*. Online. September 8, 2009.

Goldberg, Lesley. "Just One of the Guys," *Advocate*. Online. October 6, 2009.

Hernandez, Greg. "My chat with Chris Colfer, the breakout gay character of FOX's new series 'Glee'," GregInHollywood.com. August 10, 2009.

Jensen, Michael. "Interview: Chris Colfer Remembers Who Bullied Him in High School (But He's Such a Nice Guy He Answers Their Emails Anyway!)," AfterElton.com. February 23, 2010.

Milzoff, Rebecca. "Glee's Chris Colfer on Owning 'Defying Gravity' and Resembling a Hummel Figurine," *New York Magazine*. Online. November 16, 2009.

jenna ushkowitz

Cord-Cruz, Gabrielle, Maggie Cotter and Ganesh Ravichandran. "Kidsday talks with Glee's Jenna Ushkowitz," ExploreLI.com. January 9, 2010.

Gianelli, Brian. "5 Questions With Glee's Jenna Ushkowitz," Fancast.com. September 8, 2009.

"Jenna Ushkowitz Interview — JustJared.com Exclusive," JustJared.com. November 18, 2009.

Lipton, Brian Scott. "Jenna Ushkowitz Is Filled With Glee," *Theater Mania*. Online. November 3, 2009.

O'Hare, Kate. "A Little More 'Glee'," Blog.Zap2It.com. May 21, 2009.

Pastor, Pam. "From 'Sesame Street' to 'Glee'," Lifestyle.Inquirer.net. February 13, 2010.

Radish, Christina. "Exclusive Interview: Jenna Ushkowitz is Filled with GLEE," IESB.net. December 1, 2009.

Wieselman, Jarrett. "Jenna Ushkowitz: I'm rooting for Tina to join Cheerios!," *New York Post*. Online. November 18, 2009.

kevin mchale

Albiniak, Paige. "Spinning their wheels," *New York Post*. Online. November 8, 2009.

Bianculli, David. "The Musical Magic Of 'Glee'," NPR.org. September 11, 2009.

Kuhn, Sarah. "Life Stages," Backstage.com. September 3, 2009.

Radish, Christina. "Exclusive Interview with Glee's Kevin McHale," IESB.net. January 5, 2010.

Steinberg, Jamie. "Kevin McHale," *Starry Constellation Magazine*. Online. Accessed March 10, 2010.

mark salling

Atlas, Darla. "'Glee' series lets Dallas-area guys show off," DallasNews.com. August 29, 2009.

"CT Celebrity Interview With Glee's Mark Salling," *Campus Talk*. Online. November 17, 2009.

Jensen, Michael. "Mark Salling Makes 'Sweet' Music on 'Glee'," AlfterElton.com. October 22, 2009.

"Mark Salling," WendyWilliamsShow's YouTube Channel. http://www.youtube.com/WendyWilliamsShow.

Spelling, Ian. "Mark Salling Makes His Mark On Glee," News.Popstar.com. September 10, 2009.

Steinberg, Lisa. "Mark Salling," *Starry Constellation Magazine*. Online. Accessed March 10, 2010.

Sternberg, Alix. "Interview Series: Glee: Mark Salling (Puck)," TheTVChick.com. December 9, 2009.

Thomas, Rachel. "An Interview With Mark Salling (Puck, 'Glee')," TVDramas. About.com. September 2009.

Weigle, Lauren. "Mark Salling," *Music Fashion Magazine*. Online. Winter 2010.

jessalyn gilsig

Berger, Lori. "Fashion Secrets from a Glam 'Glee' Star," *Redbook*. Online. Accessed March 13, 2010.

Fienberg, Daniel. "HitFix Interview: Jessalyn Gilsig of 'Glee'," HitFix.com. September 8, 2009.

Fulkerson, Ginger. "Jessalyn Gilsig," *South Beach Magazine*. Online. Accessed March 1, 2010.

Lawson, Richard. "TV.com Q&A: Glee's Jessalyn Gilsig," TV.com. October 7, 2009.

Martin, Denise. "Love to hate or just hate? 'Glee' star Jessalyn Gilsig says tonight's episode brings Terri's moment of reckoning," *Los Angeles Times*. Online. December 2, 2009.

Sternberg, Alix. "Interview: Jessalyn Gilsig (Terri Schuester) from Glee," TheTVChick.com. October 28, 2009.

Wagner, Joan. "The Woman Glee Fans Love to Hate," Oprah.com. November 11, 2009.

iqbal theba

"Curry Bear Interviews Glee's Iqbal Theba (Principal Figgins)," CurryBear.com. Accessed March 11, 2010.

"Neal B. Exclusive: Interview with Iqbal Theba aka Principal Figgins!," NealBinNYC. wordpress.com. December 4, 2009.

Nemetz, Dave. "Interview: Glee's Iqbal Theba Rules The School," Fanpop.com. September 30, 2009.

Steinberg, Lisa. "Iqbal Theba," *Starry Constellation Magazine*. Accessed February 26, 2010.

patrick gallagher

Marchand, Francois. "B.C. actor Patrick Gallagher explores his dual nature with Glee," Vancouver Sun. Online. November 23, 2009.

Steinberg, Lisa. "Patrick Gallagher," *Starry Constellation Magazine*. Accessed February 26, 2010.

Yeo, Debra. "'Badass' who wears fanny packs," *Toronto Star*. Online. December 9, 2009.

heather morris

Kirchmyer, Lauren. "Heather Morris brings 'Glee' to Buffalo," *Buffalo Dance*

Examiner. Online. December 31, 2009.

Lydon, Kate. "The Road to 'Glee': Heather Morris Makes Her Mark in Hollywood," *Dance Spirit.* Online. May 1, 2010.

Pastor, Pam. "Glee's 'secret weapon,'" *Philippine Daily Inquirer.* Online. January 30, 2010.

"Star from Hit TV Show Visits Good Morning WNY," WWKBW.com.

Wieselman, Jarrett. "Glee's secret weapon," *New York Post.* Online. November 19, 2009.

naya rivera

"Exclusive: We Chat with Glee's Naya Rivera," NiceGirlsTV.com. March 12, 2009.

Geragotelis, Brittany. "Time Out With: Naya Rivera from 'Glee'," *American Cheerleader.* Online. September 9, 2009.

"Naya Rivera Stars in New Fox Musical Comedy 'Glee'," StarShineMag.com. March 16, 2009.

Simpson, Melody. "Get to know Naya Rivera," Examiner.com. July 16, 2009.

Simpson, Melody. "Meet Cory Monteith & Naya Rivera of Glee," HollywoodtheWriteWay.com. March 17, 2009.

harry shum jr.

"'Glee' Dancer is Waiting For His Close-Up," PopEater.com. November 10, 2009.

Lee, Angela. "Harry Shum Jr. Interview," *Portrait.* Online. October 2009.

Lin, Shannon. "Harry Shum is full of Glee," *Asiance.* Online. September 2, 2009.

Pastor, Pam. "'Kidnapping' The Other Asian," *Lifestyle Inquirer.* Online. January 9, 2010.

Radish, Christina. "Exclusive Interview: Harry Shum Jr. is Full of Glee," IESB.net. December 9, 2009.

shumbodynamedharry.tumblr.com

dijon talton

Steinberg, Lisa. "Dijon Talton," *Starry Constellation Magazine.* Online. Accessed March 10, 2010.

Twitter.com/DijonTalton

josh sussman

Elkin, Michael. "Of 'Glee' I Sing," *Jewish Exponent.* Online. June 11, 2009.

Twitter.com/JoshSussman

season one: may 2009–june 2010

"About the White House," WhiteHouse.gov. Various Biographies.

Abrams, Natalie. "Glee Gets Eve-ntful with Guest-Star Eve," *TV Guide.* Online. November 24, 2009.

AC/DC. *Highway to Hell*. Atlantic Records, 1979.

Aerosmith. *Aerosmith*. Columbia Records, 1973.

Aguilera, Christina. *Christina Aguilera*. RCA Records, 1999.

—. *Stripped*. BMG Entertainment, 2002.

Alex and Kristyn. "Dianna Agron (Quinn) PCM Interview," PopCultureMadness. com. Accessed March 13, 2010.

AllAboutMadonna.com

The All-American Rejects. *When the World Comes Down*. Interscope Records, 2008.

"All By Myself," Metacafe.com. Accessed March 20, 2010.

Allen, Lily. *Alright Still*. Regal Recordings, 2006.

AllGame.com

AllMovie.com

Anka, Paul and Odia Coates. "(You're) Having My Baby," United Artists Records. 1974.

Armstrong, Louis. *Louis Armstrong: Greatest Hits of All Time*. Burning Fire Records, 1992.

AwardsDatabase.Oscars.org

Beatles, The. *Magical Mystery Tour*. Capitol Records, 1967.

Beck. *Mellow Gold*. Geffen Records, 1994.

Bel Biv DeVoe. *Poison*. MCA Records, 1990.

Beyoncé. *I Am . . . Sasha Fierce*. Columbia Records, 2008.

Bianculli, David. "The Musical Magic Of 'Glee'," NPR.org. September 11, 2009.

BillAJones.com

Billboard.com

Bodyslamming.com

Bon Jovi. *Crush*. Island Records, 2000.

Borzillo, Carrie. "Gleeking Out With Jane Lynch & Jessalyn Gilsig," Fancast.com. March 13, 2010.

BoxOfficeMojo.com

Brandy. *Never Say Never*. Atlantic Records, 1998.

"Broadway Star Morrison Leaps To TV With 'Glee'," NPR.org. September 13, 2009.

BroadwayWorld.com

Brown, James. *It's a Man's Man's Man's World*. King Records, 1966.

Bruno, Danielle. "WWEPW Interviews Michael Hitchcock," wwepw.blogspot. com. January 16, 2010.

Bryant, Ali. "Going Ga-Ga," *Grazia*. January 15, 2010.

Burbank, Luke. "Kids Love Hot Cheetos But Schools Hate Them," NPR.org. May 9, 2006.

Carmen, Eric. *Eric Carmen*. Rhino/Arista, 1975.

"The Cast of Glee: Style Notes," Elle.com. Accessed June 2, 2010.

CharlotteRoss.com

CheyenneJackson.com

Chic. *C'est Chic*. Atlantic Records, 1978.

Chicago (Music from the Miramax Motion Picture). Sony Music Entertainment, 2002.

"Child restraint laws," Insurance Institute for Highway Safety. Online. March 2010.

"Chris & Amber's 'Atrocious' Auditions for Glee," *People*. http://www.youtube.com/people.

Cinquemani, Sal. "Review: Fearless," *Slant*. Online. December 21, 2008.

Color Me Badd, "I Wanna Sex You Up." C.M.B. Giant Records, 1991.

Conradt, Stacy. "The Quick 10: 10 Real-Life Glee Club Members," *Mental Floss*. Online. January 12, 2010.

Creedence Clearwater Revival. *Bayou Country*. Fantasy Records, 1969.

Davis, Sammy, Jr. *The Lady Is a Tramp*. One Media Publishing, 2009.

"The Deadly Ritual of Seppuku," Samauri-Weapons.net. Accessed June 11, 2010.

Dean, Jennifer. "19-year-old Riverside resident gleeful about role on new Fox series." *The Press-Enterprise*. Online. June 14, 2009.

Denver, John. *Rhymes and Reasons*. RCA Records, 1969.

Destiny's Child. *Survivor*. Columbia Records, 2001.

Diamond, Neil. *The Jazz Singer*. Capitol Records, 1980.

—. "Sweet Caroline." MCA Records, 1969.

Dion, Celine. *Falling Into You*. Epic Records, 1996.

—. *Taking Chances*. Columbia Records, 2007.

Donahue, Ann. "Glee: The Billboard Cover Story." *Billboard*. Online. April 30, 2010.

The Doors. *Waiting for the Sun*. Elektra Records, 1968.

Dos Santos, Kristin. "Five Glee Finale Secrets: That Will and Emma Kiss Wasn't Scripted!" EOnline.com. June 9, 2010.

—. "Ga-Gouch! Glee's Lea Michele Injured During Lady Gaga Dance Number," EOnline.com. April 13, 2010.

—. "Glee Cast and Creators Dish on Neil Patrick Harris, 'Puckleberry' and Lady Gaga!" EOnline.com. March 14, 2010.

Dowd, Kathy Ehrich, Diane Clehane and Steve Helling, "Exclusive: Beyoncé & Jay-Z File Signed Marriage License," *People*. Online. April 28, 2008.

Duffy. *Rockferry*. Mercury Records, 2008.

EJThomasHall.com

ESPN.com

Fancast.com

Fernandez, Maria. "How Madonna's music wound up on 'Glee'," *Los Angeles Times*. Online. March 16, 2010.

"Fictional Beer Brands," BrookstonBeerBulletin.com. Accessed March 10, 2010.

FilmReference.com

Flores, Karen. "Jollibee appears on 'Glee' episode," ABS-CBNNews.com. May 19,

2010.

Fox Broadcasting's YouTube Channel. www.youtube.com/FoxBroadcasting. Various videos.

FOX Broadcasting Company. "Glee: Behind the Scenes." www.fox.com/glee/chevy. Various videos.

FOX Broadcasting Company. "Glee." www.fox.com/watch/glee/. Various videos.

Foxsource's YouTube Channel. www.youtube.com/foxsource.

Franklin, Aretha. *I Never Loved a Man the Way I Love You.* Atlantic Recording Corporation, 1967.

Funny Girl (Original Soundtrack Recording). Sony Music Entertainment, 1968.

Gary Puckett & The Union Gap. "Young Girl." Columbia Records, 1968.

Geddes, David. *Run Joey Run.* Atlantic Records, 1975.

Ghosh, Korbi. "'Glee' creator Ian Brennan on Jane Lynch singing: 'More Sue Sylvester up in this piece'," Zap2It.com. April 22, 2010.

—. "'Glee' girl Amber Riley talks music, Mercedes & more," Zap2It.com. September 9, 2009.

Glaister, Dan. "Neil Diamond reveals secret of Sweet Caroline." *Guardian.* Online. November 21, 2007.

Glee Cast. *Glee: The Music, Journey to Regionals The Journey to Regionals.* Columbia/Epic Label Group, 2010.

—. *Glee: The Music, The Power Of Madonna.* Columbia/Epic Label Group, 2009.

—. *Glee: The Music, Volume 1.* Columbia/Epic Label Group, 2009.

—. *Glee: The Music, Volume 2.* Columbia/Epic Label Group, 2009.

—. *Glee: The Music, Volume 3 Showstoppers.* Columbia/Epic Label Group, 2010.

"The Glee Club Goes Gaga on an All-New 'Glee' Tuesday, May 25, on FOX," Fox Press Release. May 24, 2010.

Glee — Season 1, Volume 1: Road to Sectionals. DVD. Twentieth Century Fox Home Entertainment, 2009.

glee. Screenplay by Ryan Murphy and Brad Falchuk and Ian Brennan. July 21, 2008.

"Glee TV: Neil Patrick Harris Talks Glee's 'Dream On' (TV Content)," BroadwayWorld.com. Accessed March 18, 2010.

"Glee on Q TV," Qtv's YouTube Channel. www.youtube.com/Qtv

"Glee's Chris Colfer Reveals Real-Life Story Behind Kurt's Diva Moment," TVWatch. People.com. November 12, 2009.

"Glee's Heather Morris elimination from SYTYCD," Jushin3's YouTube Channel. www.youtube.com/jushin3.

GlobalSecurity.org

Godwin, Jennifer. "Glee Boss on Showmance: "We Have Some Plans to Give the People What They Want." EOnline.com. December 18, 2009.

"Going Gaga for Gaga," *Harper's Bazaar.* Online. Accessed June 3, 2010.

Goldman, Andrew. "Matthew Morrison." *Elle.* Online. December 18, 2009.

Grammy.com

GreggHenry.com

Groban, Josh. *Closer*. Reprise Records, 2003.

Guys & Dolls (Original Cast Recording). Red Sauce Records, 2005.

Gypsy (Original Cast Recording). Nonesuch Records, 1962.

Hannah Montana: The Movie (Original Motion Picture Soundtrack). Walt Disney Records, 2009.

Harding, Cortney. "Lady Gaga: The Billboard Cover Story," *Billboard*. Online. August 7, 2009.

Heart. *Bad Animals*. Capitol Records, 1987.

Hedegaard, Erik. "'Glee' Gone Wild," *Rolling Stone*. April 15, 2010.

Idol, Billy. *Don't Stop*. Chrysalis Records, 1981.

Insalata, Lillian. "Trojan Marching Band Performs With Glee," USCNews.USC.edu. April 28, 2010.

Internet Adult Film Database. IAFD.com

Internet Broadway Database. IBDB.com

Internet Movie Database. IMDb.com

Israel Kamakawiwo'ole. *Facing Future*. Mountain Apple Company, 1993.

Jaffe, Matthew. "Glee Party: Ryan Murphy and the Cast Reveal What's Ahead," TV.com. March 15, 2010.

Jensen, Michael. "Ryan Murphy and Chris Colfer Discuss 'Glee,' 'Golden Globes' and more," AfterElton.com. January 22, 2010.

JessieStJamesOnline.com

Joel, Billy. *Piano Man*. Sony Music Entertainment, 1973.

John, Elton. *Blue Moves*. MCA Records, 1976.

Jordan, Montell. *This Is How We Do It*. Def Jam Recordings, 1995.

Journey. *Departure*. Sony Music Entertainment, 1980.

—. *Escape*. Columbia/Epic Label Group, 1981.

—. *Evolution*. Columbia/Epic Label Group, 1979.

—. *Frontiers*. Sony Music Entertainment, 1983.

Katrina and the Waves. *Walking on Sunshine*. Attic Records, 1983.

"Kevin McHale Bringing Sexy Back to 'Glee,' NBCBayArea.com. April 14, 2010.

King, Joyann. "Glee's Costumer Dishes On Gaga Looks," *InStyle*. Online. May 24, 2010.

KISS. *Destroyer*. Island Def Jam Music Group, 1976.

Kraft, Nicole. "Profile: Jim & Jonathan Groff," *Hoofs Beat*. July 2007.

Lady Gaga. *The Fame*. Interscope Records, 2008.

—. *The Fame Monster*. Interscope Records, 2009.

Lauper, Cyndi. *True Colors*. Epic Records, 1986.

Lavigne, Avril. *The Best Damn Thing*. Arista Records, 2006.

Le Nguyen, Chrissy. "Chris Colfer on Crying Real 'Glee' Tears, Tattoos, and Kurt's New Boyfriend," TV.Yahoo.com. April 27, 2010.

Lee, Allyssa. "Idina Menzel on the 'Glee' Experience," TVSquad.com. May 17, 2010.

Lennon, John. *Imagine*. Apple Records, 1971.

Leopold, Todd. "The worst song of all time, part II," CNN.com. April 27, 2006.

Les Misérables (Original Broadway Cast Recording). Geffen Records, 1987.

Lim, Louisa. "Painful Memories for China's Footbinding Survivors," NPR.org. March 19, 2007.

LimaOhio.com

"Lima, Ohio," Ohio History Central. Online. www.ohiohistorycentral.org/entry.php?rec=1959.

Lipps, Inc. *Mouth to Mouth*. Casablanca NBLP 7197, 1979.

Lulu. *Greatest Hits*. Mercury Records, 2003.

Madonna. *American Life*. Warner Bros. Records, 2003.

—. *Bedtime Stories*. Warner Bros. Records, 1994.

—. *Celebration*. Warner Bros. Records, 2009.

—. *Confessions on a Dance Floor*. Warner Bros. Records, 2005.

—. *Erotica*. Warner Bros. Records, 1992.

—. *Hard Candy*. Warner Bros. Records, 2008.

—. *Like a Prayer*. Sire Records, 1989.

—. *Like a Virgin*. Sire Records, 1984.

—. *Madonna*. Sire Records, 1983.

—. *Music*. Warner Bros. Records, 2000.

—. *Ray of Light*. Warner Bros. Records, 1998.

—. *True Blue*. Sire Records, 1986.

Malkin, Marc. "An Afternoon Filled With Glee." EOnline.com. July 29, 2009.

Man of La Mancha (The New Broadway Cast Recording). BMG Entertainment, 1968.

Marky Mark and the Funky Bunch. *Music for the People*. Interscope Records, 1991.

Martin, Denise. "Lea Michele's 'Glee'-ful awakening," The Envelope: The Awards Insider. *Los Angeles Times*. Online. December 2, 2009.

MC Hammer. *Please Hammer, Don't Hurt 'Em*. Capitol/EMI Records, 1988.

Mellencamp, John. *Uh-Huh*. Island Def Jam Music Group, 1983.

Men Without Hats. *Rhythm of Youth*. Bulldog Brothers, 1982.

Miller, Gerri. "Glee Club Glory," *JVibe*. Online. August 2009.

Miller, Julie. "Kevin McHale on Glee's Wheelchair Controversy, His Dream TV Role and Celebrity Gleeks," Movieline.com. May 18, 2010.

The Monkees. *The Birds, The Bees & The Monkees*. Rhino Entertainment, 1968.

Morris, Christopher. "Keeping 'Glee' in tune," *Variety*. Online. December 4, 2009.

"Mulatto's Trip from Zero to Sixty," *Twaddle*. Online. Accessed May 10, 2010.

Myspace.com/jessiejamesmusic

Nelly. *Country Grammar*. Universal Records, 2001.

Nena. *99 Luft Balloons*. Epic Records, 1984.

Newport, Kenneth G.C. *The Branch Davidians of Waco*. Oxford University Press, 2006.

Newton-John, Olivia. *Magic: The Very Best of Olivia Newton-John*. Universal Music

Enterprises, 2001.

—. *Physical*. MCA Records, 1981.

Nguyen, Hanh. "'Glee' fashion challenges: Madonna, matching and men," Zap2It. com. April 21, 2010.

—. "'Glee' fashion scoop: 'Hell-O' to affordable looks," Zap2It.com. April 14, 2010.

—. "'Glee' fashion scoop: Take 'Home' these looks," Zap2It.com. April 27, 2010.

Nice Girls Don't Get the Corner Office. Unaired TV pilot. ABC, 2007.

"Ohio Map," *Maps of World*. Online. Accessed March 18, 2010.

Oliver!(The New Musical Cast). Big Eye Music, 2009.

"Open Sesame." Snopes.com. August 6, 2007.

"Orlandus de Lassus," NewAdvent.org. Accessed May 27, 2010.

Paige, Jennifer. *Jennifer Paige*. Hollywood Records, 1998.

Parliament. *Mothership Connection*. Island Def Jam Music Group, 1975.

Perry, Katy. *One of the Boys*. Capitol Records, 2008.

Peter, Paul and Mary. *Album 1700*. Warner Brothers, 1967.

Playbill.com

The Police. *Zenyattà Mondatta*. A&M Records, 1981.

Popular — First Season. dvd. Buena Vista Home Entertainment/Touchtone, 2004.

Popular — Second Season. dvd. Buena Vista Home Entertainment/Touchtone, 2005.

The Pretenders. *Last of the Independents*. Warner Brothers, 1994.

"Q&A: Whit Hertford on UCB, Glee, and about 501 other projects he's got going," Out-is-Through.blogspot.com. November 13, 2009.

Queen. *Queen: Stone Cold Classic*. Hollywood Records, 2006.

Ram, Archana. "'Glee' yellow dresses: Costume designer Lou Eyrich tells all," PopWatch.EW.com. October 10, 2009.

Ram, Archana. "Style Hunter: Kate Hudson's 'Nine' Glasses and More!" EW.com. January 11, 2010.

Redding, Otis. *The Very Best of Otis Redding*. Rhino/Atlantic Recording Corporation, 1992.

REO Speedwagon. *Wheels Are Turnin'*. Epic Records, 1984.

Respers France, Lisa. "'Glee' piano player happy as a 'sub-lebrity'," CNN.com. May 18, 2010.

RIAA.com

Richie, Lionel. *Can't Slow Down*. Motown Records, 1984.

Rihanna. *Good Girl Gone Bad*. Stargate, 2008.

Robert, Diamond. "Spring (Awakening) Fever: An Interview with Jonathan Groff,"

BroadwayWorld.com. January 25, 2007.

Rooksby, Rikky. *The Complete Guide to the Music of Madonna*. Omnibus Press, 2004.

Ross, Diana and Lionel Richie. *Endless Love: Original Motion Picture Soundtrack*.

Motown Records, 1981.

Rufus. *Rags to Rufus*. UMG Recordings, 1974.

"Ryan Seacrest interviews Lea Michele," PointRadio.com. Accessed June 10, 2010.

Salt-N-Pepa. *Hot, Cool & Vicious*. Next Plateau Records, 1987.

Scott, Jill. *The Real Thing: Words and Sounds Vol. 3*. Hidden Beach Recordings, 2007.

"Series 18, Episode 21," *Friday Night with Jonathan Ross*. BBC. Original Air Date: June 18, 2010.

"Shelly's Report of the 'Journey' Season Finale Taping," GleeFan.com, April 23, 2010.

"Sing it With 'Glee'," Teenfi.com. Accessed March 20, 2010.

Sisqó. *Unleash the Dragon*. Def Jam Recordings, 2000.

Sloane, Judy. "Glee — On our set visit the cast talk about the friendly competition," FilmReviewOnline.com. February 11, 2010.

Songfacts.com

Sparks, Jordin. *Jordin Sparks*. Jive Records, 2008.

Springfield, Rick. *Working Class Dog*. RCA Records, 1981.

Springsteen, Bruce & the E Street Band. *Live/1975–85*. Columbia Records, 1986.

Steinberg, Lisa. "Heather Morris," *Starry Constellation Magazine*. Online. Accessed March 10, 2010.

Sternberg, Alix. "Exclusive Interview: Jonathan Groff (Jesse St. James) from Glee," TheTVChick.com. April 20, 2010.

Streisand, Barbra. *Barbra Joan Streisand*. Sony Music Entertainment, 1971.

Style.com

Sullivan, Jazmine. *Fearless*. Arista Records, 2008.

The Supremes. *The Supremes Sing Holland-Dozier-Holland*. Motown Records, 1966.

"T4: Glee star Matthew Morrison interview," T4's YouTube Channel. www.youtube.com/user/T4.

The Time. *Ice Cream Castle*. Warner Brothers, 1984.

Tobolowsky, Stephen. "The Tobolowsky Files Ep. 16 — Dating Tips for Actors." The Tobolowsky Files. Podcast. February 12, 2010.

Top Hits of the 1930s. Goldenlane Records, 2008.

"TV," Teen.com/TV. Various videos.

TV.com

TVGuide.com

Twitter.com/chriscolfer

Twitter.com/mulattomuzik

Tyler, Bonnie. *Faster Than the Speed of Night*. Columbia Records, 1983.

U.S. Census Bureau Lima FactSheet. http://factfinder.census.gov/servlet/SAFFFacts?_event=Search&_geo.

U.S. Census Bureau QuickFacts on Lima. http://quickfacts.census.gov/qfd/states/39/3943554.html.

U2. *Achtung Baby.* Universal/Island Records, 1991.

Underwood, Carrie. *Carnival Ride.* Arista Nashville, 2008.

UrbanDictionary.com

Usher. *Confessions.* Arista Records, 2004.

Van Halen. *1984.* Warner Bros. Records, 1984.

Vanilla Ice. *To the Extreme.* Capitol Records, 1990.

VisitKingsIsland.com

Voss, Brandon, "Naya Rivera: Bring It On, Bitch!," *Advocate.* Online. May 4, 2010.

Walters, David. "Glee: 14 Exclusive Behind the Scenes Photos — Shot by Jonathan Groff!" *Details.* Online. June 4, 2010.

Warwick, Dionne. "Don't Make Me Over." Scepter Records, 1962.

—. *The Windows of the World.* Scepter Records, 1967.

Weinstein, Zack. "A Spinal Cord Injury Didn't Keep Me Off 'Glee'," TheWrap.com. May 10, 2010.

—. "Zack's not letting his injury keep him from acting (He's going to be on Glee!)," *Christopher and Dana Reeve Foundation.* Online. March 18, 2010.

West Side Story (Original Broadway Cast). Sony Music Entertainment, 1998.

West, Kanye. *Late Registration.* Roc-A-Fella/Island Def Jam, 2005.

WheelchairDance.co.uk

Wieselman, Jarett. "Chris Colfer: Oprah Winfrey smells like money," Pop Wrap. *New York Post.* Online. April 27, 2010.

Wikipedia.org

Winehouse, Amy. *Back to Black.* Island Def Jam Music Group, 2006.

The Wiz (Original Soundtrack). Geffen Records, 1978.

Wright, Gary. *The Dream Weaver.* Warner Bros. Records, 1975.

Young MC. *Stone Cold Rhymin'.* Island Records, 1989.

acknowledgments

We'd like to send out a huge thank you to everyone at ECW Press, who believed that a book about *Glee* would work, that we were the two best girls to write it, and that we could do it in only nine months. A special thanks to our editors Jennifer Hale and Jennifer Knoch, whose Emma Pillsbury–esque guidance kept us in line and on track; Sarah Dunn, our superstar publicist, who loves a good round of *Glee* karaoke as much as we do; our managing editor Crissy Boylan; and Cyanotype, whose cover and photo section designs deserve a gold star. We'd also like to thank the most amazing fandom out there: the gleeks, whose dedication makes this show come alive long after each episode is over. A special shout-out to the best *Glee* blog network out there, The Gleekdom (thegleekdom.com), whose support and suggestions for this book were invaluable. A big thank you also to everyone who participated in interviews or provided us with photos. We loved having so many gleeks involved in our book. Lastly, thank you to the creators, cast and crew of *Glee* for creating a show worth writing about. "Yay, glee! *Glee* kids, hooray!"

Erin: Thanks to my friends and family, who know all too well that I'm more like Rachel Berry than I'm willing to admit (and who tolerated my endless dispersal of *Glee* trivia for the past year). Thanks to Matt, for supporting me, even at my most obnoxious (and who now knows more about this show than any casual viewer ever should). Thanks to Suzie, for writing this book with me (and for discovering that working with me would expose her to far more crazy than an Emma/Terri showdown). But mostly, a huge thanks to my mother, who knew long before Sue Sylvester ever did that track pants and jokes about hair gel never go out of style.

Suzanne: Thank you so incredibly much to all of my family and friends who have supported me through everything. Thank you and so much love to my mom and dad, to Deb and Ryan, and to Ali and Billy for always believing in me and supporting me. And thank you to Austin, Alex, and Teddy for being able to bring a smile to my face on my most stressed-out of days. Thank you to everyone in my life who discusses *Glee* with me — you have all, in some way, influenced my thoughts on a character, a song, a scene, or an episode, and I'm indebted to all of you for that. Special thanks also to Jen for letting our apartment be taken over by *Glee* and discussing our love for JGroff at all hours of the night. Thank you to Erin for sharing this experience with me; the endless emails, the endless edits, the endless episode rewatches, and all! And lastly, thank you and all my love to Mo, because no matter what you say, I really couldn't have done this without you.

Erin Balser (left) and Suzanne Gardner are writers and editors who blog about *Glee*: Erin at gleedork.com and Suzanne at gleeksunited.wordpress .com. When they're not busy writing, you can find them singing *Glee* tunes at karaoke bars around Toronto, Ontario. This is their first book.